.NET Security

JASON BOCK, PETE STROMQUIST,
TOM FISCHER, AND NATHAN SMITH

Apress™

.NET Security

ISBN (pbk): 1-59059-053-8
Printed and bound in the United States of America 12345678910

Technical Reviewers: Brock Allen, Robert Knudson, and Chris Sells
Editorial Directors: Dan Appleman, Peter Blackburn, Gary Cornell, Jason Gilmore, Karen Watterson, John Zukowski
Managing Editor: Grace Wong
Copy Editor: Ami Knox
Compositor: Impressions Book and Journal Services, Inc.
Indexer: Valerie Haynes Perry
Cover Designer: Kurt Krames
Manufacturing Manager: Tom Debolski
Marketing Manager: Stephanie Rodriguez

Distributed to the book trade in the United States by Springer-Verlag New York, Inc., 175 Fifth Avenue, New York, NY, 10010 and outside the United States by Springer-Verlag GmbH & Co. KG, Tiergartenstr. 17, 69112 Heidelberg, Germany.

In the United States, phone 1-800-SPRINGER, email orders@springer-ny.com, or visit http://www.springer-ny.com.
Outside the United States, fax +49 6221 345229, email orders@springer.de, or visit http://www.springer.de.

For information on translations, please contact Apress directly at 2560 Ninth Street, Suite 219, Berkeley, CA 94710. Phone: 510-549-5930, Fax: 510-549-5939, Email: info@apress.com, Web site: http://www.apress.com

The information in this book is distributed on an "as is" basis, without warranty. Although every precaution has been taken in the preparation of this work, neither the author nor Apress shall have any liability to any person or entity with respect to any loss or damage caused or alleged to be caused directly or indirectly by the information contained in this work.

The source code for this book is available to readers at http://www.apress.com in the Downloads section. You will need to answer questions pertaining to this book in order to successfully download the code.

Brief Contents

Contents

About the Authors

Jason Bock is an instructor and consultant for Intertech, Inc. He has worked on a number of business applications using a diverse set of tools and technologies such as VB, COM, and Java. He is also the author of *CIL Programming: Under the Hood™ of .NET* and *Visual Basic 6 Win32 API Tutorial*, and has written articles and given presentations on technical development issues within VB. He has a bachelor's degree and a master's degree in electrical engineering from Marquette University.

When he's not developing programs, writing books, or giving presentations, Jason enjoys spending time with his wife Liz, golfing, biking, reading, listening to and playing music, and watching *The Simpsons* whenever he can. Visit his Web site at http://www.jasonbock.net.

Pete Stromquist is a consultant at Magenic Technologies (one of the nation's premier Microsoft Certified Solution Providers), specializing in Web-enabled application development using Microsoft tools and technologies. Pete has spent the last several years architecting and developing the following types of applications: intranet content management, Web-enabled training and testing software, B2B and B2C e-commerce, and Web-based telemetry and logistics. Pete has complemented his VB skills with several other technologies such as XML, XSL, COM+, IIS, ASP, and of course .NET. Pete also enjoys teaching and giving presentations on .NET technologies. Pete has a mechanical engineering background, receiving his bachelor of science from the University of Minnesota.

Tom Fischer's career spans a broad range of technologies with some of the most prestigious consulting firms in the Twin Cities. His certifications include the Sun Certified Java Programmer (SCJP), Microsoft Certified Solution Developer (MCSD), and Microsoft Certified Database Administrator (MCDBA). And as a Microsoft Certified Teacher (MCT), Tom also helps teach other developers about the latest Microsoft .NET tools and technologies.

Nathan Smith is a consultant with Spherion in Scottsdale, AZ. He holds almost every Microsoft acronym possible (all but MCT) and specializes in the development of and conversion to Web-enabled applications. Prior to the first beta release of C#, he focused primarily on Visual Basic development, which he's been involved with for approximately six years.

About the Technical Reviewers

Chris Sells is an independent consultant, specializing in distributed applications in .NET and COM, as well as an instructor for DevelopMentor. He's written several books, including *ATL Internals*, which is in the process of being updated for ATL7 as you read this. He's also working on *Essential Windows Forms* for Addison-Wesley and *Mastering Visual Studio .NET* for O'Reilly. In his free time, Chris hosts the Web Services DevCon (scheduled for November 2002 this year) and directs the Genghis source-available project. More information about Chris and his various projects is available at http://www.sellsbrothers.com.

Brock Allen is a trainer for DevelopMentor as well as an independent consultant specializing in .NET and ASP.NET. He resides in Medfield, MA, with his wife and two dogs. He can be contacted at ballen@develop.com.

Robert Knudson has been active in commercial .NET development for a year and a half. This work has included framework development for Microsoft and involvement on a large ASP.NET site. In addition, Bob has served as an editor for various .NET texts. He has been a software development consultant for eight years. Prior to his work in .NET, Bob did commercial development with C++, DCOM, and ATL technologies. Prior to his career in computer science, Bob was a college physics professor and researcher. He holds a Ph.D. in physics and master's degrees in physics and engineering from the University of Wisconsin—Madison.

Acknowledgments

ALTHOUGH THIS BOOK HAS FOUR AUTHORS' names on the cover, there are a number of people who have contributed in different ways to making this book better than it ever could have been without them.

We would all like to thank the Apress staff—they have been extremely supportive. This includes (but is not limited to) Gary Cornell, Dan Appleman, Stephanie Rodriguez, Grace Wong, Ami Knox, and anyone else at Apress who has been involved with this book—you turned our writing into a far better product than what we could've done on our own. We also thank the reviewers (Brock Allen, Robert Knudson, Chris Sells, and Nathan Smith) for their helpful comments and suggestions.

Jason would like to thank his wife Liz for her love and support (you're the best) and all of his friends and family for just being there.

Tim would like to dedicate his contributions to Theresa, Ali, and Kate. They are the greatest!

Pete would like to first thank his wife, Kris, and his son, Ethan, for all their support during the writing process. He would like to thank and give all the glory to God, since he's the one who has made all of this possible. Pete would also like to thank everyone at Magenic Technologies who has provided him the opportunities over the years to get him where he is now. He would like to thank Steve Waldner for being his mentor in this industry when he first got started. Lastly, he would like to thank Jason Bock for affording him the opportunity to write for this book.

Nathan would like to thank the members of the eternal bench crew, PZ and EL, for providing him with things to laugh about, things to gripe about, and excellent Thai food.

Introduction

"We just lost all of our JPEGs on our Web server,
and . . . um . . . we don't have a backup."

"Attention! If you have received an e-mail from Bob, do not open it."

"Could you look at this attachment? I think it's a virus. . . . "

VIRUSES. MALICIOUS E-MAIL ATTACHMENTS. Denial of service attacks. You can probably think of a number of other incidents that have happened to either you or a friend of yours on the job where a piece of unwanted code wreaked havoc on unsuspecting users. We've seen our share at the places we've worked at. In fact, all three of the quotes are from our jobs. The first incident happened when an employee opened an e-mail that contained a virus. Since he had the Web server mapped as a network drive, the images located on the server were destroyed. The second occurred when a consultant had the e-mail preview option on in Outlook and a virus was accidentally started. The company panicked, and ended up broadcasting a warning message over the intercom system. The last one happened when someone within the company triggered a virus, and management wanted one of us (Jason) to examine the attachment, as it looked like VBScript. They were hoping that they'd have a chance at understanding what kind of damage was being done to their systems.

We'd all like code to do what we want it to do. We'd all like to be able to open an attachment that appears to be an image without it e-mailing questionable Web page links to our friends and coworkers. But up until .NET, it's been rather difficult for developers to program security effectively. It's not impossible, but it's not as easy as using C++ to open a file either. Windows has always been accommodating to the user in terms of ease of use when it came to their applications. That, however, has lead to numerous security breaches and malicious executables doing their work on machines, sometimes unbeknownst to their users. In a nutshell, this has been pretty frustrating for both users and developers.

With .NET, however, Microsoft has made a concerted effort to make writing secure code a much easier endeavor that what it was. This new architecture also has the added benefit of making it easier to configure what code can and cannot do. Because the security-related classes are straightforward to use, this will help in ensuring that a corporation's machines and networks are virus free. At the same time, since .NET is a whole new ball game to everyone involved (including yours truly), it takes some time to become familiar with the classes to use them effectively. This book is an attempt to help to facilitate that learning process so you can get up to speed on .NET security programming.

Target Audience

This book is targeting the intermediate .NET developer who wants to understand how security works in .NET. Although the language of choice within this book is C#, the concepts are .NET-general and are not specific to any .NET language. A VB .NET or JScript .NET developer should be able to apply the concepts to their preferred .NET language with relative ease. We're also assuming that you know the fundamentals of .NET (for example, what an assembly is, what the difference is between a static and an instance method, and so on).

Source Code

We have created a number of small applications that we mention throughout the book. You can download the code from Apress's Web site, at `http://www.apress.com`. We have made every attempt to ensure that the code compiles and behaves as expected, but mistakes can occur. If you find a bug with the source code, or you find an erroneous statement in the book itself, please contact us at `jason@jasonbock.net`, and we'll make sure that updates are made accordingly.

CHAPTER 1

The Basics of Cryptography and Security

IN THIS CHAPTER, you'll learn the fundamental concepts of cryptography and security. I'll define what cryptography is and what it is used for, and cover the basics of ciphers and keys and how they work. I'll demonstrate the difference between symmetric and asymmetric cipher algorithms and show you how they can be used in concert for creating signatures and certificates. Finally, I'll talk about cryptography and its relation to security in general.

The Essence of Cryptography

The definition of *cryptography* is pretty straightforward: it is the science of keeping messages secure. In essence, cryptography is the study of the mathematical algorithms and functions used to secure messages. These algorithms fall into two camps: restricted and open.

Restricted Algorithms

Restricted algorithms are those created by a person or an organization and are not available to the general public. For example, this could apply to a compiled COM server from TrustUs.com, which won't give you the source code nor give you any information as to how its algorithms work.

Open Algorithms

Open algorithms are published and are available to anyone for analysis. This could take the form of an algorithm found on VerifyUs.com, where you can download white papers that document the algorithm along with a compiled

Eiffel .NET Web service and its corresponding source code that encrypts and decrypts files for you based on the algorithm.

Experience has shown that you should always go with the open algorithm. Even if it turns out that an open algorithm is not as secure as a restricted one, you as a customer of the two algorithms have no way to verify that the restricted one is better (although if the open algorithm is weak, I'd consider finding another one). And, more often than not, restricted algorithms are hacked anyway by disassembling executables, so their "security by obscurity" methodology is ineffective at best. Determining if an algorithm can withstand attacks takes lengthy analysis and testing by many qualified professionals, so it's beneficial to use an open algorithm. You can easily find out if someone has found a gaping hole in the algorithm or if it is secure.

Next, let's go over the basic terms you'll need to understand to get the most out of subsequent chapters.

Basic Terminology

This section discusses the following terms:

- Plaintext

- Ciphertext

- Hashes

- Keys

- Symmetric algorithms

- Asymmetric algorithms

- Comparison of key types

- Random number generation

I'll begin with plaintext and ciphertext.

Plaintext and Ciphertext

Plaintext describes the state of a message that can be easily read or used by any-one or anything. This can be a text file or an executable. To alter the file such that it cannot be easily read by anyone, you use an *encryption* algorithm to turn the plaintext into *ciphertext*. The encryption algorithm is simply a mathematical function that takes a message's value and from it computes another value (the ciphertext). The hope is that the resulting ciphertext cannot be converted back into the original value easily. To get the file back to a usable form, you use a *decryption* algorithm. Figure 1-1 illustrates this process.

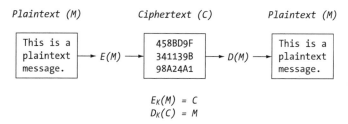

$$E_K(M) = C$$
$$D_K(C) = M$$

Figure 1-1. Encryption and decryption

The plaintext message is defined as M, and the ciphertext is C. In both situations, a function E (encryption) or D (decryption) operates on M or C, respectively, and produces the desired output.

A simple encryption algorithm that is widely known is Caesar's cipher. This takes each letter of the English alphabet and maps it to another letter. For example, one mapping would shift letters over a certain number of spaces. Therefore, a message such as "hello reader" could be changed to "ifmmp sfbefs," where each letter is shifted one letter in the cipher text.[1]

NOTE *Some books use the words* encipher *and* decipher *for* encryption *and* decryption, *respectively. I'll also use the word* ciphering *to describe the general process of changing a message from one form to another (this can be either the encryption or decryption process).*

Let's start looking at a number of encryption algorithms, beginning with hash algorithms.

---

1. This algorithm is extremely easy to break, so I wouldn't suggest using it to encrypt sensitive corporate documents.

Hashes

Hashes are used to create a unique, compact value for a message. The message, or *pre-image*, is used as input to the hash algorithm. When the algorithm is complete, you get a *hash value* on the other end, which is the unique value for the pre-image. The output of the hash is fixed-size for any input value. Figure 1-2 demonstrates how this works.

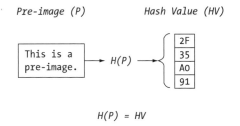

$$H(P) = HV$$

Figure 1-2. Creating a hash

Here H(P) stands for the hash algorithm that operates on the pre-image P. In this case, H will always produce a hash value (HV) 4 bytes in size. The format of the hash value is not all that important: all you care about is that the value is unique for a given pre-image. Hashes are useful when data only needs to be encrypted. Hash functions are usually very fast, and are *asymmetric*. This means that you can take a pre-image and create a hash value, but you can't take the hash value and obtain the same pre-image (at least not easily).

One common application of hashes is in storing passwords in databases. Instead of storing "somePassword", an application creates a hash of that pre-image and stores the hash value for the password. Of course, the client doesn't know (or need to know) that you've done this—he or she just enters "somePassword" and expects to be given access. However, you don't send "somePassword" over the wire. Instead, you hash this value and send it to the server, as shown in Figure 1-3, so that if someone broke into your database and grabbed your passwords, they would be worthless.[2]

---

2.   Dan Appleman wrote an article published in the January 2001 issue of *VBPJ* called "Make Passwords Secure with the Crypto API," which talks about password security in more detail. Please visit http://www.devx.com/premier/mgznarch/vbpj/2001/01jan01/da0101/da0101.asp for more information.

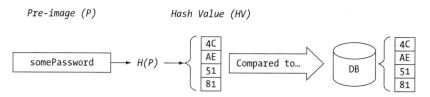

Figure 1-3. Using a hash to transmit a password

Generally speaking, creating a hash value for a pre-image is extremely easy. However, finding out the pre-image given a hash value is statistically impossible (although there's always the chance you may stumble across it via a dictionary attack—a term I'll define shortly).

Finally, you can use *salt* to add some extra data to your pre-image. Salt is random data and doesn't have any relationship to the pre-image. Its primary purpose is to act as a countermeasure against a *dictionary attack* with stored hashed passwords. A dictionary attack occurs when a hacker[3] takes a long list of common passwords, hashes their values, and compares the hash values to the ones found in a compromised database.

However, if some salt is added to the pre-image before hashing, as Figure 1-4 illustrates, the hacker now needs to add every possible salt combination to the list of passwords.

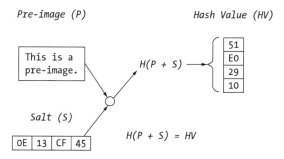

Figure 1-4. Hashing data with a random salt value

---

3. The word *hacker* has different definitions, depending on whom you talk to. I use the term to mean anyone who is trying to decrypt messages not intended for him or her.

NOTE *The addition of salt to a pre-image only protects against server compromises, as the salt value needs to be used whenever the password is hashed. If the client machine is compromised, the salt value can be discovered, but if this compromise occurs, using salt is the least of the worries for that machine's user.*

Now that you've seen how hashes work, let's investigate how keys are used in encryption algorithms.

Keys

One essential part to encryption algorithms is the *key*. Think of this just as you would a key to a safe. You can put messages into a safe, but if your enemies don't have the key or a copy of it, reading the message is a lot harder for them. In encryption algorithms, the key is used to alter the message during the encryption process, as Figure 1-5 demonstrates.

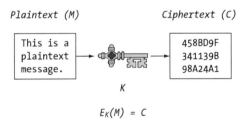

Plaintext (M)   Ciphertext (C)

$E_K(M) = C$

Figure 1-5. Encrypting data with a key

The key value (K) is used during the encryption process to produce C. The beauty in using keys is that the key can change, but the underlying algorithm remains the same. Therefore, I can use E with my key K_1 to encrypt M, which produces C_1. If you use your own key, your ciphertext will be different from mine. Granted, the analogy to a physical safe breaks down somewhat because a key doesn't (easily) change on a safe. That's even more advantageous for you, because you don't have to tear out the key assembly (or encryption algorithm, if you will) every time you want to encrypt a message with a different key. You simply create a new key and "lock" the message.

Data Formatting

Generally, when you work with keys in encryption algorithms you'll use one of the two following types of keys with the plaintext data:

- Stream ciphers

- Block ciphers

Let's take a look at each of these key types.

Stream Ciphers

Stream ciphers can take any M of any size, regardless of its length. As is seen in Figure 1-6, a stream cipher can be 5 bytes the first time, 3 bytes the next time, and 1 byte the third time.

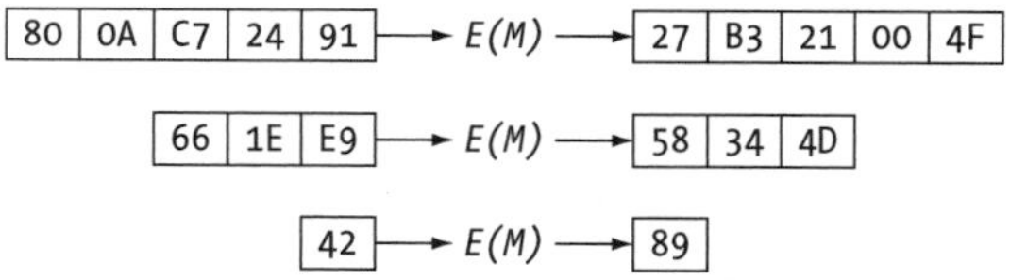

Figure 1-6. Encrypting data with a stream cipher

Ciphers that are stream based are useful when the data you need to encrypt is being received in random-sized chunks.

Block Ciphers

A *block cipher* only allows data to come in a size that is a multiple of some number. For example, if a cipher's block size was 2 bytes, both a 2-byte and a 4-byte buffer would be legal, but a 5-byte buffer would need to be padded. Figure 1-7 shows how a misaligned buffer is padded with information.

The last block is padded with a value of zero (00) before it's given to E. Once C is decrypted, though, that last byte needs to be discarded to produce the original M. [4]

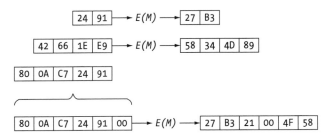

Figure 1-7. Padding input streams for block ciphers

Key Modes

There are different ways to cipher data via keys. In this section I'll describe how the following five most common modes work:

- Electronic code book (ECB)

- Cipher block chaining (CBC)

- Cipher feedback mode (CFB)

- Output feedback (OFB)

- Cipher text stealing (CTS)

Electronic Code Book

Electronic code book (ECB), shown in Figure 1-8, is used for block ciphers and simply takes the given blocks of data and ciphers each one individually.

The message M is broken up into discreet blocks such that the sizes of the blocks match the desired block length of E. Next, each block is encrypted via E, and then the blocks are combined in sequence to create C.

---

4. I'll cover different modes in the next chapter.

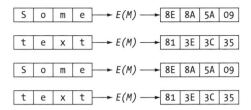

Figure 1-8. Electronic code book mode

This is computationally the easiest of the modes, but it has its problems. Note that when you use this method, you run the risk of having repeating blocks of data in the output of the cipher. As you can see in Figure 1-8, the message "Sometext" repeats itself, and their corresponding cipher blocks repeat as well. Although the process is not trivial, this information can be used to determine valuable pieces of the plaintext. Although ECB is a mode that is usually supported in most cryptographic libraries (of which .NET is no exception), I would not recommend using this mode unless you need to decrypt information from a legacy process that cannot easily be changed.

Cipher Block Chaining

Cipher block chaining (CBC) is similar to ECB, but with the addition of feedback. It takes the results from the previous cipher operation and uses these results as information for the next round of data ciphering, as illustrated in Figure 1-9.

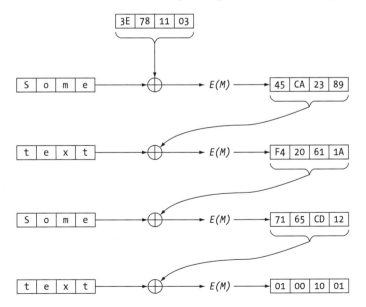

Figure 1-9. Cipher block chaining

The previous cipher block value is XORed (which is represented by the cross-hair symbol) with the current block value. This result is then encrypted to give the next cipher block, and the process is repeated until the message is encrypted. You may have noticed that the first block is XORed with a random piece of information. This is known as the *initialization vector*, or IV, and it's used to prevent the output from being the same for a given file.

With ECB, two plaintext blocks with the same information will always yield the same encryption result. In CBC, that is not the case unless the same exact information preceded the blocks. For example, if you had two files, A.TXT and B.TXT, that were both 64 bytes in length, but their first 32 bytes were the same, the encrypted output using CBC mode would be the same for the first 32 bytes. Using an IV value prevents these duplications from happening. Simply set the IV to a different value every time you encrypt the message. Whoever decrypts the message will need this value, but the IV value is not related to the message itself; it's only needed to encrypt and decrypt that message and therefore can be viewed by anyone.

NOTE *The reason the IV can be "in the clear" is that each cipherblock is conceptually just another IV block. Even if a hacker has the IV value along with the ciphertext, it doesn't help him or her in determining what the message is. Note that if you don't explicitly set the IV value, the initial block will just be a bunch of zeros, so in effect the IV is always known.*

Cipher Feedback Mode

Cipher feedback mode (CFB) is almost identical to CBC, except that the previous cipher block is encrypted first, then it is XORed with the current block value. Figure 1-10 depicts this process.

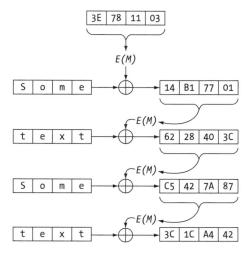

Figure 1-10. Cipher feedback mode

CFB uses the IV to initialize the first cipher block. Note that if you don't set the IV, the same plaintext will always produce the same output. By not changing the IV value, a hacker can figure out the message, so always use a different IV value.[5]

Output Feedback

Output feedback (OFB) is a stream-based mode that continually encrypts the initial seed value, and XORs that value with the plaintext. Figure 1-11 illustrates this process.

---

5.   The process by which this recovery occurs is not trivial, but it can happen.

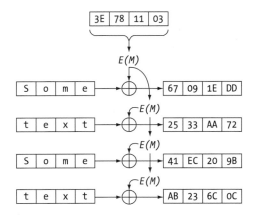

Figure 1-11. Output feedback

The encryption algorithm is never directly performed on the original message. It is only done on the seed value.

Cipher Text Stealing

Cipher text stealing (CTS) is virtually identical to CBC; however, the ciphertext produced by CTS is the same size as the plaintext. Figure 1-12 shows this process.

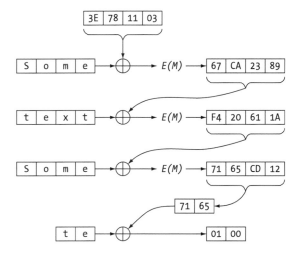

Figure 1-12. Cipher text stealing

When the last block is reached in the plaintext, the leftmost bits of the previous encrypted block are XORed with the remaining plaintext bytes.

Symmetric Algorithms

A symmetric key algorithm uses the same key to encrypt and decrypt a message as Figure 1-13 shows.

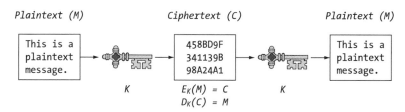

Figure 1-13. Using symmetric keys

This is different from what you saw with a hash algorithm, as the key K can be used to both encrypt M and decrypt C.

If you encrypt a message with a symmetric key, you need to ensure to the best of your abilities that no one can copy your key value. If an untrusted party copies the key value, the message is compromised, as anyone can read the contents simply by decrypting the ciphertext.

Asymmetric Algorithms

With symmetric algorithms, the same key is used for encryption and decryption. Asymmetric key-based algorithms consist of two keys that are generated by an algorithm to handle the encryption and decryption. One key is chosen to be the *private key;* the other is picked as the *public key.* A private key is similar to a symmetric key in that you should never disclose it to anyone, but a public key can be published anywhere. It doesn't matter which key is chosen to be the public or private key, but once the decision is made and you start encrypting messages with the key configuration, you can't change it (you'll see why in a moment).

To encrypt a message using an asymmetric algorithm, you use the private key. To decrypt the message, you use the public key. Figure 1-14 shows how this process works.

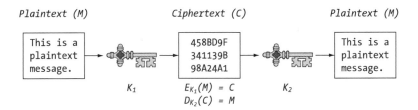

Figure 1-14. Using asymmetric keys

As the formulas show, the private key is used to encrypt M, and the public key decrypts C. Now you can see why public/private key-based cryptographic algorithms are called asymmetric. Once you've encrypted your message, you can't decrypt it with the same key.

This may sound like a disadvantage at first, but asymmetric keys are a godsend to securing systems. For example, I can create a key pair, and send the public key to my friend Scott. Scott can take my public key and encrypt a message that contains secrets about a revolutionary garbage collection algorithm he's been working on. Once he's encrypted the message, the only person who can decrypt the message is the owner of the private key (or someone who has a copy of it). As long as my private key isn't compromised (and this is a big "if"), the message is secure.

Comparing Key Types

Due to the underlying mathematics, encrypting a message with a symmetric key is usually much faster than encrypting a message with the asymmetric private key. However, using a symmetric key to share files with another party is harder than using a public/private key pair. With a symmetric key, you have to find a way to transmit the key to the party in a secure fashion. With a public/private key pair, the only key transmitted is the public key, which is something you want to do. In either case, the owner of the key(s) must ensure that either the symmetric key or his or her private key is not compromised.

Because of the strengths and weaknesses of the key types, a combination of the two algorithms is usually applied to send encrypted messages between two parties. Here's how it works. I create a symmetric key (J_s), and encrypt J_s with Scott's public key (S_{pu}). I send this result to Scott, who decrypts the message with his private key (S_{pr}). This is all laid out in Figure 1-15.

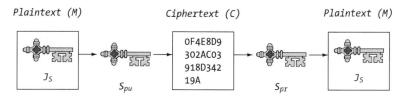

Figure 1-15. Combining symmetric and asymmetric algorithms

Because Scott is (supposedly) the only one who can decrypt the message, he now has a copy of J_s. From this point on, the public/private key pair drops out of the picture, and we use J_s to encrypt and decrypt our messages. Figure 1-16 shows this process.

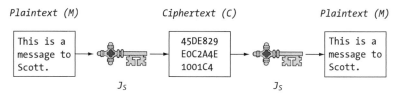

Figure 1-16. Using a symmetric key for message exchange

The beauty of this approach is that you only take the asymmetric encryption/decryption hit once. After that, you can use the faster symmetric key.

If someone intercepted a message after the session key was exchanged, all that person could do is try and break the algorithm itself.[6] This is actually an example of a *key exchange protocol* (I'll cover more protocols and how .NET relates to them in Chapter 2). There are vulnerabilities to such a protocol, and countermeasures and counter-countermeasures exist that can be used by both the friendly and non-friendly parties. I'll cover just how secure you can make your computer systems later on in this chapter in the "Crytography versus Security" section.

Before you start applying encryption algorithms to real-world scenarios, you need to address how random number generation is used in cryptography.

---

6. This is theoretically doable in the sense that you could write a program to brute-force the value of the private key, but unless you're extremely lucky you probably won't stumble across the value for a very long time.

Understanding Random Number Generators

At first glance, you may not see the relationship between cryptography and random numbers. However, *random number generators* (RNGs)—algorithms that generate a sequence of random numbers—are essential to lowering the vulnerability of a cryptographic algorithm. Let's see why.

Recall the original discussion about IVs. Their value was critical in some cipher modes to prevent the exact reproduction of an output given the same input. The problem is you need to make the IV value "random" enough such that a hacker cannot detect some kind of pattern in the IV values. Remember, IVs are not encrypted. If you use the same IV value on every cipher attempt, a hacker can use that information to make his or her attack process easier. So the trick is to make sure your IV is random.

Unfortunately, creating a random sequence on a computer is very difficult. Modern programming languages will usually have some embedded RNG, but the "randomness" is very poor. For example, Visual Basic's RNG will eventually cycle after 16 million calls. That may sound like a lot, but if a hacker knows you're using Visual Basic's RNG to fill in the IV, it makes his or her job much easier.

What you end up using is a pseudo-RNG, or PRNG. The reason these algorithms have the "pseudo" word attached is that they are not truly random. They will eventually cycle, but their cycle values are much larger than the ones you'll find in most programming languages. To be totally secure, you should use a "real" RNG. That is, the sequence should be generated off of some naturally occurring event, like the time between ticks on a Geiger counter. This is a sequence that cannot be repeated (but it's unlikely that most people have a Geiger counter connected to their computers).

NOTE *If you need some convincing that creating random seed values and having a cryptographically secure RNG is a good thing, check out* http://www-4.ibm.com/software/developer/library/playing/. *This Web page features a very good discussion on how an online poker program was hacked because the developers used a language-based RNG, which was vulnerable to attack, and how the original version of SSL was compromised.*

Plus, you also have to be concerned about the seed value for the PRNG. PRNGs will take a seed value to start a sequence generation. However, if your seed value is one that can be reverse-engineered with ease, it doesn't matter how long the cycle of your PRNG is; once the seed value is chosen, you'll always get the same generated sequence. Note that the .NET Framework provides you with PRNGs that are more secure than the ones found in standard language libraries.

Now that you understand the essential terminology, let's move on to some related cryptography concepts, starting with creating digital signatures.

Creating Digital Signatures

How many times have you gone to a public restaurant, and paid for the meal with a credit card? If you have, you probably were asked to sign the receipt, and your signature was then compared to the signature on the back of the card by the waiter or waitress (or at least it should have been). Although such a verification process is very insecure (handwritten signatures are easy to forge), signatures are currently used as one method of verification.

Such a signature can also be used in the digital world. Let's say I have finished my white paper on my new garbage collection algorithm. I want to publish it on my Web site, but I would like to have some way to prove it was me who created the paper. What I can do is create a hash value of the document. Next, I encrypt the hash value with my private key (you'll see why this is important in

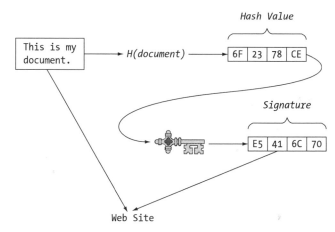

Figure 1-17. Creating a digital signature

a moment). I then publish both the paper and the encrypted hash value on my Web site, as Figure 1-17 illustrates.

Here's why this works. Someone can easily create a hash value of my document and decrypt the encrypted hash value with my public key. If they match, the signature is valid. Furthermore, no one can re-create my signature, as no one has a copy of my private key. Essentially, my private key signs the document; the hashing bit is there to speed up the process.

Of course, someone could easily steal my signature and document, put it on their Web site, and claim that the signature is theirs. The problem is that they can't re-create the signature, because they don't have my private key to encrypt the hash value. They can easily copy the signature, but they can't reproduce it.

You'll see how .NET makes digital signing an easy endeavor in the following chapter. Next, let's look at how asymmetric keys can be used as a trust-building mechanism for someone's identity.

Certificates Defined

My public key
+ CA signature (private key signed Hash)

Certificates are primarily used in secure communication to ensure that the identities at the endpoints of the communication are who they say they are. If I want someone to send a secure message to me, I can publish my public key value on my Web page, and anyone can then send me a message, secure in the knowledge that only I will be able to decrypt the message.

But how do people who want to send me a message really know that I'm the one who published the public key? Maybe someone has hacked into my Web site and has published a different public key. These people have no idea that the published key really isn't mine, so they send me, say, their garbage collection algorithm. However, they've actually encrypted a message that the hacker can decrypt, not me. From their perspective, they don't know the difference.

The issue comes down to knowing with certainty (or at least a high degree of certainty) the identity of the publisher of the key. Enter certificates. Certificates are a way to verify who has published a key. For example, I can submit my public key to a certificate authority (CA) and some other private, personal information that the CA has determined to be sufficient to prove who I am. The CA then publishes my key plus some of the personal information in a digital certificate that anyone can access and use. The CA also hashes the certificate and signs the hash with its private key, which is included as part of the certificate. This signature proves that the CA is the issuer of the certificate.

Now, there's nothing special about a certificate. Anyone can create a certificate for anyone else. The issue here is that both parties must trust the CA. If I used a CA that was notorious for leaking confidential information, it would not be wise for anyone to use my keys certified by such a company. Furthermore, if I used a CA that had a very good reputation in the industry for being ethical and highly secure, but Scott didn't trust that CA, we couldn't communicate using any keys certified by that CA.

Cryptography versus Security

When someone mentions the word *cryptography*, the word *security* is usually close behind in one's thoughts. This shouldn't surprise anyone, as cryptography is essential to having a secure system. However, simply encrypting a file on your workstation does *not* guarantee in any way that the file is secure. Some people equate encrypting messages with a bulletproof, secure system. This is not the case. Designing a system to encrypt files is much easier than ensuring that unintended parties cannot decrypt the files. Let's take a look at why the terms are related, but not synonymous.

Cryptography Is Mathematics

Consider a case where I need to exchange a message with Scott. I start by creating a 32,678 bit public/private key pair via the Unbreakable Key Algorithm (UKA).[7] I have the public key certified by Confirmation Certificates, Inc. (CCI). So far, so good—I'm certifying my public key based on an algorithm that is known to be very secure. Scott does the same thing, and we begin to exchange sensitive information.

But there's a problem. Andrew has kidnapped Scott, and Andrew is the one that I'm actually communicating with. However, I have no idea that the kidnapping has occurred—I still think it's Scott on the other end of the line.

So how do I find out if it's Scott on the other end? The fact that Scott has a certificate means nothing, as Andrew is the one in control, not Scott. I could call Scott, but Andrew may force Scott to say he's okay and that he's the one receiving and transmitting information. Maybe, though, Scott and I have set up a secret message between us to use in verbal conversation to let the other know that his identity is compromised.

This isn't as weird as it may sound—this extra code is used in home security systems. For example, if you accidentally trip the system, you need to call the home base with a disabling code so they know it was an accident, thereby preventing an unnecessary police visit. However, if a robber broke into your house and forced you to call the home base to disable the security system, you can use a "security-alert" code. From your end, it sounds like you're giving a disabling code to the home base. But the home base knows that you're giving a code that really means, "Help me!" This may give the authorities enough time to come and arrest the robber and hopefully save your life. The problem is, even if Scott and I have an agreed-upon warning message, how do we securely set up such a message in the first place? We're back to square one.

---

7. Note that all of the algorithms and companies in this section are fictitious; any similiarities to real companies or algorithms are purely coincidental.

Note that everything is working perfectly from a mathematical standpoint. Nothing has crashed, and no data has been lost. The problem is that we need a secure communication link between us where we know, beyond a shadow of a doubt, that we are both at each end of the conversation and no one is listening. But how can we do that?

Security Is Trust

About this time, you may think I might be paranoid, but this scenario brings up a very interesting issue in creating systems that are secure. The core issue that differentiates cryptography and security is trust. No matter how many layers are added between two parties, ultimately there must be trust between the two such that the following conditions can be believed:

- The person at the other end is who they say they are.

- No one has compromised the communications.

At some point, I have to trust that it's really Scott on the other end, or I either choose to send a message to an untrusted source and/or channel or I don't send the message at all. To verify such a situation may be easy or hard. The need to verify the recipient also varies—it depends on what you're sending. For example, I may want to set up a friendly golf match between Scott and me via e-mail. In this case, I probably won't send any messages with any encryption, because I really don't care if anyone knows that Scott and I want to play golf. Therefore, I simply e-mail Scott at his well-known e-mail address and I'm done. The level of security is basically none in this example. However, sending highly classified garbage collection algorithm information to Scott needs a much higher level of security.

Also, not only do we need to trust the communication channels and the parties involved in the communication, we also need time. Each cryptographic algorithm you'll find is usually based on some mathematical problem that is difficult to solve. Although the odds are against the hacker, he or she may stumble across the right values purely by accident, compromising your key. Also, if someone ever discovers a way to find two prime values for a given number, or find the pre-image given a hash value, in a computationally relative efficient manner, the algorithm is worthless. You're basically buying time when you encrypt a message. Usually, the larger the key, the larger the time window in which you message will stay secure. However, don't be lulled into thinking that, because a hacker would need 280 years to decrypt your message, the message is secure for all time. Computers get faster all the time. The knowledge base of mathematics grows every day. Your message may not be as secure in 20 years as it is today, and if the message contains sensitive information that is relevant in 20 years, that may be an issue of concern.

NOTE *You don't need a supercomputer to break cipher algorithms either. Distributed computing that uses unused CPU cycles on multiple workstations is becoming very popular to solve difficult tasks in a cost-effective manner. It's also used to break commercial cipher algorithms. See* `http://www.distributed.net/` *for more information on how the RC5 and DES algorithms are being cracked by thousands of workstations.*

Determining Security

Different people have different explanations of a "secure" system. However, after mulling over the term for a while, I came up with the following definition that I think sums it up in a concise manner: *security* is allowing the right entities to access the right information from the right resources.

In practice, operation systems will usually define the entities as users or principals, and verifying the sources can be done via the use of certificates. Unlike the Windows programming days of old, .NET changes the way code is run from a security standpoint. Users of the code need the correct permissions to run the code, but they can also verify that the code comes from a trusted source and they can limit the access of the code. The .NET security model is an improvement, but it's also different—I'll cover the security model and all of its aspects throughout this book.

Let's break this definition down a bit.

The Right Entities

"The right entities" vary from system to system, but they're whatever have been defined as being entities that can access other entities. An entity could be a person logging in to a Windows XP box, or it could be the computer itself running a task that interacts with a bunch of Web services, even if nobody is logged on. Remember, the entity doesn't have to be human; all it needs to know are the rules of the system to gain access to desired information.

The Right Information

If I log on to my bank's Web site, I hope that they've set things up on their end such that they don't allow anyone to surf to the site and casually use my checking account. Also, I don't want to visit a site and have it download a program that searches my computer for personal information. Only I should see my bank information, and only I should determine who can see what on my computer.

The Right Resources

Another hope that I have is when I visit my bank's site, it hasn't been compromised or someone isn't intercepting the communication data. I should be able to verify to a certain degree of comfort that when I access a resource, it is the expected resource—not one that is masquerading as the intended provider of information. As you saw, that can be difficult to do, and the level of trust can vary depending on what the entities are communicating about.

Summary

In this chapter, I covered the following topics:

- Terminology that defines cryptography

- Hashes and keys, and the different kinds of keys available

- Modes used during a cipher operation

- Digital signatures and certificates

- Cryptography versus security

In the next chapter, I'll dive into the `System.Security.Cryptography` namespace and demonstrate how cryptography is handled in .NET.

CHAPTER 2

Using the .NET Cryptography Classes

THIS CHAPTER WILL GO OVER the classes available in .NET that deal with cryptography. I'll cover how the classes are designed and some general rules to follow when using them. Then I'll break the discussion into different aspects of cryptography, such as hashes, keys, and certificates. Finally, I'll show you a sample application that performs encryption on object serialization streams.

Working with the System.Security.Cryptography Namespace

First off, let's take a quick look at the System.Security.Cryptography namespace, which I'll simply refer to as the Cryptography namespace from this point on. As with most of the .NET namespaces, there are a lot of members to take in at first glance. For example, this namespace has its stream classes (CryptoStream), abstract hash classes (HashAlgorithm), and symmetric algorithms (RijndaelManaged), among others. The classes were designed to make it easy for the developer to refer to an object at runtime with considerable flexibility. This design allows you to plug in different cryptographic implementations as you see fit. Furthermore, it allows you to add new implementations that either you create or other companies provide. You'll see throughout this chapter how the various classes work, starting with hash-based classes in the next section.

Cryptographic Exceptions

As you probably know, whenever you code, there's always the chance something can go wrong. .NET defines two exception classes for Cryptography: CryptographicException and CryptographicUnexpectedOperationException, with the second exception inheriting from the first exception. Unfortunately, their meanings are pretty generic when you review the software development kit (SDK). CryptographicException occurs when a processing error happens, and CryptographicUnexpectedOperationException is raised when an unexpected error occurs. Like I said, they're not that helpful, but at least you know that they can occur, so you should always include exception handling where appropriate. I'll demonstrate exception handling in the next sections.

Understanding Hash-Based Classes

HashAlgorithm is an abstract class that defines the methods that all hash algorithms should implement; it also inherits from ICryptoTransform (remember this inheritance relationship—it's important when I discuss cryptographic streaming, later in this chapter). So far, .NET has a number of abstract classes that extend the HashAlgorithm abstract class, such as KeyedHashAlgorithm, MD5 (Message Digest 5), and SHA1 (Secure Hash Algorithm-1). The main difference between SHA1 and MD5 is the hash size—MD5 produces hash values of 128 bits in length, whereas SHA1 can produce larger hash values (160 bits and higher), which makes it more resistant to brute-force attacks. Note that there are four different SHA-based abstract classes—SHA1, SHA256, SHA384, and SHA512. For the last three classes, the number defines the size in bits of the hash value; SHA1 will always produce a hash value 160 bits in length.

KeyedHashAlgorithm-based implementations work just like other hash algorithms except they use a key during the hashing process.[1] These abstract classes have corresponding concrete classes—an architecture decision that gives type distinction to each algorithm type, yet requires that at least one class exists that fully implements that abstract type. Let's spend a moment on these derived classes.

 CROSS-REFERENCE   *See Chapter 1 for a discussion of hash algorithms.*

If you look at SHA1, you'll notice that .NET defines two subclasses: SHA1CryptoServiceProvider and SHA1Managed (the other three SHA-based classes only have managed subclasses). You'll see the same naming scenario for the other derived classes (other than KeyedHashAlgorithm). What's the difference between the two? The names tell the story. If the class contains the "CryptoServiceProvider" string, it uses the classic Windows cryptographic service

---

1.   I'll give you a brief summary of the algorithms that are implemented in Cryptography in each section; I encourage the reader who desires more technical information to obtain a copy of Bruce Schneier's book, *Applied Cryptography* (John Wiley & Sons, Inc., 1996). It contains detailed descriptions of all the algorithms mentioned in this chapter.

providers, or CSPs. The "Managed" classes do all their operations within the class itself. In other words, CSP-dependent types must use unmanaged P/Invoke calls to the CryptoAPI to perform the cryptographic operation, whereas a managed type's code is completely within the safe realm of the .NET world. Therefore, a CSP-dependent type requires that the CryptoAPI libraries be on the same machine. For the first release of .NET, this shouldn't be a problem, as virtually all of the machines that run .NET will be Windows-based. However, as .NET is ported to other operation systems, this dependency may not be present, which would require the use of a managed type.

Other than the KeyedHashAlgorithm class (which adds the Key property), none of the HashAlgorithm subclasses add any new methods to HashAlgorithm. Therefore, I'd recommend binding either this interface or one of its descendants to a concrete class at construction as shown here:

```
HashAlgorithm hash = new SHA1Managed();
```

However, all of the direct subclasses of HashAlgorithm overload the Create() method, which you can use to create a class that implements a specific hashing algorithm. Here's an example:

```
try
{
    hash = SHA1.Create("SHA");
}
catch(CryptographicUnexpectedOperationException ce) {}
```

If you know that you're always going to create a specific object type, then I recommend you use the first technique. The second technique is useful if you need to perform a number of hashing operations using different implementations, because you can leverage the factory-building characteristic of Create() to return the correct instance for you.

> **NOTE** *One other potential benefit to this approach is that in future versions of .NET, "SHA1" may return a* SHA1Managed *implementation instead of a* SHA1CryptoServiceProvider *implementation, but you wouldn't care. Microsoft can eventually move the entire* Cryptography *implementation to managed space, but you would never know it, because you're simply asking for an implementation by name.*

Create() can raise a CryptographicUnexpectedOperationException exception if the Name argument is incorrect. You can also call the no-argument Create() method, which will create the default HashAlgorithm-based object. But what's the default object, and how does .NET determine if the given name is incorrect, you may ask? The answer lies in two places: CryptoConfig and machine.config.

CryptoConfig

The first place where the cryptography classes look for simple name to class name mappings is in the CryptoConfig class. This class has three static methods, but here you're interested in the overloaded CreateFromName(). This method takes a simple name and creates an instance of the class that's mapped to that name. The SDK lists the mappings—it's quite long so I won't repeat it here, but I encourage you to look up the mappings to familiarize yourself with them.[2]

The mappings only work if the object that you're calling the Create() method on is built on the base type of the algorithm you want. For example, if you ran the following code snippet:

```
HashAlgorithm hash = HashAlgorithm.Create("SHA384");
```

hash would refer to a SHA384Managed object. This next code line would also work:

```
HashAlgorithm hash = SHA384.Create("SHA384");
```

As the SHA384 class is the base of SHA384Managed, the Create() call is successful. However, if you do this:

```
HashAlgorithm hash = SHA1.Create("SHA384");
```

you would get an InvalidCastException. Since SHA1 is not the base class for SHA384Managed, this exception makes sense, but make sure that when you call Create() you're careful not to create a casting error.

---

2. Specifically, they're listed in the .NET SDK at ms-help://MS.NETFrameworkSDK/cpref/html/frlrfsystemsecuritycryptographyhashalgorithmclasscreatetopic2.htm—it's the documentation for HashAlgorithm's Create(string) method.

machine.config

You can also override the default mappings by specifying XML elements in the machine-wide configuration file, machine.config. This is an XML file that contains a lot of CLR configuration information, but in this case you're interested in how you can override the defaults if necessary. If you open up machine.config (which you can find in %runtime install path%\Config), look for the root element, <configuration>. Once you find it, you can add the following elements to <configuration>:

```
<?xml version="1.0" encoding="UTF-8" ?>

<configuration>
    <mscorlib>
        <cryptographySettings>
            <cryptoNameMapping>
                <cryptoClasses>
                </cryptoClasses>
            </cryptoNameMapping>
        </cryptographySettings>
    </mscorlib>
    <!-- other config elements go here -->
</configuration>
```

The <cryptoClasses> element will contain <cryptoClass> elements that you want to map to. Once you've finished defining the <cryptoClass> elements, you can refer to these elements in <nameEntry> elements, which either override current simple name to class name mappings in CryptoConfig, or add new mappings.

Let's go through the example in Listing 2-1 to demonstrate how this works. I'll add one mapping that overrides the simple name "SHA1" and creates a new mapping to the SHA512Managed class with a simple name of "ApressSHA".

Listing 2-1. New Cryptographic Algorithm Mappings

```
<?xml version="1.0" encoding="UTF-8" ?>

<configuration>
    <mscorlib>
        <cryptographySettings>
            <cryptoNameMapping>
                <cryptoClasses>
```

```
                        <cryptoClass
                        sha1Override="System.Security.Cryptography.SHA1Managed,
                        mscorlib, Version=1.0.3705.209,
                        Culture=neutral, PublicKey=b77a5c561934e089"/>
                        <cryptoClass
                        newApress="System.Security.Cryptography.SHA512Managed,
                        mscorlib, Version=1.0.3705.209,
                        Culture=neutral, PublicKey=b77a5c561934e089"/>
                </cryptoClasses>
                <nameEntry name="SHA1" class="sha1Override"/>
                <nameEntry name="ApressSHA" class="newApress"/>
        </cryptoNameMapping>
      </cryptographySettings>
    </mscorlib>
    <!-- other config elements go here -->
</configuration>
```

As you can see, the two `<cryptoClass>` elements contain all of the class information to create an object of that type. The only attribute of the element is used in the `<nameEntry>` elements to refer to the class description. If you add these elements to the configuration file, the following code will return a SHA512Managed object:

```
HashAlgorithm hash = (HashAlgorithm)CryptoConfig.CreateFromName("ApressSHA");
```

while this code snippet will now get a SHA1Managed object, rather than the SHA1CryptoServiceProvider:

```
HashAlgorithm hash = (HashAlgorithm)CryptoConfig.CreateFromName("SHA1");
```

You don't have to use `CryptoConfig` to get the new mappings. Any `Create()` call from any `Cryptography` class resolves to a `CreateFromName()` call, so the following code works as expected:

```
HashAlgorithm hash = HashAlgorithm.Create("ApressSHA");
```

Now if you go on to creating your own `HashAlgorithm` implementation, you know how you can make `Create()` return your objects the .NET way.

It's unlikely that the default mappings in `CryptoConfig` will be overridden in machine.config. Just remember that the mappings can be altered, so don't rely on passing in "SHA" to HashAlgorithm's `Create()` method to get a `SHA1CryptoServiceProvider` instance.

SOURCE CODE *The CryptoConfigTest project in the Chapter2 subdirectory demonstrates the XML mappings in action. I have included a text file called machine.config additions.txt in this project that contains the XML mappings discussed in the preceding text so you can copy and paste the correct XML into machine.config.*

Now that you know how to create hash objects, I'll show you how to make them work.

Hash Values

To set up the hash, you pass a byte array to the `ComputeHash()` method, like so:

```
byte[] preImage = {32, 90, 85, 46, 120, 44, 2, 202};
byte[] hashValue = hash.ComputeHash (preImage);
```

`hashValue` will contain the hash value of `preImage` when `ComputeHash()` is finished.[3]

However, before continuing with other `Cryptography` classes, notice that the `HashAlgorithm`-based object will only take data in a byte array or a `Stream` object. This complicates matters a little, especially if you're trying to hash an array of `longs` or a `String` variable. In both cases, the conversions aren't always obvious.

Let's look at how you would extract a byte array out of a `String` variable:

```
String originalPreImage = "my pre-image";
byte[] preImage = Encoding.Unicode.GetBytes(originalPreImage);
```

My original hope was that the `String` class would have a method to get its representation in a byte array. Unfortunately, the closest I could get was `ToCharArray()`, but `HashAlgorithm` won't take that. Therefore, I used the `Encoding` class (which is in the `System.Text` namespace) to get a byte array for a `String`. However, the issue isn't resolved just yet. You'll note that there are more encoders than just `Unicode`. There's `UTF7`, and `ASCII`, to name a few. This is important, as the byte array values will differ, which will lead to different hash values. If you want

---

3. If you've done CryptoAPI-based programming before, I hope you're gaining an appreciation for how easy it is to code in .NET.

to use a `Stream` object, you still have byte array issues if your data lives in a `String`:

```
String preImage = "Some Pre-Image.";
Stream preImageStream = new MemoryStream();
byte[] preImageB = Encoding.Unicode.GetBytes(preImage);
preImageStream.Write(preImageB, 0, preImageB.Length);
byte[] res = hash.ComputeHash(preImageStream);
```

You'll see in the next section how to use streams in .NET to simplify encryption.

Cryptographic Streaming

As most of the other `Cryptography` classes support streaming, I thought I'd cover how it's done with hashes first as you should be comfortable with creating hash values by this point. *Streaming* is nothing more than a way to read and write information in either a synchronous ("call-and-wait") or asynchronous ("fire-and-forget") manner. With cryptographic operations, you know that the process can take some time, depending on the size of the message and/or the key. Therefore, most of the `Cryptography` classes provide a way to stream the results of their operations.

The `CryptoStream` class derives from the `Stream` class in the `System.IO` namespace, so it has all of the methods you'd expect from a `Stream`: `Read()`, `Write()`, and so on. Also, wherever you run into a `Stream` object, you can safely substitute `CryptoStream`. `CryptoStream` defines the following custom constructor that's important for `Cryptography` users:

```
public CryptoStream(Stream stream, ICryptoTransform transform,
    CryptoStreamMode mode);
```

Because the first parameter is a `Stream` type, it's possible to chain together other `Stream`-based objects—this is useful if you want to stream the results from one cryptographic operation to another (for example, a hash algorithm's results to an asymmetric algorithm's stream object).

The second parameter must implement the `ICryptoTransform` interface. `HashAlgorithm` implements this interface, as do the return values from the `CreateEncryptor()` and `CreateDecryptor()` methods found in the symmetric and asymmetric classes. (Symmetric and asymmetric keys are examined later on in this chapter.) `CryptoStreamMode` is an enumeration that defines two values—`Read` and `Write`—and you can only use one when you call `CryptoStream`'s constructor.

The example in Listing 2-2 demonstrates hashing the contents of a file. First, you'll open a file located on disk via the `FileStream` object. Next, you'll read the entire contents of the file, and hash the results using the `SHA512Managed` class.

Listing 2-2. Hashing File Data via CryptoStream

```
String adPath = AppDomain.CurrentDomain.SetupInformation.ApplicationBase;
FileStream fin = new FileStream(adPath + @"\somefilein.txt",
    FileMode.Open, FileAccess.Read);
FileStream fhashed = new FileStream(adPath + @"\somefileout.txt",
    FileMode.OpenOrCreate, FileAccess.Write);

SHA512 sha = new SHA512Managed();
CryptoStream csSHA = new CryptoStream(fin,
    sha, CryptoStreamMode.Read);

byte[] finData = new byte[fin.Length];
csSHA.Read(finData, 0, (int)fin.Length);
fhashed.Write(sha.Hash, 0, (int)sha.Hash.Length);
fhashed.Close();
```

The file somefilein.txt should be in the same directory where the assembly that contains this code is being executed, as it's using the `ApplicationBase` property to determine the directory that the file resides.

Granted, this may seem like more work than simply calling `ComputeHash()` on the `SHA512` instance (`sha`) and obtaining the hash from the return value. If all you need to do is hash data, I'd suggest not using the `CryptoStream` class; later on, you'll see how this approach is desirable when dealing with encryption classes.

SOURCE CODE *The SimpleHashing project in the Chapter2 subdirectory creates a byte array from a* String *and uses* MemoryStream *objects to create the hash.*

Now that you've gotten your feet wet with cryptographic development in .NET, it's time to investigate the random number generation classes.

Investigating Random Number Generation Classes

Similar to what you just saw with the Hash class hierarchy, Cryptography defines an abstract class called RandomNumberGenerator, which all other random number generating classes should inherit from. Currently, .NET provides only one implementation of RandomNumberGenerator: RNGCryptoServiceProvider.[4]

RandomNumberGenerator has only two methods that you can use to generate random data: GetBytes() and GetNonZeroBytes(). Both take a byte array as their only argument, but GetNonZeroBytes() will do what its name says: none of the array elements will contain zero values. GetBytes() may contain zero values.

Here's a code snippet showing both methods in action:

```
RandomNumberGenerator rng = new RNGCryptoServiceProvider();
byte[] randomData = new byte[100];
rng.GetBytes(randomData);
byte[] randomDataWithNoZeros = new byte[50];
rng.GetNonZeroBytes(randomDataWithNoZeros);
```

The RandomNumberGenerator object will read the array's length to determine how much data it should generate.

RNGCryptoServiceProvider Custom Constructors

RNGCryptoServiceProvider has three custom constructors that allow you to pick which provider you want to use. Two of the constructors use simple data values— a byte array and a string—but right now these methods don't use the given values, and the SDK explicitly states that they should not be called by application code. The other constructor uses a CspParameters-based object. This class allows you to define which provider you want to use, along with a key container name. For example, the following code uses the RSA full provider type (defined by the PROV_RSA_FULL CryptoAPI constant, which is equal to 1):

```
const int PROV_RSA_FULL = 1;
CspParameters csp = new CspParameters(PROV_RSA_FULL);
RandomNumberGenerator rng = new RNGCryptoServiceProvider(csp);
```

---

4.   If you're looking for other RNGs for .NET, Brent Rector has released his implementations of other RNG algorithms, which you can find at http://www.wiseowl.com/downloads/downloads.aspx.

Note that the CryptoAPI constants (like PROV_RSA_FULL) are not defined in .NET; you must define them yourself. Their values can be found in the wincrypt.h file. You can also specify the provider name and key container name:

```
CspParameters csp = new CspParameters(1,
    "Microsoft Enhanced Cryptographic Provider v1.0", "Administrator");
RandomNumberGenerator rng = new RNGCryptoServiceProvider(csp);
```

If you specify invalid information, the CspParameters creation will be successful, but using it will throw an error as shown here:

```
CspParameters csp = new CspParameters(10000,
    "Microsoft Enhanced Cryptographic Provider v1.0", "Administrator");
//  This will throw an exception, as there is no 10000 provider type.
RandomNumberGenerator rng = new RNGCryptoServiceProvider(csp);
```

Formatting RNG Data

You may have already noticed that the Cryptography classes love byte arrays. For example, GetBytes() and GetNonZeroBytes() methods in RandomNumberGenerator work on byte arrays only. So does the Write() method of the HashAlgorithm abstract hash class. However, this may not be what you want. What if you need to generate a bunch of random integer values (or, more generally, System.Int32 .NET object values)? Fortunately, .NET provides some classes to help you format the byte data to other data types. For this discussion, you'll take a look at the BinaryReader class in the System.IO namespace. As BinaryReader is Stream-based, you should be able to use your knowledge of streams to get the data in the format that you want.

The best way to understand this is to take a look at the following code sample:

```
RandomNumberGenerator rng = new RNGCryptoServiceProvider();
byte[] randomData = new byte[18];
rng.GetBytes(randomData);
BinaryReader binReader = new BinaryReader(new MemoryStream(randomData));
int randomValue = binReader.ReadInt32();
```

As you can see, all you need is two lines of code to get a random value. When you call the ReadInt32() method, the stream creates a 4-byte signed integer value, and moves the current stream position 4 bytes. Note, though, the randomData byte array isn't evenly divisible by 4, so if you continually called ReadInt32(), you'd eventually run out of data. Therefore, if you want to take the results of calling GetBytes() and transform them into a bunch of random integer values, remember to catch the EndOfStreamException exception as shown here:

```
//  Assume randomData has random data.
BinaryReader binReader = new BinaryReader(new MemoryStream(randomData));
try
{
    int randomValue;
    do
    {
        randomValue = binReader.ReadInt32();
    } while(true);
}
catch(EndOfStreamException eose) {}
```

When I ran this code and displayed the contents of randomValue, I got 821499462, 1586377564, 573104213, and –772757365. I also saw that the EndOfStreamException was raised at the appropriate time—that is, when I tried to create a random number for the fifth time.

There are other formatting methods on BinaryReader, such as ReadString() and ReadDouble(), so keep this class in mind as you work with the Cryptography classes if you need to create random data of different types. Also, you can pass in different encoding strategies with another custom constructor to RandomNumberGenerator that takes an Encoding class as the second parameter.

 SOURCE CODE   *The RNGBasics project in the Chapter2 subdirectory demonstrates the use of* BinaryReader *to get random integer values.*

Extending RandomNumberGenerator

While I think it's nice that RandomNumberGenerator gives you the ability to generate data containing nonzero data, I think it could do even better. That is, it should have an overloaded GetBytes() method that takes two parameters: the byte array that will store the data and a list of values that you don't want to show up in the array. Sounds difficult? Not with the .NET Framework. First, create the following interface called FineGrainedRNG:

```
public interface FineGrainedRNG
{
    void GetBytes(byte[] data, byte[] excludedValues);
}
```

Next, create the class called ExcludingRNG that subclasses RNGCryptoServiceProvider:

```
public class ExcludingRNG : RNGCryptoServiceProvider
{
    public ExcludingRNG() : base() {}
}
```

All of the RandomNumberGenerator methods are implemented via inheritance. However, you need to handle FineGrainedRNG's GetBytes() on your own. But .NET arrays are class-based and have generic searching routines built in, so it's pretty straightforward to implement this method as follows:

```
public void GetBytes(byte[] data, byte[] excludedValues)
{
    if(null != excludedValues && excludedValues.Length > 0)
    {
        byte[] tempData = {1};
        for(int i = 0; i < data.Length; i++)
        {
            do
            {
                base.GetBytes(tempData);
            } while (Array.IndexOf(excludedValues, tempData[0]) >= 0);
            data[i] = tempData[0];
        }
```

```
    }
    else
    {
        throw new ArgumentException(
            "The excludedValues argument is invalid. ");
    }
}
```

All you do is call GetBytes() on the inner object until a value is returned that doesn't exist in excludedValues. Then, you take that value and add that to the data array. This is done until data is full. So now you can write the following code to get random bytes that don't include the values between 0 and 9 inclusive:

```
byte[] randomExcludedData = new byte[255];
byte[] excludedData = {1, 2, 3, 4, 5, 6, 7, 8, 9, 0};
FineGrainedRNG fng = new ExcludingRNG();
fng.GetBytes(randomExcludedData, excludedData);
```

As you can see, extending the .NET Framework is very easy.

 SOURCE CODE   *The ExcludingRNG project in the Chapter2 subdirectory demonstrates the use of* ExcludingRNG *to get specific random bytes values.*

In the next section, I'll talk about how keys are created in .NET, and how they are used to encrypt and decrypt data.

Creating Keys

As you saw in Chapter 1, there are two kinds of encryption algorithms: symmetric and asymmetric. In this section, I'll cover how you use both algorithm types via the .NET classes.

Symmetric Keys

Cryptography defines an abstract class called SymmetricAlgorithm that all implementations of symmetric algorithms should descend from. You use this class to
bind to object references at runtime as shown here:

```
SymmetricAlgorithm symAlg = new RijndaelManaged();
```

Currently, .NET has these four implementations of SymmetricAlgorithm:

- Data Encryption Standard (DES)

- TripleDES

- Rivest Cipher-2 (RC2)

- Rijndael (derived from the names Vincent **Rij**men and Joan **Dae**man)

RC2 has a variable-key size, whereas DES only has 56-bit keys and TripleDES
only has 112-bit keys. The Rijndael algorithm is the new government encryption
standard (sometimes denoted as AES), which may affect your algorithm decision
process depending on your project's needs. The only managed implementation
of SymmetricAlgorithm is RijndaelManaged, so this is the most "portable" choice
out of the four. Now let's take a look at the properties of the class first, and then
we'll dive into the methods.

First of all, SymmetricAlgorithm defines a set of properties that you would
probably expect for a class of this nature. If you're dealing with a block-based
algorithm instead of a stream-based algorithm, you can find out the base block
size via BlockSize, as follows:

```
int blockSize = symAlg.BlockSize;
```

You can also get and set the initialization vector (IV) for algorithms that are based
on cipher block chaining (CBC) and padding via the IV property as shown here:

```
byte[] iv = symAlg.IV;

for(int i = 0; i < iv.Length; i++)
{
    iv[i] /= 2;
}

symAlg.IV = iv;
```

CROSS-REERENCE *See Chapter 1 for discussions of IV and CBC.*

If you want to find out the key size, call the KeySize property. If you actually want the key value, call Key[5] like so:

```
byte[] keyMaterial = new byte[symAlg.KeySize];
keyMaterial = symAlg.Key;
```

You'll see in the next section, "Encrypting and Decrypting Data," how you can use these properties to perform encryption and decryption. For now, just note that you can use these properties to set up the key information before you start encrypting data. However, as you know, only certain key lengths are allowed. Also, different algorithms support different kinds of padding and modes during the encryption process. That's where the next set of properties come into play. You can use LegalKeySizes as shown in Listing 2-3 to find out if a desired key size will work or not.

Listing 2-3. Checking for a Valid Key Size

```
int desiredKeySize = 22;
KeySizes[] legalSize = symAlg.LegalKeySizes;
for(int i = 0; i < legalSize.Length; i++)
{
    if(desiredKeySize >= legalSize[i].MinSize &&
        desiredKeySize <= legalSize[i].MaxSize &&
        (desiredKeySize % legalSize[i].SkipSize) == 0)
    {
        //  Legal size.
    }
}
```

I'm not sure why SymmetricAlgorithm doesn't have an IsLegalSize() method that would figure out if a given key size is legitimate or not. You can create the KeySizesEx class shown in Listing 2-4 that would wrap a KeySizes array and add this method.

---

5. This is a vast improvement over the CryptoAPI to get the key material and to get algorithm information in general.

Listing 2-4. Making Key Size Validation Easier

```
public class KeySizesEx
{
    private KeySizes[] ks = null;
    public KeySizesEx(KeySizes[] ks)
    {
        this.ks = ks;
    }
    public bool IsValidKeySize(int DesiredSize)
    {
        bool retVal = false;
        foreach(KeySizes keySize in ks)
        {
            if(DesiredSize >= keySize.MinSize &&
                    DesiredSize <= keySize.MaxSize &&
                (DesiredSize % keySize.SkipSize) == 0)
            {
                retVal = true;
                break;
            }
        }
        return retVal;
    }
}
```

Now the following check becomes easier to maintain and use:

```
KeySizesEx kse = new KeySizesEx(symAlg.LegalKeySizes);
if(kse.IsValidKeySize(desiredKeySize))
{
    //  Size is legal.
}
else
{
    //  Size is NOT legal.
}
```

The LegalBlockSizes property works exactly the same way as LegalKeySizes, so you use the same technique demonstrated in Listing 2-4 to determine if a desired block size is legal given the current algorithm.

There are a couple of enumeration-based properties that allow you to specify the mode and padding. `Mode` returns one of the five following `CipherMode` enumeration values:

- CBC

- CFB

- CTS

- ECB

- OFB

CROSS-REFERENCE *See "Key Modes" in Chapter 1 for a discussion of cipher block chaining (CBC), cipher feedback mode (CFB), cipher text stealing (CTS), electronic code book (ECB), and output feedback (OFB).*

Similarly, `Padding` returns these `PaddingMode` enumeration values:

- None

- Public Key Cryptography Standard 7 (PKCS7)

- Zeros

SOURCE CODE *The SymmetricAlgorithmEvaluator project in the Chapter2 subdirectory retrieves all of the* `SymmetricAlgorithm` *properties.*

So now you've gone through `SymmetricAlgorithm`'s properties. How do you use the class to encrypt data? Read on to find out.

Encrypting and Decrypting Data

You use either the CreateEncryptor() or CreateDecryptor() methods with the SymmetricAlgorithm class to encrypt and decrypt information. There are two versions of this method: one that's parameterless, and one that takes two byte arrays that represent the IV and key for the encryption process. In either case, the return value is an ICryptoTransform-based object, so you can use the CryptoStream as shown in Listing 2-5 to make your job easier.

Listing 2-5. Encrypting and Decrypting Files via a CryptoStream Object

```
String adPath = AppDomain.CurrentDomain.SetupInformation.ApplicationBase;
FileStream fin = new FileStream(adPath + @"\somefilein.txt",
    FileMode.Open, FileAccess.Read);
MemoryStream mout = new MemoryStream();
byte[] finData = new byte[fin.Length];

SymmetricAlgorithm rijn = Rijndael.Create();
CryptoStream coutenc = new CryptoStream(mout, rijn.CreateEncryptor(),
    CryptoStreamMode.Write);
fin.Read(finData, 0, (int)fin.Length);
coutenc.Write(finData, 0, (int)fin.Length);
coutenc.FlushFinalBlock();

FileStream fdec = new FileStream(adPath + @"\somefileout.txt",
    FileMode.OpenOrCreate, FileAccess.Write);

CryptoStream coutdec = new CryptoStream(fdec, rijn.CreateDecryptor(),
    CryptoStreamMode.Write);
coutdec.Write(mout.GetBuffer(), 0, (int)(mout.Length));
coutdec.Close();
```

This code looks almost identical to what you saw in Listing 2-2. However, there's an issue that should be addressed. First, after all of the file data is written (and encrypted) to mout, I don't call Close(); I call FlushFinalBlock(). There's a couple of reasons why I do this. The first, and more obvious one is that I need the buffer stored in mout to decrypt the data. If I call the Close() method to close the memory stream, I can't get at that data anymore.

The second reason isn't as apparent. Remember that encryption algorithms can be block- or stream-based. Rijnadel is block-based (the block size is 128 bits), so it used padding (PKCS7 is the default) to make sure the block size matches up. When you decrypt the memory stream's buffer, you need to make sure that the decryption has that "extra" padding so the resulting file is the same size as the original. When you call the `FlushFinalBlock()` method, the memory stream `Length` property will be equal to the length of the original buffer plus the size of the padding. The memory buffer will actually be twice the size of the original file, so you don't have to worry about going past the size of the buffer by calling `Length` (which will be equal to or larger than the original size of the file).

SOURCE CODE *The SymmetricAlgorithmEncryptor project in the Chapter2 subdirectory encrypts and decrypts a file via the* `CryptoStream` *class.*

In the next section, you'll see how you can create the same symmetric key based on a password.

Deriving Symmetric Keys with a Password

For key exchange scenarios, you need to create a session key. If you run into a scenario where you need to derive the exact same key given some initialization data (that is, a password), you can use the `PasswordDeriveBytes` class. This class allows you to define the password and salt value on construction. The following code snippet demonstrates `PasswordDeriveBytes` in action:

```
RNGCryptoServiceProvider rng = new RNGCryptoServiceProvider();
byte[] rngData = new byte[8];
rng.GetBytes(rngData);

PasswordDeriveBytes pwdDerive = new PasswordDeriveBytes(
    "SuperSecretPassword", rngData);

byte[] ivData = new byte[8];
rng.GetBytes(ivData);

byte[] RC2Key =
    pwdDerive.CryptDeriveKey("RC2", "SHA",
    128, ivData);
```

`CryptDeriveKey()` is using the CryptoAPI to create the key, so it needs to employ the service providers. If you specify an algorithm that is not implemented in the provider being used, you'll get a `NullReferenceException` as shown here:

```
//  This will throw an exception,
//  as none of the MS providers
//  implement Rijndael.
byte[] RijndaelKey =
    pwdDerive.CryptDeriveKey("Rijndael", "SHA",
    128, ivData);
```

SOURCE CODE   *The PNGSample project in the Chapter2 sub-directory demonstrates* PasswordDeriveBytes *in action.*

Although using SymmetricAlgorithm-based classes is pretty easy, things get a bit trickier when you want to use an asymmetric algorithm. Read on for details.

Asymmetric Keys

Similar to what you saw in the previous sections, all asymmetric algorithms derive their implementations from the abstract class AsymmetricAlgorithm. Currently, .NET defines two abstract implementations of AsymmetricAlgorithm: Rivest, Shamir, and Adleman (RSA) and Digital Signature Algorithm (DSA). The RSA algorithm is able to both perform encryption and create digital signatures; DSA can only be used for signatures. However, signing with DSA is faster than in RSA.

Each abstract class has a CryptoServiceProvider implementation. However, this is where the similarities stop. For one thing, no properties exist for obtaining the private key material directly. You have properties like KeySize and LegalKeySize, which work as expected, but there's no PrivateKey property. However, there is an indirect way to find out the key sizes—I'll explain how in the next section.

I'll present a code snippet in a moment to show you how you can use an asymmetric algorithm to encrypt and decrypt data. However, before I do, I need to point out that there are no CreateEncryptor() or CreateDecryptor() methods when you use an AsymmetricAlgorithm-based object. The way you can use a key pair is to call methods on the AsymmetricAlgorithm-derived classes. For example, the RSACryptoServiceProvider class has the Encrypt() and Decrypt() methods. This breaks the pattern you've seen so far—that is, you never need to touch the actual object that implements the abstract class or interface. In this case, you don't have a choice—you need to call methods specific to an implementing class. This may sound odd at first, but remember that not all asymmetric algorithms are used primarily to handle encryption (like DSA). Therefore, these methods must be defined on the derived classes and not on the base classes.[6]

To make the issues clearer, take a look Listing 2-6, which creates a RSA key pair, and encrypts and decrypts a file.

Listing 2-6. Encrypting and Decrypting Files via an Asymmetic Algorithm

```
String adPath = AppDomain.CurrentDomain.SetupInformation.ApplicationBase;
FileStream fin = new FileStream(adPath + @"\somefilein.txt",
    FileMode.Open, FileAccess.Read);
FileStream fdec = new FileStream(adPath + @"\somefileout.txt",
    FileMode.OpenOrCreate, FileAccess.Write);

RSACryptoServiceProvider rsa = (RSACryptoServiceProvider)RSA.Create();
int len = 0, readBytes = 0, dataSize = 0;
if(1024 == rsa.KeySize)
{
    dataSize = 16;
}
else
{
    dataSize = 5;
}
byte[] finData = new byte[dataSize], rsaEncrypt = null,
    rsaDecrypt = null;

while(readBytes < fin.Length)
{
    len = fin.Read(finData, 0, dataSize);
    readBytes += len;
    rsaEncrypt = rsa.Encrypt(finData, false);
    rsaDecrypt = rsa.Decrypt(rsaEncrypt, false);
    fdec.Write(rsaDecrypt, 0, (int)rsaDecrypt.Length);
}
fdec.Close();
```

---

6. I would argue that the design should have included an IAsymmetricCipherAlgorithm inter-
    face that would define Encrypt() and Decrypt(). Then, asymmetric algorithms that can be
    used for encryption would implement this interface. Unfortunately, that's not the way
    things were done.

As you can see, I have to make a cast to get the proper type reference, as I'm calling a method directly from the RSACryptoServiceProvider class. Then, it's just a matter of calling Encrypt() and Decrypt() at the correct times.

You may be wondering why I use the KeySize property to determine the size of the data chunk I grab out of the file. The SDK states that if you use PKCS#1 v1.5 padding (which is what you get when you set the second parameter to false), you can only pass data arrays that have no more than 16 bytes if you have the high encryption pack installed (the maximum is 5 if you don't). The high encryption pack refers to the Enhanced Provider for the CryptoAPI. If the KeySize is 1024, this means you have the high encryption pack installed; otherwise, you need to encrypt data in 5-byte chunks.

Although it isn't as explicit as the KeySize-Encrypt() scenario I mentioned in the last paragraph, you also have to be careful about the size of the data chunk that's decrypted. You should only decrypt the data with the same size chunks as what you got when you encrypted it. The chunk size should be the same as KeySize in bytes, so when you decrypt the data, only use data chunks that are no bigger than KeySize/8 bytes in length. In the previous example, I'm immediately decrypting the encrypted data chunk, so I know the array size is correct; in a production system, though, you probably won't have this luxury.

If you decide to encrypt and decrypt data using an asymmetric algorithm, remember that it is painfully slow to execute, even if the source file is only 10KB in size. Symmetric algorithms are much faster than asymmetric algorithms, so if you want to encrypt an entire file using an asymmetric algorithm, you may want to do it in another thread so your users don't get impatient waiting for a form that appears hung.

SOURCE CODE   *The AsymmetricAlgorithmEncryptor project in the Chapter2 subdirectory encrypts and decrypts a file using the* RSACryptoServiceProvider *class.*

In the next section, you'll see how you can retrieve public and private key material.

XML Strings and Parameter Classes

Recall that there's no property on AsymmetricAlgorithm to get the private key. This is important if you need to store the key pair into a key management system, or if you need to persist the key value for future use. However, there are a couple of indirect ways to retrieve the key value. First, let's look at the ToXMLString() method. This takes one argument: a Boolean value that if you set to true returns all of the key algorithm information. Here's a code snippet that extracts this information to a file:

```
RSACryptoServiceProvider rsa =
    (RSACryptoServiceProvider)RSA.Create();
String adPath = AppDomain.CurrentDomain.SetupInformation.ApplicationBase;
FileStream frsaTrue = new FileStream(adPath + @"\rsaXMLTrue.xml",
    FileMode.OpenOrCreate, FileAccess.Write);
byte[] rsaData = Encoding.ASCII.GetBytes(rsa.ToXmlString(true));
frsaTrue.Write(rsaData, 0, (int)rsaData.Length);
frsaTrue.Close();
```

If you open up rsaXMLTrue.xml, you'll see something like this:

```
<RSAKeyValue>
    <Modulus>mWquxr2m634o...</Modulus>
    <Exponent>AQAB</Exponent>
    <P>zC/ZVO+HdIBpUE...</P>
    <Q>wFjCvqjA+1xuqOsSQ...</Q>
    <DP>oOOJZfKDxNsGXxmw...</DP>
    <DQ>bGMYClwJsxsY+HLOb...</DQ>
    <InverseQ>vpHpPVGnXKOkd...</InverseQ>
    <D>eUmiS3T8VgkzHDX7uL+2mW...</D>
</RSAKeyValue>
```

I've deleted some of the element contents for brevity's sake. With this information, you could derive the precise value for the private key value, but as it would take multiple-precision arithmetic, I'll leave that as an exercise for you.

If you simply want to publish the "public" parts so a friend could use your public key to decrypt a file you encrypted with the related private key, simply set includePrivateParameters to false. You'll then get an XML string that looks like this:

```
<RSAKeyValue>
    <Modulus>mWquxr2m634oYmO...</Modulus>
    <Exponent>AQAB</Exponent>
</RSAKeyValue>
```

Remember that if you export the entire contents, you're responsible for ensuring that the string's data is kept secret at all times. Exposing this information is a risk to a certain degree, so I'd suggest that you only call ToXMLString(true) if you have to know what the private key value is.

Once you have the XML string, you can use FromXMLString() to set the key value on the given asymmetric algorithm object. However, if you exported only the public key information, you'll only be able to use the resulting RSA-based object to perform encryption; it won't have enough information to do decryption as the following example shows:

```
RSACryptoServiceProvider rsa = (RSACryptoServiceProvider)RSA.Create();
String xmlPublic = rsa.ToXmlString(false);
RSACryptoServiceProvider rsaLoad = (RSACryptoServiceProvider)RSA.Create();
rsaLoad.FromXmlString(xmlPublic);
byte[] baseData = {65, 54, 65, 2, 110, 30, 53, 40, 59, 20};
byte[] rsaEncrypt = rsa.Encrypt(baseData, false);
byte[] rsaDecrypt = rsaLoad.Decrypt(rsaEncrypt, false);
```

The Decrypt() call will throw a CryptographicException with the message, "Bad Key." However, if you use rsaLoad to encrypt the data, the asymmetric algorithm will be able to decrypt it like so:

```
// Assume rsa and rsaLoad are set up the same.
byte[] baseData  = {65, 54, 65, 2, 110, 30, 53, 40, 59, 20};
byte[] rsaEncrypt = rsaLoad.Encrypt(baseData, false);
byte[] rsaDecrypt = rsa.Decrypt(rsaEncrypt , false);
```

There's another way you can get at and set the key information via ExportParameters() and ImportParameters(). ExportParameters() works just like ToXmlString() in that it takes a Boolean to determine if you want to get all of the key information. However, ExportParameters() returns a Parameters class for the current algorithm in use. For example, if you were using a DSACryptoServiceProvider object, ExportParameters() would return a DSAParameters class.

```
DSACryptoServiceProvider dsa = (DSACryptoServiceProvider)DSA.Create();
DSAParameters dsaParams = dsa.ExportParameters(false);
```

Note that ExportParameters() and ImportParameters() are not defined in AsymmetricAlgorithm, whereas the ToXmlString() and FromXmlString() methods are. The reason is that each algorithm class has to define its own Parameters class, as the key makeup can be different for each algorithm.

Both the DSAParameters and RSAParameters classes have their key values as public fields. If you look carefully, you'll also see that some of the fields are marked as nonserialized. This means that the field will not be added to the serialization process if the object is serialized. This is desirable, as you probably don't want the private key information to travel around networks without your approval.

SOURCE CODE   *The KeyXMLStrings project in the Chapter2 subdirectory shows the difference in exporting public and public/private XML key information.*

Let's move on to using AsymmetricAlgorithm-based objects to create signatures.

Signatures and Verification

There are two ways to use AsymmetricAlgorithm-based objects to create signatures. One way is to use SignData() and VerifyData() methods. These methods are defined in both RSA and DSA; since DSA automatically employs the SHA1 algorithm, you don't have to specify the hash algorithm used. RSA allows you to define the hash algorithm, so its second argument is a HashAlgorithm.

Here's a code snippet demonstrating how you use RSACryptoServiceProvider to sign and verify data:

```
byte[] someData = {56,34,25,61,55,20,90,50,44};
RSACryptoServiceProvider rsa = new RSACryptoServiceProvider();
RSACryptoServiceProvider rsaSign = new RSACryptoServiceProvider();
RSACryptoServiceProvider rsaVerify = new RSACryptoServiceProvider();
SHA1 sha = new SHA1Managed();
rsaSign.FromXmlString(rsa.ToXmlString(true));
byte[] sig = rsaSign.SignData(someData, sha);
//sig[0] /= 2;
rsaVerify.FromXmlString(rsa.ToXmlString(false));
bool isValid = rsaVerify.VerifyData(someData,
    sha, sig);
```

If you uncomment the commented line of code, the isValid Boolean value will be false after the VerifyData() method is done because the signature is now corrupted.

The other way to use AsymmetricAlgorithm-based objects to create signatures is to implement CreateSignature() and VerifySignature() on any DSA-based class. Therefore, you could use either a DSACryptoServiceProvider instance or DSASignatureFormatter to make a DSA PKCS #1 signature, and DSASignatureDeformatter to verify it.

Here's a code snippet demonstrating how you would use DSASignatureFormatter and DSASignatureDeformatter:

```
DSACryptoServiceProvider dsaKey = new DSACryptoServiceProvider();
DSASignatureFormatter dsaSigForm = new DSASignatureFormatter();
dsaSigForm.SetKey(dsaKey);
byte[] dsaSignature = dsaSigForm.CreateSignature(sha.ComputeHash(someData));
//dsaSignature[0] /= 2;
DSASignatureDeformatter dsaSigDeform = new DSASignatureDeformatter(dsaKey);
bool isValid = dsaSigDeform.VerifySignature(sha.ComputeHash(someData),
dsaSignature);
```

Either way, you're going to get the same results, so it's your choice (that is, use one object type or two).

SOURCE CODE   *The SignaturesSample project in the Chapter2 subdirectory signs and verifies data using all four methods:* SignData(), VerifyData(), CreateSignature(), *and* VerifySignature().

Now that you're comfortable using key information, let's see how you can exchange keys with another party in a secure manner.

Key Exchange Classes

Recall in Chapter 1 that I talked about using a symmetric key as a session key between two parties. Each party creates a public/private key pair, and transmits the session key using the key pairs. There's also a way to prevent sending over the symmetric key itself—you encrypt some random data with one party's public key. Then the party decrypts the data, and creates the key. Since the first party already has the key, that's all it takes to exchange the key as both parties can generate the session key with the random data. There are more complex variations on this theme, but essentially they all work the same (more or less).

The Cryptography namespace defines two abstract classes, AsymmetricKeyExchangeFormatter and AsymmetricKeyExchangeDeformatter, which you can use to create the key exchange data. So far, there are four RSA-based implementations of this class:

- RSAPKCS1KeyExchangeFormatter

- RSAOAEPKeyExchangeFormatter

- RSAPKCS1KeyExchangeDeformatter

- RSAOAEPKeyExchangeDeformatter

For the interested reader, OAEP stands for Optimal Asymmetric Encryption Padding, and PKCS stands for Public Key Cryptography Standard. You need to use the same one on the deformatting side as you do on the formatting side. I'll use the RSAPKCSKeyExchangeXXX classes in Listing 2-7 to demonstrate how key exchange works.

Listing 2-7. Exchanging a Session Key

```
RSACryptoServiceProvider bobKeyPair = new RSACryptoServiceProvider();
RSACryptoServiceProvider aliceKeyPair = new RSACryptoServiceProvider();

Rijndael bobKeyExch = new RijndaelManaged();
bobKeyExch.KeySize = 128;
bobKeyExch.GenerateKey();
```

```
RSAPKCS1KeyExchangeFormatter bobKeyFormatter =
    new RSAPKCS1KeyExchangeFormatter();
RSACryptoServiceProvider alicePublicKey =
    new RSACryptoServiceProvider();
alicePublicKey.FromXmlString(aliceKeyPair.ToXmlString(false));
bobKeyFormatter.SetKey(alicePublicKey);
byte[] bobKeyExchData =
    bobKeyFormatter.CreateKeyExchange(bobKeyExch.Key);

RSACryptoServiceProvider alicePrivateKey =
    new RSACryptoServiceProvider();
alicePrivateKey.FromXmlString(aliceKeyPair.ToXmlString(true));
RSAPKCS1KeyExchangeDeformatter aliceKeyDeformatter =
    new RSAPKCS1KeyExchangeDeformatter();
aliceKeyDeformatter.SetKey(alicePrivateKey);
byte[] aliceKeyExchData =
    aliceKeyDeformatter.DecryptKeyExchange(bobKeyExchData);

Rijndael aliceKeyExch = new RijndaelManaged();
aliceKeyExch.KeySize = 128;
aliceKeyExch.Key = aliceKeyExchData;
```

I use a 128-bit Rijndael key, as CreateKeyExchange() won't throw an
exception with that key size given the default values of an RSA public/private
key pair. Once Bob has the data in bobKeyExchData, he can ship it to Alice, who
can create the key on the other side. Now they have a session key to
communicate with.

SOURCE CODE *The KeyExchangeSample project in the
Chapter2 subdirectory transmits a session key between two
parties.*

In the next section, you'll see the level of support that .NET has for
certificates.

Working with the System.Security.Cryptography.X509Certificates Namespace

As with most things in life, there's always an exception or two. Although most of the cryptographic operations exist with System.Security.Cryptography, there's one other namespace that you need to know about: System.Security.Cryptography.X509Certificates. This namespace contains classes that are related to viewing X.509 certificate information. Before you begin looking at these classes, I need to fill you in on certificate creation.

Creating Test Certificates

As you'll see in a moment, the X509Certificate class doesn't actually make a certificate; it only examines a certificate file. Fortunately, with .NET you don't need a certificate authority (CA) to get a certificate file; it ships with the Certificate Creation Tool (makecert.exe). To make a certificate file, run the following code from the command line:

```
makecert "c:\somedirectory\simpleCertificate.cer"
```

This will create the file in the given directory. There are a lot of options available for makecert.exe.[7] For example, you can set the certificate's subject name via the -n switch:

```
makecert -n "CN=Some Company" simpleCertificate.cer
```

You can also specify the date when this certificate is no longer valid via the -e switch:

```
makecert -e 03/09/2020 simpleCertificate.cer
```

---

7. For all available options, please review the following document in the SDK: ms-help://MS.NETFrameworkSDK/cptools/html/cpgrfcertificatecreationtoolmakecertexe.htm, or look up makecert.exe.

NOTE *The docs explicitly state that makecert.exe should be used for testing purposes only, so I wouldn't use the generated certificates in a production system, as they are not verified via a certificate authority. If you want to get a trusted certificate, you can purchase one from the following sites:* http://www.verisign.com, http://www.thawte.com, *and* http://www.entrust.net.

Once you have the certificate in place, you can view its contents via the X509Certificate class, which is discussed next.

X509Certificate Class

This class has two static methods that allow you to view certificate information: CreateFromCertFile() and CreateFromSignedFile(). The names are a bit misleading as they don't actually create a certificate; they create a X509Certificate object that contains the certificate information in the file.

Once you have the object, you can use a number of read-only methods to get certificate information, such as GetIssuerName() and GetEffectiveDateString(). You can also get the raw byte information for certain parts of the certificate, like GetCertHash() and GetPublicKey(), as follows:

```
String adPath = AppDomain.CurrentDomain.SetupInformation.ApplicationBase;
X509Certificate x509 = X509Certificate.CreateFromCertFile(
    adPath + @"\simpleCert.cer");
String x509Name = x509.GetName();
byte[] x509PublicKey = x509.GetPublicKey();
```

If necessary, you can also create an X509Certificate object from another one:

```
String adPath = AppDomain.CurrentDomain.SetupInformation.ApplicationBase;
X509Certificate x509 = X509Certificate.CreateFromCertFile(
    adPath + @"\simpleCert.cer");
X509Certificate x509Derived = new X509Certificate(x509.GetRawCertData());
```

For the sake of completeness, I should mention that there's also the following X509CertificateCollection class that inherits from CollectionBase, so it acts like a type-safe collection for X509Certificate objects:

```
String adPath = AppDomain.CurrentDomain.SetupInformation.ApplicationBase;
X509Certificate x509 = X509Certificate.CreateFromCertFile(
    adPath + @"\simpleCert.cer");
X509Certificate x509Derived = new X509Certificate(x509.GetRawCertData());
X509CertificateCollection x509Col = new X509CertificateCollection();
x509Col.Add(x509);
x509Col.Add(x509Derived);
foreach(X509Certificate cert in x509Col)
{
    String issuerName = cert.GetIssuerName();
}
```

SOURCE CODE   *The X509Info project in the Chapter2 subdirectory displays all of the information in a certificate file.*

Let's take all that you've learned so far and wrap up the chapter with an example that allows you to encrypt serialized object data.

Exploring Serialized Objects and Cryptography

To finish off this chapter, let's go through an example that will allow you to sign an object's serialized state as well as encrypting (or sealing) it, so the serialized content can be safely stored to memory or disk. Start by looking at the design of the classes, and then move on to their implementations.[8]

.NET Design

The two classes that you'll need to create are SignedObject and SealedObject. SignedObject will take an object and sign or verify its serialized data. SealedObject will take an object and encrypt or decrypt its serialized data. Sounds simple enough, right? There's only a couple of requirements you need to keep in mind. Both classes need to be serializable—that is, they must provide a mechanism to take the current object's state and persist it—as one can be passed into the other. Both can only take objects that are serializable; if a given

---

8.   If you're a Java developer, the following design may look a little familiar.

object is not serializable, the object should throw a `NotSerializableException` custom exception.

However, as with any component design, there are some caveats. Recall that there's no way to call the `SignData()` method on either a DSA- or RSA-based object in a polymorphic manner because those methods are defined in the subclasses, not in `AsymmetricAlgorithm`. Therefore, you should make `SignedObject` and `SealedObject` abstract, and only define a couple of methods and properties on the abstract classes that are common, like `Object`. Each subclass will define their own `Verify()` and `Sign()` methods that take XML parameter strings or parameter classes for the given algorithm.

It would be nice to also have some kind of compression scheme in place to give the user the option to make the internal storage smaller. For example, if you use `SealedObject`, you might be able to save a lot of space and encryption time by compressing the given object's serialization stream. You take a hit during the compression process, but compression allows the user to streamline the resulting `SealedObject` data space. When the object is decrypted, it's also decompressed before it's deserialized and given back to the client via `Object`. Unfortunately, there's nothing in the .NET Framework to do this, so you'll have to hold off on this feature for now.

> **NOTE** *Technically, there are the* `Compress()` *and* `Decompress()` *methods on the* `PassportIdentity` *class, but I don't want to get into the Passport world at the moment. If you'd like to add this feature yourself, a company called XceedSoft (`http://www.xceedsoft.com`) provides a compression component that you can purchase. Note that J# will have the* `ZipInfo` *classes in its runtime, so if you have that language installed you can use those as well.*

What's nice about these two objects is that you can use them in concert to ensure secure communication between parties. One party, Joe, signs his object, which allows the other party, Jane, to determine that it was Joe who signed the object. Joe also seals the object with Jane's public key, ensuring that Jane will be the only one who can open it. This scenario is depicted in Figure 2-1.

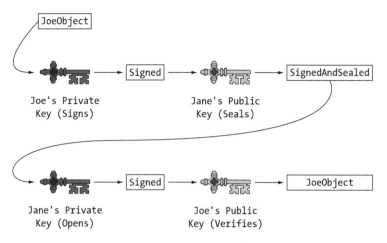

Figure 2-1. Signing and sealing an object

As Figure 2-1 shows, Joe takes an object, serializes it, and signs that data with his private key. Jane wants to receive this signature, so Joe encrypts the signature result with Jane's public key. When Jane receives this data, she decrypts the data and verifies that the original object data did come from Joe. Note that this process can be reversed—that is, Joe could encrypt his object data first with Jane's public key and then sign that result. Jane would then verify that the encrypted data came from him, and then decrypt the object data.

Before I move on to talking about implementing the two classes, you need to know how an object is serialized in .NET, so I'll address that next.

Object Serialization in .NET

It's not that hard if you want .NET to handle serialization for you—just add the [Serializable] attribute to your class as follows:

```
[Serializable]
public class SignAndSeal
{
    //...
}
```

When SignAndSeal is serialized, all the fields of the class instance will be added to the stream. If you don't want to have a field serialized for whatever reason, add the [NonSerialized] attribute as shown here:

```
[Serializable]
public class SignAndSeal
{
    private String internalData = null;
    [NonSerialized]
    private int temporaryData = 0;
}
```

However, there may be circumstances where you need control over the serialization process. In these cases, you can inherit from the ISerializable interface. This allows you to fine-tune the serialization process as you see fit, like so:

```
[Serializable]
public class SignAndSeal : ISerializable
{
    private String internalData = null;
    private SignAndSeal(SerializationInfo si, StreamingContext ctx) {}
    public void GetObjectData(SerializationInfo si, StreamingContext ctx) {}
}
```

When you implement ISerializable, you must create a custom constructor with the arguments shown to set the object's state to the given serialization data. You add object data to the serialization stream via the AddValue() method on SerializationInfo. Also, you have to implement GetObjectData() to set the object's state appropriately. You can retrieve the object's data via a number of GetXXX() methods that return the value as a specific type (for example, GetInt32()). Finally, you still need to mark the class as [Serializable] as the runtime looks for that attribute as a marker for a class that can be serialized. If you simply add the ISerializable interface without the [Serializable] attribute, a SerializationException will be thrown.[9]

Whether or not you use ISerializable, the real issue with object serialization is not how you set up the class, but how you format the serialization stream. .NET comes with two formatters: BinaryFormatter and SoapFormatter (although you need to reference the System.Runtime.Serialization.Formatters.Soap.dll assembly to use the SoapFormatter). The following code demonstrates how an object is serialized and deserialized using the two formatters:

---

9. For a complete discussion of object serialization, please read Chapter 11, "Input, Output, and Object Serialization," from Andrew Troelsen's book, *C# and the .NET Platform* (Apress, 2001).

```
using System.Runtime.Serialization.Formatters.Binary;
using System.Runtime.Serialization.Formatters.Soap;
SignAndSeal sas = new SignAndSeal("Some data. ");
MemoryStream msBin = new MemoryStream();
BinaryFormatter binFormat = new BinaryFormatter();
binFormat.Serialize(msBin, sas);
msBin.Position = 0;
SignAndSeal newSASBin = binFormat.Deserialize(msBin) as SignAndSeal;
MemoryStream msSOAP = new MemoryStream();
SoapFormatter soapFormat = new SoapFormatter();
soapFormat.Serialize(msSOAP, sas);
msSOAP.Position = 0;
SignAndSeal newSASSoap = soapFormat.Deserialize(msSOAP) as SignAndSeal;
```

If you look at the data that is stored in the two MemoryStream objects after each Serialize() method call, you'd see that they're vastly different. Therefore, you have to take into consideration the format in which the client would like you to serialize and deserialize the object. As all formatting classes descend from IFormatter, you can take in an IFormatter-based object in the constructors of

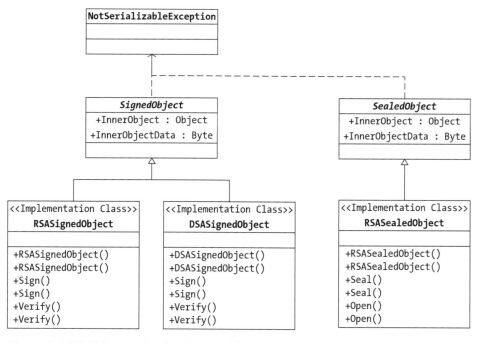

Figure 2-2. UML layout for the Sign and Seal design

SignedObject and SealedObject. Figure 2-2 shows a Unified Modeling Language (UML) diagram that lays out the class design.

The abstract classes SignedObject and SealedObject provide the contract semantics via the Sign(), Verify(), Seal(), and Open() methods that a class must implement to sign and/or seal an object. That's what RSASignedObject, DSASignedObject, and RSASealedObject do. The abstract classes also have two properties, InnerObject and InnerObjectData, that are used to retrieve object data.

Now that the design is in place, let's start coding. You'll tackle the SignedObject first.

SignedObject Implementation

The abstract base class of SignedObject is pretty straightforward, as you can see in Listing 2-8.

Listing 2-8. The Abstract Base Class of SignedObject

```
public abstract class SignedObject
{
    protected IFormatter m_formatStrategy = null;
    protected byte[] m_signature = null;
    protected byte[] m_wrappedObjectData = null;

    public SignedObject() : base() {}

    public SignedObject(Object ObjectToWrap, IFormatter FormatStrategy)
    {
        int hasSerializableAttrib = (int)ObjectToWrap.GetType().Attributes &
            (int)TypeAttributes.Serializable;

        if(0 == hasSerializableAttrib)
        {
            throw new NotSerializableException(
                "The given object is not serializable.");
        }

        MemoryStream ms = new MemoryStream();
        this.m_formatStrategy = FormatStrategy;
        this.m_formatStrategy.Serialize(ms, ObjectToWrap);
        this.m_wrappedObjectData = ms.GetBuffer();
        ms.Close();
```

```
        }

        public SignedObject(Object ObjectToWrap) :
            this(ObjectToWrap, new BinaryFormatter()) {}

        public Object InnerObject
        {
            get
            {
                return(this.m_formatStrategy.Deserialize(
                    new MemoryStream(this.m_wrappedObjectData)));
            }
        }

        public byte[] InnerObjectData
        {
            get
            { return(this.m_wrappedObjectData); }
        }
    }
```

All SignedObject does is implement the general InnerObject and
InnerObjectData properties that both RSASignedObject and DSASignedObject
need. Also, SignedObject's constructor checks to see that the given object is
marked for serialization. If it isn't, you can't sign it, so the custom exception
NotSerializationException is thrown.

Now, let's look at RSASignedObject in Listing 2-9. As DSASignedObject is virtually identical, I'll only cover one here. First, I'll show you the object construction
and initialization routines.

Listing 2-9. SignedObject Initialization and Setup

```
[Serializable]
public sealed class RSASignedObject : SignedObject, ISerializable
{
    private HashAlgorithm m_hash = nu;;
    private RSACryptoServiceProvider m_rsa = null;

    private RSASignedObject(SerializationInfo si, StreamingContext stc)
    {
        this.Initialize();
        String hashAlg = (String)si.GetValue("HashAlgorithm",
            typeof(System.String));
```

```csharp
        if("" != hashAlg)
        {
            this.m_formatStrategy =
                (IFormatter)Activator.CreateInstance(
                Type.GetType(hashAlg));
        }
        this.m_formatStrategy =
            (IFormatter)Activator.CreateInstance(
            Type.GetType((String)si.GetValue("FormatterStrategy",
            typeof(System.String))));
        this.m_signature = (byte[])si.GetValue("Signature",
            typeof(System.Byte[]));
        this.m_wrappedObjectData = (byte[])si.GetValue("ObjectData",
            typeof(System.Byte[]));
    }

    private RSASignedObject() : base()
    {
        this.Initialize();
    }

    public RSASignedObject(Object ObjectToWrap, IFormatter FormatStrategy)
        : base(ObjectToWrap, FormatStrategy)
    {
        this.Initialize();
    }

    public RSASignedObject(Object ObjectToWrap)
        : base(ObjectToWrap)
    {
        this.Initialize();
    }

    private void Initialize()
    {
        m_rsa = new RSACryptoServiceProvider();
    }
```

You need to "serialize" m_formatStrategy, but IFormatter is not serializable. Therefore, you store the type name in GetObjectData(), and when the object is deserialized, use CreateInstance() on Activator to create the correct serializer. This is also the case for m_hash, although you have to be careful here because the object may have been serialized before the algorithm was given. The rest of the methods don't do much other than ensure that all of the private fields are initialized.

Finally, take a look at the two methods that handle the signature processing:

```
private void Sign(HashAlgorithm Hash)
{
    this.m_signature = m_rsa.SignData(this.m_wrappedObjectData, Hash);
    this.m_hash = Hash;
}

private bool Verify(HashAlgorithm Hash)
{
    return m_rsa.VerifyData(this.m_wrappedObjectData,
        Hash, this.m_signature);
}
```

The signature data is stored in m_signature when a signature is requested, and it is verified via VerifyData(). Also, when Sign() is called, the given HashAlgorithm is stored to be used when a verification is needed. This is nice, as the client doesn't have to remember what hash algorithm was used to sign the data. Both these methods are used by the public methods—they simply forward the call to these methods as the following code snippet demonstrates:

```
public void Sign(String KeyXMLString, HashAlgorithm Hash)
{
    m_rsa.FromXmlString(KeyXMLString);
    this.Sign(Hash);
}
public bool Verify(RSAParameters KeyParameters)
{
    m_rsa.ImportParameters(KeyParameters);
    return this.Verify();
}
```

The only difference between DSASignedObject's and RSASignedObject's implementations is that the client doesn't have a choice for the hash algorithm with DSASignedObject because it always uses SHA1.

Now that you have the signing implementation done, let's work on the sealing process.

SealedObject Implementation

RSASealedObject is pretty much the same as RSASignedObject. The only real difference is that you're encrypting and decrypting data. I'll show you four methods in Listing 2-10: two private methods that RSASealedObject uses to handle the ciphering (Encrypt() and Decrypt()), and two public methods that use these private methods (Seal() and Open()).

Listing 2-10. Implementing SealedObject

```
private void Encrypt()
{
    int bytesProcessed = 0;
    int maxDataSize = this.MaxDataSize;
    int newChunkSize = 0;
    byte[] dataChunk = new byte[this.MaxDataSize];
    byte[] encryptedDataChunk = null;
    MemoryStream ms = new MemoryStream();

    do
    {
        newChunkSize = (this.m_wrappedObjectData.Length - bytesProcessed)
            < maxDataSize ? this.m_wrappedObjectData.Length -
            bytesProcessed : maxDataSize;
        Array.Copy(this.m_wrappedObjectData, bytesProcessed,
            dataChunk, 0, newChunkSize);
        encryptedDataChunk = m_rsa.Encrypt(dataChunk, false);
        ms.Write(encryptedDataChunk,
            0, (int)encryptedDataChunk.Length);
        bytesProcessed += newChunkSize;
    } while (bytesProcessed < this.m_wrappedObjectData.Length);

    ms.Position = 0;
    this.m_wrappedObjectData = new byte[ms.Length];
    Array.Copy(ms.GetBuffer(), 0,
        this.m_wrappedObjectData, 0, (int)ms.Length);
    ms.Close();
}
private void Decrypt()
{
    int bytesProcessed = 0;
    int maxDataSize = this.m_rsa.KeySize / 8;
    int newChunkSize = 0;
```

```
            byte[] dataChunk = new byte[this.m_rsa.KeySize / 8];
            byte[] encryptedDataChunk = null;
            MemoryStream ms = new MemoryStream();

            do
            {
                newChunkSize = (this.m_wrappedObjectData.Length - bytesProcessed)
                    < maxDataSize ? this.m_wrappedObjectData.Length -
                    bytesProcessed : maxDataSize;
                Array.Copy(this.m_wrappedObjectData, bytesProcessed,
                    dataChunk, 0, newChunkSize);
                encryptedDataChunk = m_rsa.Decrypt(dataChunk, false);
                ms.Write(encryptedDataChunk,
                    0, (int)encryptedDataChunk.Length);
                bytesProcessed += newChunkSize;
            } while (bytesProcessed < this.m_wrappedObjectData.Length);

            ms.Position = 0;
            this.m_wrappedObjectData = new byte[ms.Length];
            Array.Copy(ms.GetBuffer(), 0,
                this.m_wrappedObjectData, 0, (int)ms.Length);
            ms.Close();
        }
        public void Seal(String KeyXMLString)
        {
            m_rsa.FromXmlString(KeyXMLString);
            this.Encrypt();
        }
        public void Open(RSAParameters KeyParameters)
        {
            m_rsa.ImportParameters(KeyParameters);
            this.Decrypt();
        }
```

This approach is pretty straightforward. Encrypt the serialized object when Seal() is called, and then decrypt it on Open(). The only tricky part about this is making sure you encrypt and decrypt data using the correct chunk size and that you move through the plaintext's or ciphertext's byte data according to valid key sizes.

Now that you've got your objects, you're going to put them through a test run.

Examples

Let's say that you have two people—Joe and Steve—who want to sign a SignAndSealTest object. However, Steve wants to send the object to Carol in a secure fashion. Therefore, the following actions must take place:

1. Joe creates a SignAndSealTest object and signs it with his private DSA key.

2. Steve takes Joe's signed object and signs it with his private RSA key.

3. Steve encrypts the object with Carol's public key and e-mails her the serialized RSASignedObject object.

4. Carol deserializes the stream and decrypts Steve's signed object with her public key.

5. Carol verifies that Steve signed the object via his public key and extracts Joe's signed object.

6. Carol verifies that Joe signed the object via his public key and extracts the SignAndSealTest object.

This sounds like a lot of code, but it's not. Let's look at the first part in Listing 2-11—signing the object twice and sealing the results.

Listing 2-11. Signing and Sealing an Object

```
SignAndSealTest joesObject = new SignAndSealTest("Joe's original data.");
DSACryptoServiceProvider joesKeys = new DSACryptoServiceProvider();
DSASignedObject joesSig = new DSASignedObject(joesObject);
DSAParameters joesPrivateKey = joesKeys.ExportParameters(true);
joesSig.Sign(joesPrivateKey);

RSACryptoServiceProvider stevesKeys = new RSACryptoServiceProvider();
RSASignedObject stevesSig = new RSASignedObject(joesSig);
RSAParameters stevesPrivateKey = stevesKeys.ExportParameters(true);
stevesSig.Sign(stevesPrivateKey, new SHA1Managed());

RSACryptoServiceProvider carolsKeys = new RSACryptoServiceProvider();
String carolsPublicKey = carolsKeys.ToXmlString(false);
RSASealedObject carolsLock = new RSASealedObject(stevesSig);
carolsLock.Seal(carolsPublicKey);
```

```
MemoryStream ms = new MemoryStream();
IFormatter ifrm = new BinaryFormatter();
ifrm.Serialize(ms, carolsLock);
ms.Position = 0;
```

At this point, both Steve and Joe have signed the object, and Steve has sealed everything with Carol's public key. The sealed object is now serialized and can be saved to disk to e-mail to Carol (if so desired). Listing 2-12 reverses the process.

Listing 2-12. Opening and Verifying a Signed-and-Sealed Object

```
RSASealedObject carolsUnlock = (RSASealedObject)ifrm.Deserialize(ms);
ms.Close();
RSAParameters carolsPrivateKey = carolsKeys.ExportParameters(true);
carolsUnlock.Open(carolsPrivateKey);

RSASignedObject stevesVerify = (RSASignedObject)carolsUnlock.InnerObject;
String stevesPublicKey = stevesKeys.ToXmlString(false);
bool isSteveOK = stevesVerify.Verify(stevesPublicKey);

if(true == isSteveOK)
{
    DSASignedObject joesVerify = (DSASignedObject)stevesVerify.InnerObject;
    DSAParameters joesPublicKey = joesKeys.ExportParameters(false);
    bool isJoeOK = joesVerify.Verify(joesPublicKey);
    if(true == isJoeOK)
    {
        SignAndSealTest joesOriginal = (SignAndSealTest)joesVerify.InnerObject;
    }
}
```

If all goes well, `joesOriginal` should contain the string, "Joe's original data."

 SOURCE CODE *The SignAndSeal project in the Chapter2 sub-directory contains all of the classes discussed in this section along with the demonstration code.*

Summary

In this chapter, I covered the following topics:

- Cryptography classes in .NET

- Creation of hashes, sign data, and encrypt data with symmetric and asymmetric algorithms

- Extensions to the classes to make small improvements to the underlying framework

- Cryptographic object serialization framework using the Cryptography classes

In the next chapter, you'll learn about XML encryption and signatures.

CHAPTER 3

XML Encryption and Signatures

IN THIS CHAPTER, I'll talk about the Extensible Markup Language (XML) Encryption and Signatures specifications. These specifications are important for cryptography developers, as XML is now used in business data exchange and system interoperability protocols. This chapter will demonstrate how you can use .NET classes to help you sign and encrypt XML documents. Before you see how these classes work, let's start with a (very) brief tour of XML.

Locking Down XML

You've probably noticed that XML has become one of the biggest buzzword abbreviations in recent years. XML is a standard for marking up textual information in a consistent way such that any language in any environment can parse it with relative ease. For example, take a look at the following text document:

```
John Smith, 37
Jane Smith, 35
```

The document contains information, but there's no way to determine what the information means. Although we as human readers may be able to deduce what the meaning of the comma-separated values are (for example, the first value is a name, the second value is an age), our deductions may turn out to be wrong. Now, take a look at the same information in XML form:

```
<Golfers>
    <Golfer FirstName="John" LastName="Smith" >
        <AverageRound>37</AverageRound>
    </Golfer>
    <Golfer FirstName="Jane" LastName="Smith" >
        <AverageRound>35</AverageRound>
    </Golfer>
</Golfers>
```

Granted, we guessed right on the first value, but the second value has an entirely different meaning in the XML document[1] than what we surmised in the comma-separated document.[2]

Now, it's probably not a big deal if someone you don't know stumbles across this document and it contains your average golf score. But take a look at this document:

```
<Order>
    <Items>
        <Item ID="123456789">
            <Description>SuperEfficient GC</Description>
            <Price>0.99</Price>
        </Item>
    </Items>
    <Payment Method="Credit" Type="HighInterest">
        <Number>7890123456789012</Number>
        <ExpirationDate>12/12/2003</ExpirationDate>
    </Payment>
</Order>
```

This document describes your order for an efficient garbage collection (GC) algorithm that you want to plug into .NET.[3] Now, wouldn't you be a bit concerned if this document got passed across the wire in the clear? But it doesn't stop there either. With e-commerce servers such as BizTalk in the picture, XML-based information may get passed to a number of servers and components well after you clicked the Submit Order button on a Web page running over HTTPS. Furthermore, what if you want to sign the Payment element to indicate that it truly came from you and nobody else?

This isn't a new problem—people have been passing order information through business channels for a while now in a secure fashion. The issue with XML is, how do you secure the data in a standard way such that you can sign or encrypt an element so another program could verify the signature or decrypt it

---

1. This doesn't mean XML is self-describing, because it really isn't. Adding column names to the original text document would've helped out just as well. XML Schemas help in defining what a document means, but delving into Schemas is beyond the scope of this book.

2. To be fair, there's a lot more to XML than just marking up text. A whole slew of specifications have popped up around XML, such as XML Protocols (or SOAP), and XML Schemas, that make the XML world a bit more difficult to understand than what the last example may lead you to believe.

3. Technically, you can't "plug in" a new GC algorithm into .NET (at least not with version 1) but let's assume that you could implement your own GC if you were a glutton for punishment.

regardless of the language of the sending program or the platform that program was running on? Furthermore, how can you do this such that other programs can still read information from the XML document that isn't encrypted?

Fortunately, the World Wide Web Consortium (W3C) is aware of these issues. Currently, there are two specifications in the works that define how you can encrypt and sign XML data—they are called XML Signatures and XML Encryption (information on which can be found at `http://www.w3.org/TR/xmldsig-core/` and `http://www.w3.org/TR/xmlenc-core/`, respectively). Let's take a look at how each of these work.[4]

XML Signatures

The XML Signatures specification allows a client to sign a data object. This data object can be an element within the document itself, or it can be an external resource, such as a file located on a Web server. Essentially, the layout of the Signature element looks like what you see in Listing 3-1.

Listing 3-1. Signature Element Layout

```
<Signature>
    <SignedInfo>
        <CanonicalizationMethod>
            <SignatureMethod>
                (<Reference URI=)?>
                    (<Transforms>)?
                    <DigestMethod>
                    <DigestValue>
                </Reference>)+
    </SignedInfo>
    <SignatureValue>
    (<KeyInfo>)?
    (<Object>)*
</Signature>
```

where "?" means zero or one occurrence, "+" means one or more occurrences, and "*" means zero or more occurrences.

---

4. As of the writing of this book, the Signatures spec was in the "Proposed Recommendation" stage, whereas the Encryption spec had just entered the "Last Call" stage. In either case, changes may have occurred after the book went to print, so please refer to the given URLs for up-to-date information.

The Signing Process

Rather than describe what each element is used for in detail, take a look at how you would sign the `Payment` element in the order document to demonstrate how the specification drives the signing process. First, you need to create a `Reference` element as follows:

```
<Reference URI="Order/Payment">
    <DigestMethod Algorithm="http://www.w3.org/2000/09/xmldsig#sha1"/>
    <DigestValue>WC9IRkF6TUFNbkwxUE...</DigestValue>
</Reference>
```

The optional `URI` (Uniform Resource Identifier) attribute defines the source of the resource to be signed. In this case, it's the `Payment` element underneath the `Order` element (which I reference with an XPath expression), but the resource could also be a file:

```
<Reference URI="http://www.apress.com/orderFile.xml">
```

It can also identify the element that contains the signature:

```
<Reference URI="#paymentSig">
```

The `DigestMethod`'s `Algorithm` attribute can be any value, although the specification only defines the `sha1` value. The `DigestValue` is the hash value of the Base64-encoded encrypted data.

The Transforms Element

One element that I didn't list in this example under the `Reference` element is the `Transforms` element. This element is optional, but if it's listed it will contain at least one `Transform` element. Each `Transform` element must have the `Algorithm` attribute; they can also have `MimeType` and `Charset` attributes. The `Algorithm` attribute defines what kind of transformation was done to the original data before it was digested (that is, hashed). For example, say you wanted to only sign the `Number` element information after a Base64 transform was performed. In this case, the `Reference` element would look like Listing 3-2.

Listing 3-2. Adding Transformation to the Signing Process

```
<Reference URI="Order/Payment">
    <Transforms>
        <Transform Algorithm="http://www.w3.org/TR/1999/REC-xpath-19991116">
            <XPath>Number</XPath>
        </Transform>
        <Transform Algorithm="http://www.w3.org/2000/02/xmldsig#base-64"/>
    </Transforms>
    <DigestMethod Algorithm="http://www.w3.org/2000/09/xmldsig#sha1"/>
    <DigestValue>WC9IRkF6TUFNbkwxUE...</DigestValue>
</Reference>
```

NOTE   *The order of the* Transform *elements is important. If I had listed the Base64 transform first, the XPath query would not have been possible.*

Adding Reference to SignedInfo

Now, continue with the signing process. The next step is to add the Reference element to a SignedInfo element as shown in Listing 3-3.

Listing 3-3. The SignedInfo Element

```
<SignedInfo xmlns="http://www.w3.org/2000/09/xmldsig#">
    <CanonicalizationMethod Algorithm=
        "http://www.w3.org/TR/2001/REC-xml-c14n-20010315"/>
    <SignatureMethod Algorithm=
        "http://www.w3.org/2000/02/xmldsig#rsa-sha1"/>
    <Reference URI="Order/Payment">
        <DigestMethod Algorithm="http://www.w3.org/2000/02/xmldsig#sha1"/>
        <DigestValue>WC9IRkF6TUFNbk...</DigestValue>
    </Reference>
</SignedInfo>
```

The CanonicalizationMethod element defines the algorithm used to canonicalize the SignedInfo element. As the textual representations of a data stream in XML may differ, this method standardizes, or canonicalizes, the output. For example, the following two documents are logically the same, but if they were hashed they would give different values due to the extra </subNode1> element:

```
<node1>
    <subNode1/>
</node1>

<node1>
    <subNode1></subNode1>
<node1>
```

There are standard algorithms that will format the two documents so that they are physically the same.[5]

The other element, SignatureMethod, defines which algorithm was used to sign the data. The XML Signatures specification defines two algorithms that can be used to sign XML information: DSA (dsa) and PKCS1 (rsa-sha1). Of course, you can define your own signing algorithm—just make sure that the document recipients will be able to understand the algorithm type you specify.

The KeyInfo Element

The next stage is to create the KeyInfo element, which contains the public key information shown in Listing 3-4.

Listing 3-4. KeyInfo Element Example

```
<KeyInfo xmlns="http://www.w3.org/2000/09/xmldsig#">
    <RSAKeyValue xmlns="">
        <Modulus>60GTY9xdOS9s...</Modulus>
        <Exponent>AQAB</Exponent>
    </RSAKeyValue>
</KeyInfo>
```

---

5. Of the two documents, the second one is in canonical format according to the Canonical XML specification, which can be found at http://www.w3.org/TR/xml-c14n.

The RSAKeyValue XML structure is surprisingly similar to the exported XML that you saw in Chapter 2 for the RSACryptoServiceProvider class—in fact, it's exactly the same. Of course, if you were using DSA, then the appropriate information would be contained in the KeyInfo element.

You can also include X.509 certificate information in this KeyInfo element via an embedded X509Data element as shown here:

```
<KeyInfo xmlns="http://www.w3.org/2000/09/xmldsig#">
    <X509Data xmlns="http://www.w3.org/2000/09/xmldsig#">
        <X509Certificate>MIIBgzCCAS2gAwIBA...</X509Certificate>
    </X509Data>
</KeyInfo>
```

Using a certificate is advantageous because the receiver of the document can put more trust semantics into the signature, as anyone can generate a public/private key pair.

 CROSS-REFERENCE   *This is actually a very key point when it comes to strong naming an assembly, which I'll cover in Chapter 4.*

The Signature Element

Finally, you need to create the Signature element, which will include SignedInfo, KeyInfo, and the signature value of SignedInfo (which will be contained in a SignatureValue element). Listing 3-5 shows you how.

Listing 3-5. Signature Element Example

```
<Signature xmlns="http://www.w3.org/2000/09/xmldsig#">
    <SignedInfo>
        <CanonicalizationMethod
            Algorithm="http://www.w3.org/TR/2001/REC-xml-c14n20010315"/>
        <SignatureMethod
            Algorithm="http://www.w3.org/2000/02/xmldsig#rsa-sha1"/>
        <Reference URI="Order/Payment">
            <DigestMethod
                Algorithm="http://www.w3.org/2000/02/xmldsig#sha1"/>
            <DigestValue>WC9IRkF6TUFN...</DigestValue>
        </Reference>
    </SignedInfo>
```

```
<SignatureValue>HiKXeLuav4FHk/...</SignatureValue>
    <KeyInfo>
        <RSAKeyValue xmlns="">
            <Modulus>vmOnBv/...</Modulus>
            <Exponent>AQAB</Exponent>
        </RSAKeyValue>
    </KeyInfo>
</Signature>
```

Now you can include the Signature element into the order XML document as shown in Listing 3-6.

Listing 3-6. Including a Signature Element in an XML Document

```
<Order>
    <Items>
        <Item ID="123456789">
            <Description>SuperEfficient GC</Description>
            <Price>0.99</Price>
        </Item>
    </Items>
    <Payment Method="Credit" Type="HighInterest">
        <Number>7890123456789012</Number>
        <ExpirationDate>12/12/2003</ExpirationDate>
    </Payment>
    <Signature xmlns="http://www.w3.org/2000/09/xmldsig#">
        <!--  details omitted for brevity...>
    </Signature>
</Order>
```

A recipient of this XML document could verify that you signed the Payment element information. Of course, in a real-world situation, certificates would probably be used, but the idea is the same.

 NOTE *In this document, the recipient(s) can deduce that the payment information is valid relative to the entity that signed it, but the items ordered may or may not be what the entity wants. Such business logic resolution is ultimately up to the business, but one response would be to reject the order as there is no way to know if the items ordered are really what the signer wanted.*

In this case, the `Signature` element is enveloped, or contained, by the original document. This element would also be valid if the signature were enveloping the document as shown here:

```
<Signature xmlns="http://www.w3.org/2000/09/xmldsig#">
    <!--  details omitted for brevity...>
    <Order>
        <!--  details omitted for brevity...>
    </Order>
</Signature>
```

You could also create a separate XML file like the following that referenced the original document—this is known as a *detached* signature:

```
<Signature xmlns="http://www.w3.org/2000/09/xmldsig#">
    <!--  details omitted for brevity...>
    <Reference URI="file://c:\myorder.xml">
        <!--  details omitted for brevity...>
    </Reference>
</Signature>
```

Now you know how to sign XML information. But how do you encrypt it? That's what I'll cover in the next section.

XML Encryption

As you saw in the last example, the `Payment` element information is still in the clear even though you signed it. Personally, I'd like to be able to encrypt my credit card information with a business's public key so I know they're the only ones who can decrypt it. You'll see how this is accomplished by following the XML Encryption specification in Listing 3-7 to encrypt the `Payment` element.

Listing 3-7. Encrypting XML Information

```
<Order>
    <Items>
        <Item ID="123456789">
            <Description>SuperEfficient GC</Description>
            <Price>0.99</Price>
        </Item>
    </Items>
```

```
<EncryptedData Type="http://www.w3.org/2001/04/xmlenc#Element">
    <CipherData>
        <CipherValue>ahK++gYSxAA1MoZC77D...</CipherValue>
    </CipherData>
</EncryptedData>
</Order>
```

It looks a little easier than what you had to deal with in XML Signatures. The EncryptedData's Type attribute specifies what the cipher data is. In this case, it's element data (#Element), but it could also be an element's content information (#Content) as shown here:

```
<EncryptedData Type="http://www.w3.org/2001/04/xmlenc#Content">
```

or it could also be an entire XML document:

```
<EncryptedData Type=
"http://www.isi.edu/in-notes/iana/assignments/media-types/text/xml">
```

No matter what the type, you'll end up replacing the EncryptedData element with the decrypted results. The Type attribute is just a hint as to what the format of the decrypted information should look like. If it's #Element, you know the first character should be "<"; if it's #Content, the first character may be "<", but there's no guarantee that this will always be the case.

The CipherValue element contains the encrypted data. All the client has to do is decrypt the Base64-encoded data, and replace the EncryptedData element with whatever shows up in the results. However, it's possible that the CipherData element contains a CipherReference element instead as in this example:

```
<CipherData>
    <CipherReference URI="http://www.somesite.com/ciphervalues.xml">
        <Transforms>
            <Transform Algorithm="http://www.w3.org/TR/1999/REC-xpath-19991116">
                <XPath>CipherValue[@id="paymentinformation]</XPath>
            </Transform>
        </Transforms>
    </CipherReference>
</CipherData>
```

In this case, the recipient would have to download the ciphervalues.xml document, find the CipherValue element whose id attribute is equal to paymentinformation, and decrypt that element's value.

Also, while `EncryptedData` elements cannot be parents or children of other `EncryptedData` elements, the decryption of `CipherValue`'s text value may end up being another `EncryptedData` element. This is called *super-encryption* in the specification. So remember that if you're searching XML documents for `EncryptedData` elements, you may need to do the decryption process recursively.

Of course, whenever there's encryption, key information is close at hand—let's see how key material is represented in XML.

Key Information

If you review the XML example shown in Listing 3-1, you may wonder, where's the key information? In this case, the assumption is that the sender and recipient have already negotiated a shared symmetric key. In other words, this is *out-of-band* information. It's assumed that the parties who are using this document have the same key, so transmitting it is not necessary. Of course, the two parties may have multiple shared secret keys in storage. To tell the parties which key they should use, you add a `KeyInfo` element as shown in Listing 3-8.

Listing 3-8. Adding Key Material to an XML Document

```
<Order>
    <Items>
        <Item ID="123456789">
            <Description>SuperEfficient GC</Description>
            <Price>0.99</Price>
        </Item>
    </Items>
    <EncryptedData Type="http://www.w3.org/2001/04/xmlenc#Element">
        <EncryptionMethod Algorithm=http://www.w3.org/2001/04/xmlenc#aes256-cbc>
        <ds:KeyInfo xmlns:ds="http://www.w3.org/2000/09/xmldsig#">
            <ds:KeyName>Jane's Key</ds:KeyName>
        </ds:KeyInfo>
        <CipherData>
            <CipherValue>ahK++gYSxAA1MoZC77D...</CipherValue>
        </CipherData>
    </EncryptedData>
</Order>
```

The definition of `KeyInfo` comes from the XML Signatures Schema definition.

It's also possible that the key exchange did not take place before the document was sent to the other parties. In this case, you can send an XML document that contains nothing more than an EncryptedKey element that specifies an asymmetric algorithm. Listing 3-9 provides an example of this.

Listing 3-9. Transmitting a Public Key in XML

```
<EncryptedKey CarriedKeyName="Jane's Key">
    <EncryptionMethod Algorithm="http://www.w3.org/2001/04/xmlenc#rsa-1_5"/>
    <ds:KeyInfo xmlns:ds="http://www.w3.org/2000/09/xmldsig#">
        <ds:KeyName>Jane's Private Key</ds:KeyName>
    </ds:KeyInfo>
    <CipherData>
        <CipherValue>dv2jGeLAD5unDt3nGUAZZ/9vU...</CipherValue>
    </CipherData>
</EncryptedKey>
```

The recipient needs to be able to find key material referenced by the name, "Jane's Private Key". All the sender is doing is providing some kind of identifier with the KeyName element; it's up to the receiver to translate the name into a valid key. The key should be an RSA private key, as the Algorithm attribute of the EncryptionMethod element defines. The encrypted information in CipherValue is the symmetric key, which should be referenced by the value found in CarriedKeyName, "Jane's Key".

You now know the essentials of cryptography in XML—next let's see what .NET has provided in terms of support for these XML standards.

Understanding the Relationships between .NET, Cryptography, and XML

.NET has already started to address the XML standards relating to cryptography via the System.Security.DLL assembly—specifically, those classes that belong to the System.Security.Cryptography.Xml namespace, which I'll refer to as Cryptography.Xml from this point on. These classes make it easy to work with XmlElement-based objects, and they abstract some of the intricacies in the specifications away. In this section, you'll take a look at how you can use these classes to sign XML information.[6]

---

6. You'll see why I don't include encryption in this sentence when you get to the "Encrypting XML" section.

Signing XML

To see how you use the Cryptography.Xml classes for signature purposes, sign the Payment element with a private RSA key and then envelope the signature with the document. The first thing you need to do is get the Payment element out of the document itself. Fortunately, .NET provides extensive support for XML document processing, so all you need to do is use the System.Xml namespace and you have all the classes you need. Here's the example:

```
String appPath = Application.StartupPath;
XmlDocument xmlDoc = new XmlDocument();
xmlDoc.Load(appPath + @"\Order.XML");
XmlNodeList paymentElems = xmlDoc.SelectNodes("Order/Payment"));
```

Now that you have the node list (which in this case will contain only one element), you can let the classes do all the work. First, create the SignedXml object, which will contain your payment information within a data object:

```
SignedXml signedXml = new SignedXml();
System.Security.Cryptography.Xml.DataObject paymentInfo =
    new System.Security.Cryptography.Xml.DataObject();
paymentInfo.Data = paymentElems;
paymentInfo.Id = "OrderPayment";
signedXml.AddObject(paymentInfo);
```

Next, add a Reference element that refers to the data object:

```
Reference reference = new Reference();
reference.Uri = "#OrderPayment";
signedXml.AddReference(reference);
```

Finally, add a generated key to the SignedXml object, and create the signature:

```
RSA rsaKey = RSA.Create();
signedXml.SigningKey = rsaKey;
KeyInfo keyInfo = new KeyInfo();
keyInfo.AddClause(new RSAKeyValue(rsaKey));
signedXml.KeyInfo = keyInfo;
signedXml.ComputeSignature();
```

At this point, if you would get the XML from signedXml, it would look like Listing 3-10 (the key and signature information have been truncated).

Listing 3-10. Signature Element Results

```
<Signature xmlns="http://www.w3.org/2000/09/xmldsig#">
    <SignedInfo>
        <CanonicalizationMethod
        Algorithm="http://www.w3.org/TR/2001/REC-xml-c14n-20010315"/>
        <SignatureMethod Algorithm="http://www.w3.org/2000/09/xmldsig#rsa-sha1"/>
        <Reference URI="#OrderPayment">
            <DigestMethod Algorithm="http://www.w3.org/2000/09/xmldsig#sha1"/>
            <DigestValue>DoC7GhTuQk8H...</DigestValue>
        </Reference>
    </SignedInfo>
    <SignatureValue>lzFitF4ebqOh...</SignatureValue>
    <KeyInfo>
        <KeyValue xmlns="http://www.w3.org/2000/09/xmldsig#">
            <RSAKeyValue>
                <Modulus>sDmqsYcveGWG...</Modulus>
                <Exponent>AQAB</Exponent>
            </RSAKeyValue>
        </KeyValue>
    </KeyInfo>
    <Object Id="OrderPayment">
        <Payment Method="Credit" Type="HighInterest" xmlns="">
            <Number>7890123456789012</Number>
            <ExpirationDate>12/12/2003</ExpirationDate>
        </Payment>
    </Object>
</Signature>
```

Now you need to insert the `Signature` element into the original document:

```
xmlDoc.DocumentElement.InsertAfter(xmlDoc.ImportNode(signedXml.GetXml(), true),
    xmlDoc.DocumentElement.FirstChild);
```

Because the `Signature` element wasn't part of the original document, you need to import it, and then insert it after the document root element's first child element.

To verify the signature is just as easy, as you see here:

```
XmlDocument signedDoc = new XmlDocument();
signedDoc.LoadXml(xmlDoc.OuterXml);
SignedXml sigs = new SignedXml(signedDoc);
XmlNodeList sigElems = signedDoc.GetElementsByTagName("Signature");
sigs.LoadXml((XmlElement)sigElems[0]);
MessageBox.Show(sigs.CheckSignature().ToString());
```

If everything works, you should see a message box with the word "True" in it. In this case, there's only one `Signature` element, so you only need to make one check. With other documents, you should loop through each element in the node list returned by `GetElementsByTagName()`. To check each signature, simply call `CheckSignature()`—a return value of true signals success.

Now, if you wanted to sign the document itself and create a detached signature file, you could eliminate a fair amount of code, like so:

```
SignedXml signedXml = new SignedXml();
Reference reference = new Reference();
reference.Uri = @"file://" + Application.StartupPath +
    @"\Order.XML";
signedXml.AddReference(reference);
RSA rsaKey = RSA.Create();
signedXml.SigningKey = rsaKey;
KeyInfo keyInfo = new KeyInfo();
keyInfo.AddClause(new RSAKeyValue(rsaKey));
signedXml.KeyInfo = keyInfo;
signedXml.ComputeSignature();
```

You have no need to load the target document, nor do you need to create a `DataObject`, since the entire document (whose location is specified via the URI property) will be signed. Verifying the signature is the same as before, except this time use the signature data's to create the document to verify as shown here:

```
XmlDocument signedDoc = new XmlDocument();
signedDoc.LoadXml(signedXml.GetXml().OuterXml);
SignedXml sigs = new SignedXml(signedDoc);
XmlNodeList sigElems = signedDoc.GetElementsByTagName("Signature");
sigs.LoadXml((XmlElement)sigElems[0]);
MessageBox.Show(sigs.CheckSignature().ToString());
```

SOURCE CODE *The XMLSignaturesTest project in the Chapter3 subdirectory contains the code used in this section to sign an XML element via a number of* Cryptography.Xml *classes.*

Now that I've covered XML signatures in .NET, let's see how XML encryption works.

Encrypting XML

While .NET has supporting classes for the XML Signatures specification, it has nothing for XML Encryption. However, just because .NET does not explicitly support XML Encryption doesn't mean you can't encrypt XML elements via the Cryptography classes you used in the previous chapter.[7] Let's see what it would take to encrypt the Payment element.

Assuming that no session key exists, the first thing you need to do is exchange a key. To do this, you need to create a symmetric key, encrypt it, and then make the result Base64 encoded. Listing 3-11 shows this process.

Listing 3-11. Encrypting XML Key Information

```
Rijndael rKey = new RijndaelManaged();
RSACryptoServiceProvider rsa = new RSACryptoServiceProvider();
MemoryStream encryptedData = new MemoryStream();

int start = 0;
do
{
    byte[] keyMaterial = new byte[16];
    Array.Copy(rKey.Key, start, keyMaterial, 0, 16);
    byte[] encryptedSessionKey = rsa.Encrypt(keyMaterial, false);
    encryptedData.Write(encryptedSessionKey, 0,
        (int)encryptedSessionKey.Length);
    start += 16;
} while(start < rKey.Key.Length);
```

---

7. Along those same lines, one could argue that it's possible to use the Cryptography classes to sign XML data per the XML Signatures specification. However, I'd recommend you use the Cryptography.Xml classes, as I think it makes the signature processing easier.

```
encryptedData.Position = 0;
String rToBase64 = Convert.ToBase64String(encryptedData.GetBuffer(),
    0, (int)encryptedData.Length);
```

Once you have the session key encrypted, it becomes a matter of creating the right XmlElement objects at the right time so you can generate the appropriate encryption elements. Listing 3-12 shows this code.

Listing 3-12. Setting up XML Key Exchange

```
XmlDocument keyExchDoc = new XmlDocument();
XmlElement encryptedKey = keyExchDoc.CreateElement("EncryptedKey");
keyExchDoc.AppendChild(encryptedKey);
XmlAttribute carriedKeyName = keyExchDoc.CreateAttribute("CarriedKeyName");
carriedKeyName.Value = "Jane's Session Key";
encryptedKey.Attributes.Append(carriedKeyName);

XmlElement encryptionMethod = keyExchDoc.CreateElement("EncryptionMethod");
encryptedKey.AppendChild(encryptionMethod);
XmlAttribute encryptionAlgorithm = keyExchDoc.CreateAttribute("Algorithm");
encryptionAlgorithm.Value = "http://www.w3.org/2001/04/xmlenc#rsa-1_5";
encryptionMethod.Attributes.Append(encryptionAlgorithm);

XmlElement keyInfo = keyExchDoc.CreateElement("ds", "KeyInfo",
    "http://www.w3.org/2000/09/xmldsig#");
encryptedKey.AppendChild(keyInfo);

XmlElement keyName = keyExchDoc.CreateElement("ds", "KeyName", null);
keyName.InnerText = "Jane's Private Key";
keyInfo.AppendChild(keyName);

XmlElement cipherData = keyExchDoc.CreateElement("CipherData");
encryptedKey.AppendChild(cipherData);

XmlElement cipherValue = keyExchDoc.CreateElement("CipherValue");
cipherValue.InnerText = rToBase64;
cipherData.AppendChild(cipherValue);
```

At this point, calling `OuterXml` on `keyExchDoc` yields the following XML document:

```
<EncryptedKey CarriedKeyName="Jane's Session Key">
    <EncryptionMethod Algorithm="http://www.w3.org/2001/04/xmlenc#rsa-1_5"/>
    <ds:KeyInfo xmlns:ds="http://www.w3.org/2000/09/xmldsig#">
        <KeyName>Jane's Private Key</KeyName>
    </ds:KeyInfo>
    <CipherData>
        <CipherValue>CQu3/R138mrMDuLuY74C1....</CipherValue>
    </CipherData>
</EncryptedKey>
```

Jane needs to decrypt the result with her private key named "Jane's Private Key". Once she has the key material, she needs to refer to that key as "Jane's Session Key".

Okay, let's assume Jane received this document and transformed and decrypted `CipherValue`'s text. Now you can send Jane the XML order document with the `Payment` element encrypted by using the code in Listing 3-13.

Listing 3-13. Encrypting XML Information

```
String appPath = Application.StartupPath;
XmlDocument paymentDoc = new XmlDocument();
paymentDoc.Load(appPath + @"\Order.XML");
XmlElement paymentElem =
    (XmlElement)paymentDoc.SelectSingleNode("Order/Payment");


byte[] paymentXmlInfo = Encoding.Unicode.GetBytes(paymentElem.OuterXml);
MemoryStream ms = new MemoryStream();
CryptoStream csBase64 = new CryptoStream(ms,
    new ToBase64Transform(),
    CryptoStreamMode.Write);
CryptoStream csRijndael = new CryptoStream(csBase64,
    rKey.CreateEncryptor(),
    CryptoStreamMode.Write);
csRijndael.Write(paymentXmlInfo, 0,
    (int)paymentXmlInfo.Length);
csRijndael.FlushFinalBlock();
String base64enc = Encoding.ASCII.GetString(ms.GetBuffer(),
    0, (int)ms.Length);
```

At this point, you have the payment information encrypted. Now you need to create the `EncryptedData` element and add the key information along with the encryption results. Listing 3-14 provides this code.

Listing 3-14. Adding XML Encryption Information to an XML Document

```
XmlElement encryptedData = paymentDoc.CreateElement("EncryptedData");
XmlAttribute encryptedType = paymentDoc.CreateAttribute("Type");
encryptedType.Value = "http://www.w3.org/2001/04/xmlenc#Element";
encryptedData.Attributes.Append(encryptedType);

XmlElement keyInfo = paymentDoc.CreateElement("ds", "KeyInfo",
    "http://www.w3.org/2000/09/xmldsig#");
encryptedData.AppendChild(keyInfo);

XmlElement keyName = paymentDoc.CreateElement("ds", "KeyName", null);
keyName.InnerText = "Jane's Session Key";
keyInfo.AppendChild(keyName);

XmlElement cipherData = paymentDoc.CreateElement("CipherData");
encryptedData.AppendChild(cipherData);

XmlElement cipherValue = paymentDoc.CreateElement("CipherValue");
cipherValue.InnerText = base64enc;
cipherData.AppendChild(cipherValue);

XmlElement orderElem =
    (XmlElement)paymentDoc.SelectSingleNode("Order");

orderElem.ReplaceChild(encryptedData, paymentElem);
```

You replace the `Payment` element from the original document with the encrypted information.

The end result of this code is the XML document shown in Listing 3-15.

Listing 3-15. XML Encryption Results

```
<Order>
    <Items>
        <Item ID="123456789">
            <Description>SuperEfficient GC</Description>
            <Price>0.99</Price>
        </Item>
    </Items>
    <EncryptedData Type="http://www.w3.org/2001/04/xmlenc#Element">
        <ds:KeyInfo xmlns:ds="http://www.w3.org/2000/09/xmldsig#">
            <KeyName>Jane's Session Key</KeyName>
        </ds:KeyInfo>
        <CipherData>
            <CipherValue>lupcw1DYZ9kOTr1rX2TN...</CipherValue>
        </CipherData>
    </EncryptedData>
</Order>
```

Once Jane receives this document, she can retrieve the key material named "Jane's Session Key". That key decrypts the text found in `CipherValue`. The resulting information replaces the `EncryptedData` element, and she can process the document normally. Here's how you can accomplish this decoding processing:

```
XmlDocument docToDecrypt = new XmlDocument();
docToDecrypt.LoadXml(orderElem.OuterXml);
XmlElement encryptedElem =
    (XmlElement)docToDecrypt.SelectSingleNode("Order/EncryptedData");
XmlElement cipherDataElem =
    (XmlElement)encryptedElem.SelectSingleNode("CipherData/CipherValue");
byte[] cipherDataRes = Convert.FromBase64String(cipherDataElem.InnerText);
```

At this point, `cipherDataRes` contains the encrypted data. Now you need to use the Rijndael-based key to decrypt it:

```
MemoryStream msDec = new MemoryStream();
CryptoStream csRijndaelDec = new CryptoStream(msDec,
    rKey.CreateDecryptor(),
    CryptoStreamMode.Write);
csRijndaelDec.Write(cipherDataRes, 0,
    (int)cipherDataRes.Length);
csRijndaelDec.FlushFinalBlock();
String finalResult = Encoding.Unicode.GetString(msDec.GetBuffer(),
    0, (int)msDec.Length);
```

CROSS-REFERENCE   *See "Symmetric Keys" and "Encrypting and Decrypting Data" in Chapter 2 for discussions of the Rijndael algorithm.*

The last step is to replace the `EncryptedData` node with the decrypted information:

```
XmlNode encryptedParentElem = encryptedElem.ParentNode;
XmlDocumentFragment xdf = docToDecrypt.CreateDocumentFragment();
xdf.InnerXml = finalResult;
encryptedParentElem.ReplaceChild(xdf, encryptedElem);
MessageBox.Show(docToDecrypt.OuterXml);
```

The `XmlDocumentFragment` class makes it easy to load "free-floating" XML and stuff them into a document. If all goes well, the message box should display the original document.

SOURCE CODE   *The XMLEncryptionTest project in the Chapter3 subdirectory contains the code used in this section to encrypt an XML element.*

....

Decrypting XML and Validation

It's interesting to note that encrypting and decrypting data using the XML format has a nice side-effect with regards to the verification process. Let's say that you received an order document with encrypted information. You decrypt it, replace the `EncryptedData` element, and begin to process the document via an `XmlDocument` class instance. However, as soon as you call `Load()`, you get an exception. In this case, something went wrong in the decryption phase. If you know that your decryption and element replacement logic is sound, you can deduce that you were sent a document that did not come from the sender who gave you a session key. Why? If the decryption process produced output like this:

```
<Order>
    <Items>
        <Item ID="123456789">
            <Description>SuperEfficient GC</Description>
            <Price>0.99</Price>
        </Item>
    </Items>
*$JD(()#MFHI#$O)C<SKDFLE  K3..O9)Du993Osk
</Order>
```

> XmlDocument won't be able to load it. Therefore, you could halt the order fulfillment processing before it even starts.

....

Before I finish this chapter, I wanted to briefly touch on another specification in the works at the W3C: Decryption Transform for XML Signatures.[8]

Decryption Transform for XML Signatures

This specification deals with the problem of determining what the order of decryption and signature verification should be in an XML document. For example, let's say that I wanted to sign my Payment element to prove that I added the credit card information. However, I also want to encrypt the Number element, as I don't want that to be seen by just anyone. Therefore, the SignatureValue element will contain a signature that includes the encrypted Number element. If the recipient of this document were to try to decrypt the element before the signature is verified, the verification would fail.

Essentially, this specification defines another transformation type. This Transform element may have DataReference elements that specify which elements should not be decrypted to verify a signature. In the scenario described in the preceding paragraph, I would list the Number element as an element not to decrypt until the verification process is complete.

Keep this draft specification in mind if you're going to do a lot of XML signature verification and decryption. You may need to find all of the Transform elements that list such a transformation type to ensure the processing steps are carried out correctly.

---

8.   You can find information about this specification at http://www.w3.org/2001/04/decrypt#.

NOTE *Throughout this chapter, I've made mention of session keys and key exchange. As you saw in Chapter 2, key exchange is essential when trying to transport session keys. The W3C is aware of the need for a standard way to exchange key material via XML, so the XML Key Management Specification (or XKMS 2.0) has been established (http://www.w3.org/TR/xkms2/). However, the specification is considered a work in progress, so the details may change significantly from their current form.*

Summary

In this chapter, I covered the following topics:

- Fundamentals of the XML Signatures and Encryption specifications

- Signing and encrypting XML information in conformance with these specifications

In the next chapter, you'll start to dive into the layers of .NET security.

CHAPTER 4

Code Access Security

IN THIS CHAPTER, I'll introduce you to Code Access Security (CAS) as well as how permissions and evidence factor into the picture. This will include discussions on what policy levels are, how evidence affects assemblies loaded into application domains, and how the evidence they submit affects the permissions they are granted. Then I'll cover permissions and how they work in .NET. Finally, I'll demonstrate how you can create your own custom permissions.

Understanding Code Access Security

The CAS mechanism in .NET allows for tighter control over code usage of resources by the user of a particular machine. For example, let's say I bought a component object model (COM) server from a component vendor that has one coclass called CCompletelySafe that implements the IItsOK interface. This interface has one method called NothingBadWillHappen(). To get this to run, I add the reference to my VB application, and start coding away, like so:

```
Dim oOK As IItsOK
Set oOK = CreateObject("TrustMe.CCompletelySafe")
oOK.NothingBadWillHappen()
```

Unfortunately, in no time at all I've e-mailed everyone in the company a bunch of links that will probably get me fired. Plus, my files are being deleted at a furious rate, and my computer is also creating a bunch of HTTP traffic. The real problem here is that I can't determine what that method call will do until I invoke it.[1]

Authenticode helped this situation out, but it didn't address the core problem. For example, let's say I create a malicious COM server that would appear to work as documented, but after a certain number of method calls, it performs all sorts of tasks that a user would not expect. I go through the process of signing my code with Authenticode, and you download and use my code. Although you get all sorts of information about me as the author of the component, you don't

---

1. Of course, security based on interface and method names is not a policy that I recommend anyone follow in the near and distant future.

know what the underlying implementation is going to do. Unless you try to disassemble the code or you're very careful about monitoring resource usage on your machine, you'll never know that the COM server is malicious.

Clients want to let components do as little as necessary. If you don't think a grid component should have access to the hard drive, you should be able to set that policy up. Conversely, if the designer of the component really needs access to a particular subdirectory, he or she should be able to at least make the request in a way that a client could discover this request and determine if that particular component should have permission to use the subdirectory. With the CAS model, this is possible. A developer can use attributes to state that he or she wants to write files to a specific directory, which will be stored in the assembly as metadata (data that describes the assembly's members). Also, a user can decide via policy configuration whether to grant that access or not.

Before looking at how CAS works in .NET, I'd like to cover the namespaces that contain the classes used throughout this chapter (all of the classes within these namespaces are defined in mscorlib.dll). The System.Security namespace contains the base interface definitions for the security classes you'll use, such as IPermission. System.Security.Permissions contains all of the .NET-defined permission classes, like UIPermission. Finally, System.Security.Policy classes deal with policy management and evidence.

 CROSS REFERENCE *If you look at the SDK, you'll notice that there's also a* System.Security.Principal *namespace. The classes within that namespace will be covered in Chapter 5.*

Covering the Essentials

Let's continue by looking at the top level of CAS: policies, code groups, and evidence.

Policies and Evidence

In a nutshell, *policies* determine what an assembly can and cannot do. Whenever an assembly is loaded and its code is executed, the runtime looks at certain pieces of information called *evidence* and determines what permissions are granted such that the code can use certain resources. This evidence is based on a number of attributes of an assembly. Table 4-1 lists the different pieces of evidence that the runtime is aware of.

Table 4-1. Evidence Items

NAME	DESCRIPTION
ApplicationDirectory	The directory where the application is installed
Hash	Hash value of an assembly
Publisher	The Authenticode signer of the code
Site	Origin of the code, such as `http://www.apress.com`
StrongName	Cryptographically strong name of the assembly
URL	URL of assembly location
Zone	Zone of assembly location (for example, MyComputer)

Each of these pieces of evidence can be used to grant or deny access to resources based on their presence. However, it's up to you to decide how much trust you put in this evidence. For example, a strong name is a good indicator that an assembly has not been tampered with, so you can verify that mscorlib.dll hasn't been altered because the hacker would need access to Microsoft's private key to re-sign the assembly. Keep in mind that a strong name does not have any way to identify where the assembly came from, whereas the presence of a certificate (that is, the publisher) does. (I'll show you what the difference is between these two pieces of evidence in the section "Adding Evidence.") After I cover code groups in this section, I'll show you how you can use a piece of evidence to grant an assembly certain privileges.

There are four levels of policy that the runtime automatically knows about at installation time:

- Enterprise

- Machine

- User

- AppDomain

What's nice about this approach is it allows you to make decisions at different levels. Furthermore, these decisions can be overridden at a lower level. For example, let's say your enterprise decided that any code that's loaded has the ability to use reflection. However, if you specify at the machine policy level that any code cannot use the reflection classes, all code on the machine will not have this ability. There are some subtleties as to how access is calculated based on how the code group is set up—you'll see how this is calculated in detail in the section "Permission Sets" later in the chapter.

Code Groups

Each of the policies just mentioned contains a number of *code groups*. A code group allows you to define what loaded code can do depending on the evidence that it presents. Remember, code groups use evidence to determine the level of trust—this is called "satisfying the membership condition." These groups have a named permission set associated with it—I'll explain permission sets when I cover how permissions work later on in the chapter.

You can add code groups as subcode groups to other code groups if you'd like. For example, the default code group setup for the Machine policy level has a root code group of All_Code, and it contains five subgroups: My_Computer_Zone, LocalIntranet_Zone, Internet_Zone, Restricted_Zone, and Trusted_Zone. This gives you the ability to have fine-grain control over what resources are granted and denied.

Code groups can have two attributes associated with them that are not mutually exclusive. The first one is called Exclusive. If a code group has this value, it means that whatever access it allows or denies to code within a policy level is the limit. For example, let's say the runtime determines that an assembly satisfies the membership conditions of two code groups within a policy level. One of the code groups allows access to five resources; the other allows access to three of these five resources, but it has the Exclusive attribute. Therefore, the runtime will not grant the two extra resources from the first code group. Note that this Exclusive restriction extends across all of the policies. It is possible to belong to Exclusive code groups in other policy levels, but you can only belong to one Exclusive code group within a policy.

The second attribute is called LevelFinal. This states that no code groups should be evaluated for any policy levels under the current one (this restriction does not hold for the AppDomain policy level). For example, let's alter the example slightly. You have one code group in the Enterprise level with the LevelFinal attribute and another code group in the Machine level, both of which have the membership conditions satisfied. In this case, the code group in the Machine level will never be touched.

Controlling Evidence in Application Domains and Assemblies

Applications run in app domains under the control of a host. These hosts (shell, browser, server, or custom-designed) have access to the assembly code. A host can provide evidence to the runtime about the assembly. Once an application is up and running, it can also create other app domains and pass evidence information to these new app domains.

Take a look at how you can create an AppDomain that has a certain set of evidence items and how it's transferred to assemblies within the AppDomain. To start, create the class shown in Listing 4-1 in an assembly called Book.dll.

Listing 4-1. The Book.dll Assembly

```
using System;
using System.Collections;
using System.Security.Policy;
using System.Reflection;

namespace BookImpl
{
    public class Book : MarshalByRef
    {
        private string m_Author = null;
        private string m_Title = null;

        public Book() : base() {}

        public Book(string Author, string Title)
        {
            this.m_Author = Author;
            this.m_Title = Title;

            IEnumerator adEvidence =
                AppDomain.CurrentDomain.Evidence.GetEnumerator();
            while(adEvidence.MoveNext())
            {
                object adevid = adEvidence.Current;
                Console.WriteLine("AppDomain Evidence:  " + adevid.ToString());
            }
```

```
            IEnumerator assemblyEvidence =
                Assembly.GetExecutingAssembly().Evidence.GetEnumerator();
            while(assemblyEvidence.MoveNext())
            {
                object assemblyevid = assemblyEvidence.Current;
                Console.WriteLine("Assembly Evidence:  " +
                    assemblyevid.ToString());
            }
        }

        public string Author
        {
            get
            { return this.m_Author; }
            set
            { this.m_Author = value; }
        }

        public string Title
        {
            get
            { return this.m_Title; }
            set
            { this.m_Title = Title; }
        }
    }
}
```

It's a simple class that defines the author and title of a book. Okay, it's not that interesting and the model isn't a very accurate description of a real-world scenario, but the interesting code is in the custom constructor. Note that you'll iterate through the evidence from both the current AppDomain and Assembly—you'll see why you iterate through both in a moment. Once you've created the assembly, put the DLL into a common directory, which you'll use throughout the rest of the project. I used C:\assembly, but you can use whatever you want.

Now create a console application that generates some evidence, passes that into a new AppDomain, loads the assembly, and creates an instance of the Book type. Listing 4-2 provides this code.

Listing 4-2. Creating a Book Instance

```csharp
using System;
using System.Collections;
using System.Reflection;
using System.Runtime.Remoting;
using System.Security;
using System.Security.Cryptography.X509Certificates;
using System.Security.Permissions;
using System.Security.Policy;
using BookImpl;

namespace EvidenceTest
{
    class ETest
    {
        static void Main(string[] args)
        {
            try
            {
                X509Certificate x =
                    X509Certificate.CreateFromCertFile(
                    @"C:\assembly\simpleCert.cer");
                Publisher p = new Publisher(x);
                Url u = new Url(@"file:///C:/assembly");
                Zone z = new Zone(SecurityZone.MyComputer);
                object[] e = {p, u, z};
                Evidence eSet = new Evidence(e, null);
                AppDomain newAD = AppDomain.CreateDomain(
                    "ApressDomain", eSet,
                    @"C:\assembly", null, false);

                IEnumerator es = newAD.Evidence.GetEnumerator();
                while(es.MoveNext())
                {
                    object evid = es.Current;
                    Console.WriteLine("Evidence:   " +
                        evid.ToString());
                }

                string[] ctorArgs = {"Jason Bock", "Some Book"};
```

```
                AssemblyName bookAssemblyName =
                    AssemblyName.GetAssemblyName(
                    @"C:\assembly\Book.dll");

                Assembly bookAssembly = newAD.Load(
                    bookAssemblyName, eSet);
                Book aBook = bookAssembly.CreateInstance(
                    "BookImpl.Book", false,
                    BindingFlags.CreateInstance,
                    null, ctorArgs, null, null) as Book;

                Console.WriteLine("Author is " + aBook.Author);
                Console.WriteLine("Title is " + aBook.Title);
            }
            catch(Exception ge)
            {
                Console.WriteLine("Exception:   " +
                    ge.GetType().Name + " " + ge.Message);
                 Console.WriteLine(ge.StackTrace);
            }
            finally
            {
                Console.WriteLine("Press the return key to continue...");
                Console.Read();
            }
        }
    }
}
```

First, create the three pieces of evidence. For the `Publisher` class, all you
need is a certificate file, which you created in Chapter 2 if you followed along
with the examples. Once you have your three `Evidence` objects, you add them to
an array and pass the array into `CreateDomain()`. After that's done, print what the
`AppDomain` has for its evidence. Next, load the assembly into the new `AppDomain`,
get an object reference via `CreateInstance()` (passing in the two constructor values), and read the two properties.

Now, before you run this code, what do you expect will happen in the console
window? The results, which appear in Listing 4-3, surprised me the first time
I ran it.

Listing 4-3. Evidence Results

```
Evidence:   <System.Security.Policy.Publisher version="1">
    <X509v3Certificate>30820183....</X509v3Certificate>
</System.Security.Policy.Publisher>
Evidence:   <System.Security.Policy.Url version="1">
    <Url>file:///C:/assembly</Url>
</System.Security.Policy.Url>
Evidence:   <System.Security.Policy.Zone version="1">
    <Zone>MyComputer</Zone>
</System.Security.Policy.Zone>

AppDomain Evidence:   <System.Security.Policy.Zone version="1">
    <Zone>MyComputer</Zone>
</System.Security.Policy.Zone>
AppDomain Evidence:   <System.Security.Policy.Url version="1">
    <Url>file:///C:/assembly/EvidenceSample.exe</Url>
</System.Security.Policy.Url>
AppDomain Evidence:   <System.Security.Policy.Hash version="1">
    <RawData>4D5A9000...</RawData>
</System.Security.Policy.Hash>

Assembly Evidence:   <System.Security.Policy.Zone version="1">
    <Zone>MyComputer</Zone>
</System.Security.Policy.Zone>
Assembly Evidence:   <System.Security.Policy.Url version="1">
    <Url>file:///C:/assembly/book.DLL</Url>
</System.Security.Policy.Url>
```

When you iterate through the evidence in your code, you see all three items. However, in the Book object, the evidence is different. For example, your Publisher evidence item is nowhere to be found.

The reason for this is very subtle. When you get the Assembly object reference back from Load(), the assembly is loaded into the AppDomain, but it's marshaled-by-value into the current default domain. So when you create an instance of the Book class, you're actually doing it in your own domain, on the ApressDomain domain. In fact, add the following line of code to Book's custom constructor:

```
Console.WriteLine("Current AppDomain Name:  " +
    AppDomain.CurrentDomain.FriendlyName);
```

Now the console window should show this in the output stream:

```
Current AppDomain Name:  BookTest.exe
```

To get the assembly to "see" the evidence, you need to change the object creation code a bit, as follows:

```
ObjectHandle aBookOH = newAD.CreateInstance(
    bookAssemblyName.Name, "BookImpl.Book",
    false, BindingFlags.CreateInstance,
    null, ctorArgs, null,
    null, eSet);

Book aBook = aBookOH.Unwrap() as Book;
```

In this case, you're creating the object directly from the new AppDomain. When you run your test application, you'll see that the Book object now has the expected AppDomain name, and the evidence iterations contain your three items.

When you create the object with CreateInstance(), you have to pass in the evidence list, even though you set that when you created the AppDomain via CreateDomain(). In fact, set the last argument in CreateInstance() to null. You'll see that you lose your evidence items.

SOURCE CODE   *The Book project in the Chapter3 subdirectory contains the definition of the* Book *class, and the EvidenceSample solution creates the* AppDomain *and* Assembly *with a specific evidence set. Make sure you put the assemblies and the test certificate into the correct directories.*

Adding Evidence

In Chapter 3, I briefly mentioned that I would cover the difference between strong-naming an assembly and adding certificate information to an assembly. Now I'll demonstrate how these two pieces of evidence are added to an assembly and why they are different.

Say you have a class called EvidenceInfo, which resides in the EvidenceDemo assembly, like so:

```
public class EvidenceInfo {}
```

EvidenceInfo doesn't do much, and in this example, it doesn't need to as I'm more concerned with the evidence that will be attached to the assembly rather than what EvidenceInfo can do.

First, add the strong name. To do this, you need to create a public/private key pair, which is done with the Strong Name tool (sn.exe):

```
sn -k EvidenceDemo.snk
```

Once you have the file, you can update the AssemblyKeyFile attribute that is always present in the AssemblyInfo.cs file whenever you create a VS .NET C# project. Here's how to do this:

```
[assembly: AssemblyKeyFile(@"..\..\EvidenceDemo.snk")]
```

Whenever an assembly is strong-named, the signature in the assembly can be verified with sn as well by using the -vf option as shown here:

```
sn -vf EvidenceDemo.dll
```

That's all you need to do to strong-name an assembly. Adding a certificate file is a bit more involved. The first piece of information you need is the certificate file, which can be created with the makecert tool I mentioned in Chapter 2. Here's an example:

```
makecert -sv EvidenceDemo.pvk EvidenceDemo.cer
```

The -sv option creates a private key file that will be used in a moment. When you run this tool, you'll get two dialog boxes asking for password information. Remember these passwords—you'll need them again very soon.

Once the certificate file is created, you need to convert it into another format via the Software Publisher Certificate Test tool (cert2spc.exe) as shown here:

```
cert2spc EvidenceDemo.cer EvidenceDemo.spc
```

This step is necessary for the final step where the assembly is signed with the certificate. You accomplish this with the File Signing tool (signcode.exe), which will only take files in the spc format. Here's an example:

```
signcode -spc EvidenceDemo.spc -v EvidenceDemo.pvk EvidenceDemo.dll
```

When you run this tool, you'll get another dialog box asking for the password you gave in the makecert process. If all goes well, your assembly will be signed. You can verify an assembly signature with the Certificate Verification tool (chktrust.exe), like so:

```
chktrust EvidenceDemo.dll
```

If the signature is valid, the Certificate Verification tool will return a message that looks like this:

```
Assembly 'EvidenceDemo.dll' is valid
```

At this point, you have an assembly strong-named with a certificate. The main difference between the certificate and the strong name is the former can be verified, whereas the latter cannot. Recall that a strong name is a great way to ensure that an assembly has not been tampered with, as the verification with makecert would fail if the assembly's binary information was altered. However, the strong name itself doesn't say anything about who published it. With a certificate, you get this identification information—in fact, you can use the `CreateFromSignedFile()` method on the `X509Certificate` class to extract the certificate from the signed assembly so you can view the certificate's information, such as the issuer name, the serial number, and the expiration date. You can't do that with a strong name.

I would suggest that if you need to give assemblies access to resources via the developer's identity, you should use evidence based on certificate information. That doesn't mean I think strong-naming an assembly is a bad idea; far from it. Just make sure you understand the differences between the two, especially when it comes to altering policy for new assemblies, a subject I'll cover in the next section.

SOURCE CODE   *The EvidenceDemo project in the Chapter3 subdirectory contains the* EvidenceInfo *class along with all of the strong name and certificate-related files. If you want to use the .pvk file in the certificate process, you'll need the password, which is "yuihjk".*

Creating Custom Code Groups

Before diving into the details of permissions, I'll go through a simple example to illustrate how policies, evidence, and code groups work in concert. Let's say I expand EvidenceInfo's implementation such that it extensively uses the Reflection classes (the classes that allow you to gather type information at run-time). I ship the assembly to my friend Sheila. She trusts that my assembly would never use the Reflection classes in a destructive manner, so she creates a code group called Sheila_Certificate_Check. This is easily done with the .NET Admin MMC snap-in tool[2] as follows:

1. Start the .NET Framework Configuration administration tool (which can be found in Adminstrative Tools in the Control Panel applet). Drill down to the All_Code code group by choosing Runtime Security Policy ➤ Machine ➤ Code Group. The All_Code code group is highlighted in Figure 4-1.

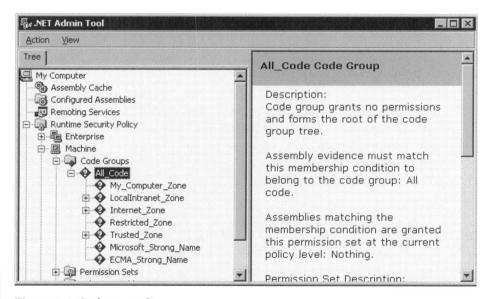

Figure 4-1. Code group list

---

2. You could also use caspol.exe to achieve the same effect; I personally gravitate toward tools that are not command-line driven.

2. To add the new code group, right-click the All_Code group and select New as Figure 4-2 illustrates.

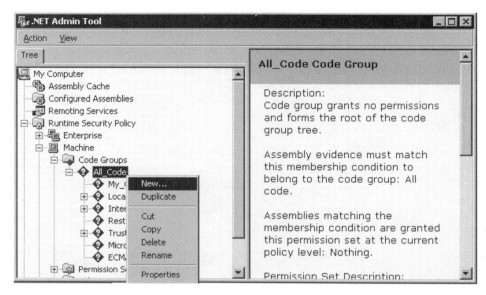

Figure 4-2. Adding a new code group

3. You'll now see a set of dialog boxes for the Create Code Group Wizard. The first one allows you to name the new code group and give it a description as shown in Figure 4-3.

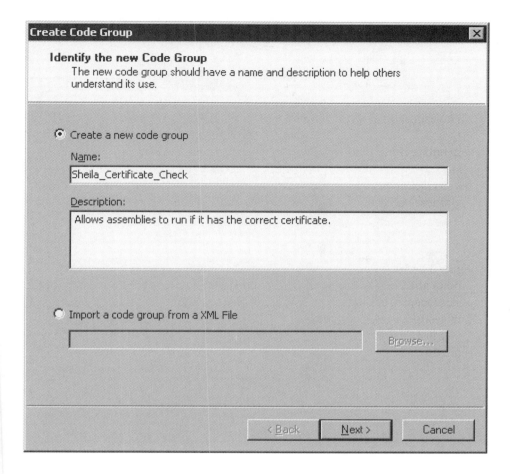

Figure 4-3. Initial code group definition

4. Once you define the code groups, a window appears asking you to spec-
    ify the evidence that this code group will use. When you select Publisher,
    UI elements appear below this combo box that allow you to specify attri-
    butes like the public key (which is required), name, and version, along
    with an Import button to get the certificate information from an assem-
    bly, like EvidenceDemo (see Figure 4-4).

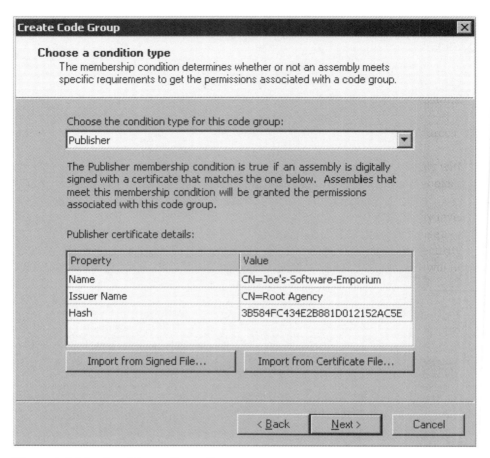

Figure 4-4. Membership configuration

5.   After choosing the publisher set up, you can select which permission set you'd like code to have if it matches the strong name as shown in Figure 4-5. Pick the FullTrust group as it contains the permission to use reflection. (Permissions are discussed in the next section.)

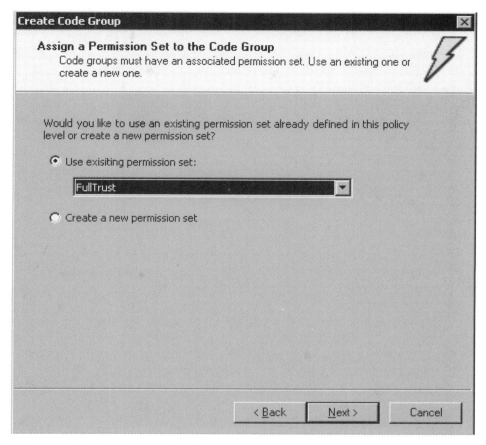

Figure 4-5. Permission set selection

You'll get one more window in which you need to press a Finish button to confirm creation of the code group. Now, whenever the EvidenceDemo assembly is loaded, it'll have the ability to perform reflection, as it is signed with the desired certificate.[3]

Now that you have a general understanding of what policies do to outline what an assembly can do, I'll next turn your attention to permissions and how they define the resource usage of an assembly.

---

3. Granted, all locally running code has this permission by default, but you didn't hurt anything by what you just did either.

Managing Permissions

A *permission* is a class that defines what a client can do to a securable resource. This class must implement the `IPermission` interface (which exists in `System.Security`) as shown here:

```
using System.Security;
public class CustomerPermission : IPermission {}
```

As you can tell from its name, `CustomerPermission` allows (or denies) clients access to information about a customer. You'll see how this works later on in the "Creating Custom Permissions" section.

.NET defines these three types of permissions:

- *Code access permissions.* These permissions allow code to access different resources, such as files (`FileIOPermission`), and UI (`UIPermission`), and perform reflection on components (`ReflectionPermission`).

- *Identity permissions.* These permissions allow the code to perform actions based on the evidence that they present. For example, `URLIdentityPermission` allows you to state that assemblies that originated from a certain place, like `http://www.somewebsite.com/secureassemblies`, can use certain resources.

- *Role-based security permissions.* There is only one class here—`PrincipalPermission`—and it allows you to access resources depending on the current identity. I'll address this permission in Chapter 5.

Before I continue, I must stress one important fact: *code can never grant itself a permission to access a resource.* Repeat that to yourself a couple of times so you don't forget it. The only time permissions are granted or denied is when the code is loaded. After that, if it's been determined that you can't read the Registry, nothing in your code will make it otherwise. Some of the wording with methods on permission objects may suggest that you can add permissions at runtime, but none of them will grant permissions you don't have.

Permission Requests

Now that you know what a permission is in theory, I'm sure you're wondering how these permission classes actually work. There are two ways you can ensure safe access to a resource. The first way is to add an attribute to your class that defines the permission that you want.[4] This is known as *declarative security*. For example, Listing 4-4 shows how you state that you want all code within the assembly to have the ability to read from c:\apress\securedirectory but not from the c:\apress\unsecuredirectory.

Listing 4-4. Adding Declarative Security

```
[assembly: FileIOPermissionAttribute(SecurityAction.RequestMinimum,
    Read=@"c:\apress\securedirectory")]
[assembly: FileIOPermissionAttribute(SecurityAction.RequestRefuse,
    Read=@"c:\apress\unsecuredirectory")]
namespace APress.DotNetSecurity.Chapter4.FileIO
{
    public class FileIOPermissionTest {}
}
```

Before I add more functionality to this class, I'll show you the other method to obtain the same effect. You can make the request during code execution by creating the permission object—this is called *imperative security*. Listing 4-5 shows what the previous code snippet would look like if I used the FileIOPermission object instead of the attribute.

Listing 4-5. Using Imperative Security

```
public class FileIOPermissionImperative : Directories
{
    public void ReadSecureDirectory(string FileName)
    {
        FileIOPermission ioPerm = new FileIOPermission(
            FileIOPermissionAccess.Read, @"c:\apress\securedirectory");
        ioPerm.Demand();
        FileStream fs = new FileStream(@"c:\apress\securedirectory\" + FileName,
            FileMode.Open);
        fs.Close();
    }
```

---

4. Note that a permission does not have to create an attribute to allow you to use declarative syntax, so it's possible with some permissions that you won't be able to perform declarative security.

```
public void ReadUnsecureDirectory(string FileName)
{
    FileIOPermission ioPerm = new FileIOPermission(
        FileIOPermissionAccess.Read, @"c:\apress\unsecuredirectory");
    ioPerm.Deny();
    FileStream fs = new FileStream(@"c:\apress\unsecuredirectory\" + FileName,
        FileMode.Open);
    fs.Close();
}
}
```

Technically, both approaches achieve the same effect—that is, they will prevent a client from accessing the unsafe directory.[5] However, there are differences with each approach, and I'll cover these now.

With attributes, you can state what kind of access level you want with the specified resource. For example, Listing 4-4 used the `RequestMinimum` and `RequestRefuse` values from the `SecurityAction` enumeration. `RequestMinimum` states that, for any code within your assembly, you must have this permission available. (Note that any `RequestXXX` value can only be made at the assembly level.) If the runtime decides for whatever reason that your assembly cannot have this permission, none of your code will run. `RequestRefuse` states the opposite: none of the code within the assembly can use this permission.

There's also a third kind of request: `RequestOptional`. This states that you would like access to the associated resource, but if it's not there, your code will be able to work around that possible restriction. You may not be able to do everything you want, but it's no big deal if you can't. For example, you may make logging to a file optional via a `RequestOptional` action:

```
[assembly: FileIOPermissionAttribute(SecurityAction.RequestOptional,
Write=@"c:\apress\logging\baseLogFile.txt")]
namespace APress.DotNetSecurity.Chapter4.FileIO
{
    public class FileIOPermissionTest {}
}
```

If any errors occur within the code where logging is prohibited by the runtime because this permission was not granted, core functionality will still work as expected.

---

5. In this case, the imperative example is not making a request; it's making a demand. Although the results are the same, a demand and a request are different. I'll explain why later on in the chapter.

In some cases, though, adding security through attributes may be overkill. Take a look at the following code:

```
[FileIOPermissionAttribute(SecurityAction.Demand,
    Read=@"c:\")]
public void FileReadConditional(bool ReadFile)
{
    if(ReadFile)
    {
        FileStream fs = new FileStream(@"c:\apress\unsecuredirectory\afile.txt",
            FileMode.Open);
        fs.Close();
    }
}
```

In `FileReadCondition()`, afile.txt will only be opened if `ReadFile` is true. However, if it's false, there's no reason to check to see if I have the permission necessary to read the file. Security checks require processing time, and in this case I could optimize the method such that it only demands the permission if I need to access the file.

In general, I would try to use declarative security over imperative. One main reason that I like declarative security is that it's much easier to find out what an assembly wants to do. The command-line .NET tool called permview, accessed as follows, allows you to see all of the declarative permissions from an assembly:

```
permview /decl Book.dll
```

If you use imperative security, you're pretty much out of luck when trying to figure out what a purchased assembly wants to do, unless you're willing to do method call graphs and find out when a method on a permission object is called (which can get quite time-consuming).[6] Also, you can only make a request via the declarative approach; there is no way to request permissions imperatively.

You can choose from a total of nine security actions. Table 4-2 lists all these actions and describes how they work.

---

6. Of course, an assembly can have a mixture of declarative and imperative security, so permview is not the true answer in figuring out what an assembly wants to do from a security standpoint. But it's better than nothing.

Table 4-2. Security Actions

NAME	ACTION IMPLEMENTATION	TARGET
Assert	Runtime	Class, method
Demand	Runtime	Class, method
Deny	Runtime	Class, method
InheritanceDemand	Load time	Class, method
LinkDemand	JIT	Class, method
PermitOnly	Runtime	Class, method
RequestMinimum	Grant time	Assembly
RequestOptional	Grant time	Assembly
RequestRefuse	Grant time	Assembly

I'll cover how the others work later on in the sections "Demanding Permissions," "Asserts," and "Limiting Permissions."[7]

As you can see, this is a very powerful concept. You can state the resources you think your code will need to run in metadata. In fact, if you use the Intermediate Language Disassembler tool (ILDasm) to look at an assembly with declarative security , you'll see these attributes. Figure 4-6 shows what it looks like when you view the assembly in ILDasm.

In this case, a declarative security attribute was added at the assembly level. This information is captured in the byte array defined by the `.permissionset` directive. The `reqmin` attribute states that `RequestMinimum` is the desired security action, so if the permission in the permission set is denied, the assembly will not load. I'll cover this directive in more detail in the section "Link Demands."

---

7. Technically, there are more actions that can be used, but these are the only ones available via standard coding techniques. See Section 21.11 of Partition II for definitions of these additional actions.

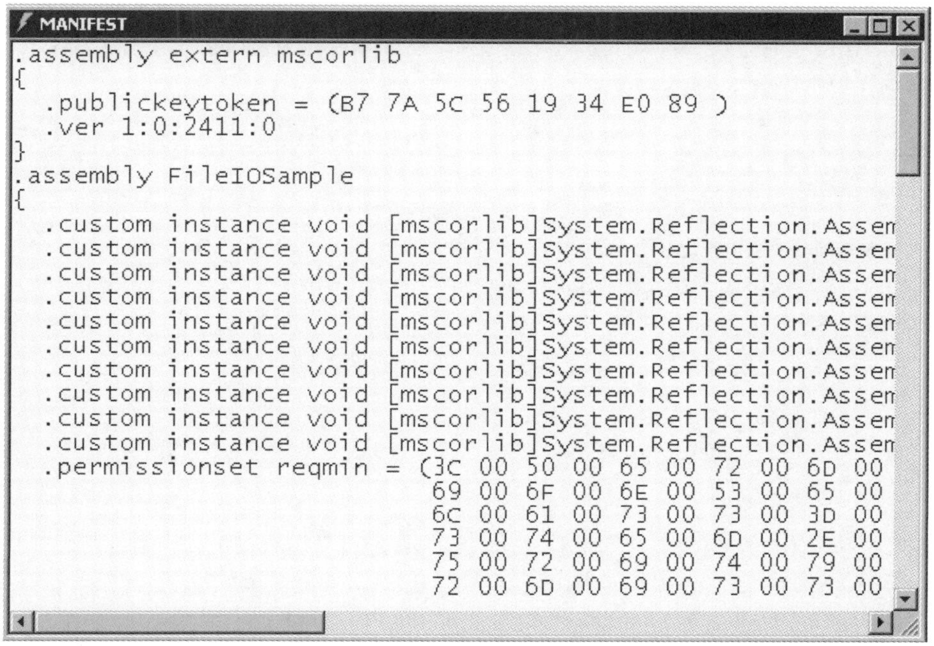

```
 MANIFEST                                    _ □ X
.assembly extern mscorlib
{
  .publickeytoken = (B7 7A 5C 56 19 34 E0 89 )
  .ver 1:0:2411:0
}
.assembly FileIOSample
{
  .custom instance void [mscorlib]System.Reflection.Assem
  .custom instance void [mscorlib]System.Reflection.Assem
  .custom instance void [mscorlib]System.Reflection.Assem
  .custom instance void [mscorlib]System.Reflection.Assem
  .custom instance void [mscorlib]System.Reflection.Assem
  .custom instance void [mscorlib]System.Reflection.Assem
  .custom instance void [mscorlib]System.Reflection.Assem
  .custom instance void [mscorlib]System.Reflection.Assem
  .custom instance void [mscorlib]System.Reflection.Assem
  .permissionset reqmin = (3C 00 50 00 65 00 72 00 6D 00
                           69 00 6F 00 6E 00 53 00 65 00
                           6C 00 61 00 73 00 73 00 3D 00
                           73 00 74 00 65 00 6D 00 2E 00
                           75 00 72 00 69 00 74 00 79 00
                           72 00 6D 00 69 00 73 00 73 00
```

Figure 4-6. Security attributes in an assembly

Permission Sets

Now that you know a bit about permissions, I'll cover *permission sets*. Recall that they determine what your code can do. This set is the union of all allowable permissions that an assembly can have. Remember, a number of different policies exist, each with different code groups that the assembly's evidence can satisfy. It's possible that you may get the ability to use the Registry (`RegistryPermission`) from a lot of different locations in the code groups; you'll only see this permission listed once in the permission set.

Take a look at how you can get the current permission set for running code. To do this, you need to use the following objects in concert—SecurityManager and Assembly—as shown here:

```
using System.Reflection;
using System.Security;
PermissionSet ps = SecurityManager.ResolvePolicy(
    Assembly.GetExecutingAssembly().Evidence);
Console.WriteLine("Permission set count is " + ps.Count);
IEnumerator perms = ps.GetEnumerator();
while(perms.MoveNext())
{
    IPermission p = perms.Current as IPermission;
    Console.WriteLine(p.ToString());
}
```

ResolvePolicy() takes an Evidence object and returns the set of permissions granted for the presented evidence. Getting this evidence isn't hard, since the Assembly object has the Evidence property available. You just need to get the assembly for the code that is currently running, which GetExecutingAssembly() returns.

Now, when I run this code from an assembly, I get two permissions, UrlIdentityPermission and ZoneIdentityPermission. As there are only three pieces of evidence that my assembly presents to the runtime—Zone, Url, and Hash—this makes sense. If I strong-name the assembly, I would get StrongNameIdentityPermission as well.

Using Named Permission Sets

The permission set returned to you when you use the evidence from the executing assembly does *not* contain all of the permissions that are granted to you by the code groups. For example, I could've used the FileStream object with no problem, but the FileIOPermission object didn't show up in the permissions set. To find out all of the permissions takes a bit more work; specifically, you need to get a list of all the permissions from a number of named permissions sets.

A *named permission set* is nothing more than a permission set with a name. You can make up a named permission set on the fly if you'd like:

```
NamedPermissionSet nps =
    new NamedPermissionSet("MyPermissionSet");
nps.SetPermission(new FileIOPermission(
    FileIOPermissionAccess.Read, @"c:\somedirectory"));
```

You can also persist a named permission set so it can be associated with a policy level. (I'll show you how to do this later in the section "Creating Custom Permissions.") In this case, the name only has to be unique within the policy, so it's possible to have two named permission sets with the same name in the Enterprise and User policy levels.

Six named permission sets come with .NET, and Table 4-3 lists these sets.

Table 4-3. Named .NET Permission Sets

NAME	DESCRIPTION
Everything	All permissions (except SkipVerification) are granted.
Execution	Code can run, but no other permissions are granted.
FullTrust	Full access is granted to resources that can be unrestricted.
Internet	Permissions are granted to code running from an Internet site.
LocalIntranet	Permissions are granted to code running from an enterprise's internal site.
Nothing	Code is unable to run.

Of these sets, only the Internet, LocalIntranet, and Everything sets are modifiable.

You can request permissions via a named permission set either declaratively or imperatively. Note that you can only do this with the nonmodifiable named permissions sets: Nothing, Execution, and FullTrust. Custom permission sets and/or modifiable built-in sets cannot be used, as these can vary from machine to machine.

Now I'll go back to the problem I talked about at the beginning of this section to see how to work with named permission sets associated with code groups.[8] The goal is to get and subsequently walk through the code groups where the evidence matches its membership conditions. Again, judicious use of the classes and methods that .NET provides as demonstrated in Listing 4-6 will make this pretty easy.

Listing 4-6. Permission Discovery via Code Groups and Named Permission Sets

```
private static bool isLevelFinal = false;
private static CodeGroup exclusiveCodeGroup = null;

private static void GetPermissions()
```

---

8.   This discussion will also cover how you need to deal with Exclusive and LevelFinal code groups, something I mentioned I'd eventually get to near the beginning of this chapter.

```
    {
        Evidence e = Assembly.GetExecutingAssembly().Evidence;
        PermissionSet allPS = new PermissionSet(null);
        IEnumerator policies = SecurityManager.PolicyHierarchy();
        while(policies.MoveNext())
        {
            PolicyLevel pl = policies.Current as PolicyLevel;
            CodeGroup cg = pl.ResolveMatchingCodeGroups(e);
            isLevelFinal = false;
            exclusiveCodeGroup = null;
            WalkCodeGroup(cg);

            IEnumerator perms = null;
            if(exclusiveCodeGroup == null)
            {
                PolicyStatement ps = pl.Resolve(e);
                perms = ps.PermissionSet.GetEnumerator();
            }
            else
            {
                perms =
                    exclusiveCodeGroup.PolicyStatement.PermissionSet.GetEnumerator();
            }

            while(perms.MoveNext())
            {
                IPermission exp = perms.Current as IPermission;
                allPS.SetPermission(exp);
            }

            if(isLevelFinal)
            {
                break;
            }
        }

        IEnumerator allPerms = allPS.GetEnumerator();
        while(allPerms.MoveNext())
        {
            IPermission ps = allPerms.Current as IPermission;
        }
    }
```

The two static variables (isLevelFinal and exclusiveCodeGroup) are needed for the WalkCodeGroup() method. As its implementation uses recursion, you need to keep track of Exclusive and LevelFinal conditions in the code groups. I'll show what this method does in a moment.

When you get your evidence, you receive a list of policies via PolicyHierarchy(). Listing 4-7 shows how you walk through the policies, getting all of the code groups via ResolveMatchingCodeGroups; these groups are traversed by WalkCodeGroup().

Listing 4-7. Resolving Code Groups in the Policy Levels

```
private static void WalkCodeGroup(CodeGroup cg)
{
    PolicyStatementAttribute psa = cg.PolicyStatement.Attributes;

    int res = (int)(psa & PolicyStatementAttribute.LevelFinal);
    if(0 < res)
    {
        isLevelFinal = true;
    }

    res = (int)(psa & PolicyStatementAttribute.Exclusive);
    if(0 < res && exclusiveCodeGroup == null)
    {
        exclusiveCodeGroup = cg;
    }

    IList cgChildren = cg.Children;
    if(null != cgChildren && 0 < cgChildren.Count)
    {
        IEnumerator cgChilds = cgChildren.GetEnumerator();
        while(cgChilds.MoveNext())
        {
            CodeGroup cgChild = cgChilds.Current as CodeGroup;
            WalkCodeGroup(cgChild);
        }
    }
}
```

Each code group is checked to see if it's either Exclusive or LevelFinal. If it's Exclusive, this is the only code group within the policy that will be used. If it's LevelFinal, set isLevelFinal to true to signal the fact that you don't have to traverse any other lower policy levels.

Once the recursion is done, check to see what `WalkCodeGroup()` found. If there was an `Exclusive` group, only its permissions are added to `allPS`. Otherwise, you get all of the permissions for this policy. In this case, I use `Resolve()` to figure out what the `PolicyStatement` looks like, where I can grab the complete `PermissionSet`. If you had a `LevelFinal` code group, you would break out of the policy walk. Once you're done processing the policies, walk through the resulting set of permissions to see what you've got.

Note that in all of this code, you don't have to check to see if there's more than one code group within a policy level that's marked as `Exclusive`. Figure 4-7 shows the friendly reminder that you'll get from the runtime if this condition occurs.

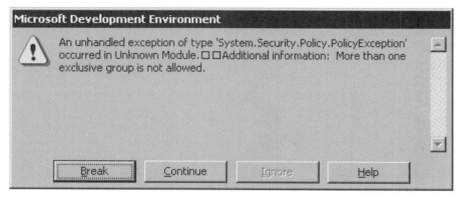

Figure 4-7. Multiple exclusive code group error

Subtleties with the FullTrust Permission Set

If you tried to run the code from the last section from your computer, you probably didn't see any permissions listed. The reason is that all of the permission sets that were found for the assembly were `FullTrust`. You'll notice that the `FullTrust` permission set doesn't have any permissions listed with it. As a sanity check, run the following code snippet from any .NET assembly:

```
long fullTrustPSCount = 0;

IEnumerator ftPoliciesSearch = SecurityManager.PolicyHierarchy();

while(ftPoliciesSearch.MoveNext())
{
    PolicyLevel pl = ftPoliciesSearch.Current as PolicyLevel;
    if("Enterprise" == pl.Label)
```

```
    {
        NamedPermissionSet fullTrustPS =
            pl.GetNamedPermissionSet("FullTrust");
        fullTrustPSCount = fullTrustPS.Count;
        break;
    }
}
```

You'll notice that `fullTrustPSCount` is 0 after the code breaks out of the while loop. Why is this? The `FullTrust` permission set by definition gives access to all unrestricted resources, so why are there no permissions associated with the set? The reason is a kind of catch-22. The .NET runtime assemblies that evaluate policy for other assemblies cannot examine their own policy. Therefore, all .NET Framework assemblies are signed with a strong name from Microsoft. If any assembly has this strong name, it is automatically given access to any resource it desires.

NOTE *This could be considered a security risk. If someone is able to obtain the private key from Microsoft, that person could load assemblies that will get access to any resource. However, to do this, one would need to either get someone to give up the private key, or brute-force it. Both tasks are not trivial to complete, so I think the risk is minimal.*

SOURCE CODE *The PermissionSetSample solution in the Chapter3 subdirectory shows you how you can walk code groups and permission sets. A PS.snk file exists so you can sign the assembly and create code groups with specific permissions to see them listed in the console results.*

Demanding Permissions

What does it mean to "demand" a permission? At first glance, this may sound like a security leak—that is, you can demand any permission to any resource you want. Although the wording may seem odd at first, this does not mean that you can "demand" a permission at runtime that you do not have.[9] Simply put, this is a way to ensure that callers have the permission that you've demanded. If they don't, they can't call your code.

Demands can be declarative or imperative. In either case, the highest level that you can make the demand is at the class. Also, the runtime doesn't check the currently executing code to see if it has the permission to use the resource; it only checks the callers in the call stack.

Now take a look at how you would make a demand with both approaches. First, use the following attribute to demand that users of a class have the permission to use the Registry:

```
[type: RegistryPermissionAttribute(SecurityAction.Demand,
    Read=@"HKEY_LOCAL_MACHINE\SomeKey")]
public class SomeClass
{
    public void NoSecurityNeeded() {}
    public void SecurityNeeded() {}
}
```

You can make this a bit more specific. For example, if you want any user to be able to invoke NoSecurityNeeded() even if he or she doesn't have Registry access, you can modify this code as follows:

```
public class SomeClass
{
    public void NoSecurityNeeded() {}
    [method: RegistryPermissionAttribute(SecurityAction.Demand,
        Read=@"HKEY_LOCAL_MACHINE\SomeKey")]
    public void SecurityNeeded() {}
}
```

With the declarative approach, the demand is verified at load time, although this can vary depending on where the demand is made. In the first case, the check is made when the code is loaded for SomeClass. The second case delays

---

9. Remember what I said earlier—code can *never* grant itself permission to any resource.

the demand until SecurityNeeded() is invoked. In the second case, it's possible that the check is never made if that method is never invoked. Imperative demands are always done at runtime, and as you saw before, the check may not occur if the demand is dependent on code logic.

If you want to avoid raising a SecurityException by demanding a permission, you can use IsGranted() on the SecurityManager object as shown here:

```
public void SecurityNeeded() {
    RegistryPermission rp = new RegistryPermission(
        RegistryPermissionAccess.Read,
        @"HKEY_LOCAL_MACHINE\SomeKey");
    if(true == SecurityManager.IsGranted(rp))
    {
        rp.Demand();
    }
}
```

 NOTE IsGranted() *only checks the immediate caller, so this is not a guarantee that all callers have the permission.*

There are two specific kinds of demands available in .NET: *link demands* and *inheritance demands*. I'll discuss these next.

Link Demands

Link demands look something like this:

```
[ReflectionPermissionAttribute(SecurityAction.LinkDemand,
    ReflectionEmit=true)]
```

This demand works just like the regular permission demand, but the runtime does not perform a full stack walk to ensure that all callers in the stack have the permission. Only the immediate client of the class or method needs the demanded permission.

What's nice about this demand is that you can create classes that only certain callers can either create and/or invoke methods on. For example, let's say you design the following class:

```
public class LDT
{
    [StrongNameIdentityPermission(SecurityAction.LinkDemand,
        PublicKey="fe833...")]
    [StrongNameIdentityPermission(SecurityAction.LinkDemand,
        PublicKey="ba901...")]
    public void MethodOne() {}

    [StrongNameIdentityPermission(SecurityAction.LinkDemand,
        PublicKey="ba901...")]
    public void MethodTwo() {}
}
```

In this case, only clients signed with the two strong names given can call MethodOne(). However, MethodTwo() can only be called by one client.

Now, before you run off and start coding classes to have this kind of calling access, there is one big caveat you should keep in mind. Say you have two console applications, CallerA and CallerB. CallerA is signed with the first public key ("fe833 . . . ") and CallerB is signed with the second one ("ba901 . . . "). Both call the code in the same way, as demonstrated in Listing 4-8.

Listing 4-8. Calling Code with a LinkDemand

```
using System;
using LinkDemandTest;

namespace CallerA
{
    class CA
    {
        static void Main(string[] args)
        {
            try
            {
                LDT ldt = new LDT();
                Console.WriteLine("Calling MethodOne().");
                ldt.MethodOne();
                Console.WriteLine("MethodOne() complete.");
                Console.WriteLine("Calling MethodTwo().");
                ldt.MethodTwo();
                Console.WriteLine("MethodTwo() complete.");
            }
```

```
        catch(Exception e)
        {
            Console.WriteLine(e);
        }
        finally
        {
            Console.WriteLine("Press any key to continue...");
            Console.ReadLine();
        }
    }
  }
}
```

Now, what do you think will happen when CallerA and CallerB are executed? CallerB will be able to call both MethodOne() and MethodTwo(). However, CallerA will fail, *not* when it tries to call MethodTwo(), but when it tries to create an instance of LDT. This is because a link demand is not resolved at runtime but when the class is JIT (Just-In-Time) compiled. This is when the assembly's code is translated into native assembly code for the target processor. So if a class has methods that are protected with LinkDemand security actions, you as a developer need to make sure you don't call the unavailable method, even if you may not even call it due to logical code results at runtime.

SOURCE CODE *The LinkDemandSample folder in the Chapter3 subdirectory contains the LinkDemandTest, CallerA, and CallerB solutions described in the preceding text.*

Expected and Actual Results

There's another, more insidious problem with the link demands on MethodOne(). While it looks like the only type that is signed with the CallerA or CallerB public keys, that's not the case. If I call this method from a console application called CallerC that is not signed, I'll be able to call MethodOne(). Why is that? The reason is not obvious. You have to open up the LDT type in ILDasm and look at MethodOne()'s Common Intermediate Language (CIL) code:

```
.method public hidebysig instance void  MethodOne() cil managed
{
  .permissionset linkcheck = ()
  // Code size         1 (0x1)
  .maxstack  0
  IL_0000:  ret
} // end of method LDT::MethodOne
```

The permission set, which is defined by the `.permissionset` directive, is empty. This seems odd, but you'll have some insight into this result if you read up on how this security metadata is added to an assembly by a compiler.[10] Essentially, a compiler needs to look at all of the permission attributes added to an assembly, add them all to a permission set, and then put the resulting XML that defines the permission set into a `.permissionset` directive. Now see what happens when you try to perform these actions in code:

```
FileStream fs1 = new FileStream(@"CallerA.snk", FileMode.Open);
StrongNameKeyPair snkp1 = new StrongNameKeyPair(fs1);
StrongNamePublicKeyBlob p1Blob =
    new StrongNamePublicKeyBlob(snkp1.PublicKey);
StrongNameIdentityPermission s1 =
    new StrongNameIdentityPermission(p1Blob, "CallerA", new Version());

FileStream fs2 = new FileStream(@"CallerB.snk", FileMode.Open);
StrongNameKeyPair snkp2 = new StrongNameKeyPair(fs2);
StrongNamePublicKeyBlob p2Blob =
    new StrongNamePublicKeyBlob(snkp2.PublicKey);
StrongNameIdentityPermission s2 =
    new StrongNameIdentityPermission(p2Blob, "CallerB", new Version());

PermissionSet psSNAdd = new PermissionSet(PermissionState.None);
psSNAdd.AddPermission(s1);
Console.WriteLine("With just s1:  " + psSNAdd.ToXml().ToString());
Console.WriteLine("Count = " + psSNAdd.Count);
psSNAdd.AddPermission(s2);
Console.WriteLine("With both:  " + psSNAdd.ToXml().ToString());
Console.WriteLine("Count = " + psSNAdd.Count);
```

---

10.   See Section 21.11 in the Partition II ECMA document.

I'm using two classes called StrongNameKeyPair and StrongNamePublicKeyBlob. They're essentially helper classes to extract key data out of files and then pass that information into a StrongNameIdentityPermission object. Anyway, if you run this code, you'll see that after the first StrongNameIdentityPermission is added to psSNAdd, the count will be 1. When the second one is added, the count suddenly drops to 0, and the resulting XML contains nothing as shown here:

```
<PermissionSet class="System.Security.PermissionSet" version="1"/>
```

This behavior is different from what happens if two FileIOPermissions are combined, like this:

```
FileIOPermission f1 =
    new FileIOPermission(FileIOPermissionAccess.Read, @"C:\Program Files");
FileIOPermission f2 =
    new FileIOPermission(FileIOPermissionAccess.Write, @"C:\ADirectory");
PermissionSet psFileAdd = new PermissionSet(PermissionState.None);
psFileAdd.AddPermission(f1);
Console.WriteLine("With just f1:  " + psFileAdd.ToXml().ToString());
Console.WriteLine("Count = " + psFileAdd.Count);
psFileAdd.AddPermission(f2);
Console.WriteLine("With both:  " + psFileAdd.ToXml().ToString());
Console.WriteLine("Count = " + psFileAdd.Count);
```

After both are added, the permission count in psFileAdd is 1, but both permissions are in the XML as displayed here:

```
<PermissionSet class="System.Security.PermissionSet" version="1">
   <IPermission class="System.Security.Permissions.FileIOPermission,
      mscorlib, Version=1.0.3300.0,
      Culture=neutral, PublicKeyToken=b77a5c561934e089"
      version="1"
      Read="C:\Program Files"
      Write="C:\ADirectory"/>
</PermissionSet>
```

This is another good argument for using the security tools during the post-build process. permview will show that MethodOne() has a permission set associated with it, but there's nothing in it. Make sure you always check the results in the generated assembly every way you can—they may not be what you expect!

SOURCE CODE   *The LinkDemandPermissionSetTest folder in the Chapter3 subdirectory contains the LinkDemandPSTest project that shows how permission sets are calculated.*

Link Demands and Interfaces

There is a way to get around link demands if you are implementing interfaces. Consider Listing 4-9.

Listing 4-9. Interfaces and Link Demands in the Implementing Class

```
public interface IPhone
{
    bool Dial(string PhoneNumber);
}

public class Phone : IPhone
{

    public Phone() {}

    [method:  StrongNameIdentityPermission(SecurityAction.LinkDemand,
        PublicKey="0024...")]
    public bool Dial(string PhoneNumber)
    {
        bool retVal = false;

        if(PhoneNumber.Equals("555-1212"))
        {
            retVal = true;
        }

        return retVal;
    }
}
```

Phone is implementing the IPhone interface, but its Dial() implementation has a LinkDemand based on a public key value. However, if I call the method via IPhone's Dial() method in an assembly that does not have that public key value for its strong name, like this:

```
IPhone p = new Phone();
Console.WriteLine("Dialing 555-9999...");
Console.WriteLine(p.Dial("555-9999"));
Console.WriteLine("Dialing 555-1212...");
Console.WriteLine(p.Dial("555-1212"));
```

I won't get an exception because the call is on IPhone, not Phone. Unfortunately, moving the link demand on IPhone's Dial() doesn't solve anything, as the client would just use a Phone instance to call Dial(). Although interface-based coding has its advantages, be careful if you decide to throw link demands on methods, as the only way to ensure a caller can't get around the link demand security check is to have it on all methods within the class inheritance hierarchy.

> **SOURCE CODE** *The InterfacesAndLinkDemands folder in the Chapter3 subdirectory contains two projects: AvoidLinkDemand, which contains* IPhone *and* Phone, *and AvoidLinkDemandTest, which demonstrates how to get around the link demand.*

Inheritance Demands

Inheritance demands only allow classes to inherit from a class if it meets the demand. An inheritance demand can also be made on a method—in this case, the overriding method must have the correct permissions. Although this definition sounds simplistic enough, you need to be aware of when the check is made.

Take a look at a base class that exists within its own assembly:

```
using System;
using System.Security.Permissions;

namespace IDBaseClass
{
    public class BaseClass
    {
        [method: ReflectionPermission(
            SecurityAction.InheritanceDemand,
            Flags=ReflectionPermissionFlag.ReflectionEmit)]
        public virtual void SomeMethod()
```

```
        {
            Console.WriteLine("BaseClass.SomeMethod()...");
        }
    }
}
```

In this example, I've stated that any classes that wish to override SomeMethod() must have the permission to emit code at runtime. Now, create a subclass in another assembly that will not have this permission:

```
using System;
using System.Security.Permissions;
using IDBaseClass;

[assembly: ReflectionPermission(SecurityAction.RequestRefuse,
    Flags=ReflectionPermissionFlag.ReflectionEmit)]
namespace IDDerivedClass
{
    public class DerivedClass : BaseClass
    {
        public override void SomeMethod()
        {
            Console.WriteLine("DerivedClass.SomeMethod()...");
        }
    }
}
```

If I try to run the following code from a console application:

```
static void Main(string[] args)
{
    DerivedClass dc = new DerivedClass();
    dc.SomeMethod();
}
```

I won't even make it into Main(). Figure 4-8 shows the resulting message box.

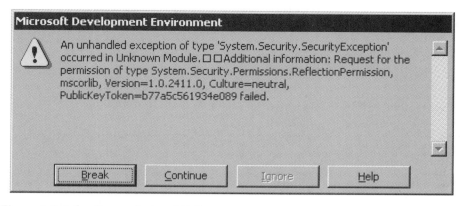

Figure 4-8. Inheritance demand failure

Even though the inheritance demand was at the method level, it's resolved when the type is loaded, not when the method is called. If the derived class did not override SomeMethod(), no error would occur.

This is an interesting way to prevent clients of your classes from overriding your method implementations. If they don't have the correct permissions, they either cause an error to occur at runtime, or end up using the default implementation.

SOURCE CODE   *The InheritanceDemandSample solution in the Chapter3 subdirectory demonstrates how inheritance demands work. The subdirectories IDBaseClass and IDDerivedClass contain the base and derived classes in their own assemblies, and IDTest shows how an inheritance demand works.*

Asserts

Asserts allow you to let objects perform an action regardless of whether they have permission to do so.[11] For example, say you want to provide a general service to read the first 10 bytes of any file on the machine. It's possible that a caller may not have that permission, but you do, and you don't want an exception to be raised even if the caller can't access certain files. This is risky to do and should be done only when absolutely necessary, as this opens up the possibility of a luring attack. Make sure that if you use an assert, you don't open yourself up to performing actions on behalf of a client who really shouldn't be able to do what you're letting them do.

You can make an assertion with either declarative or imperative syntax. With declarative syntax, asserts have the same scope as demands. Listing 4-10 shows that they can be made at either the type or method level.

Listing 4-10. Asserting a Permission

```
[type: UIPermissionAttribute(SecurityAction.Assert,
    Window=UIPermissionWindow.AllWindows)]
public class SomeClass
{
    public void NoSecurityNeeded() {}
    [method: FileIOPermissionAttribute(SecurityAction.Assert,
        Read=@"c:\apress\securedirectory")]
    public void SecurityNeeded() {}
}
```

Similarly, imperative security looks like this:

```
public class SomeClass
{
    public SomeClass() : base()
    {
        UIPermission uip = new
            UIPermission(UIPermissionWindow.AllWindows);
        uip.Assert();
    }
```

---

11. You cannot assert permissions that you do not have; this only affects permissions that you already have but that objects in the call stream may not.

```
public void NoSecurityNeeded() {}
public void SecurityNeeded()
{
    FileIOPermission fip = new
        FileIOPermission(FileIOPermissionAccess.Read,
        @"c:\apress\securedirectory");
    fip.Assert();
}
}
```

Assertions limit the traversal of a stack walk. Remember, if you make a security assertion, you're basically saying to the runtime that you don't care what the permission set looks like for any of the callers of your code. If you have five callers in the call chain, and the fourth one makes an assertion for a specific permission, the stack walk will not check the first three callers for that permission if the fifth caller demands it. Figure 4-9 shows how the call stack works in this case.

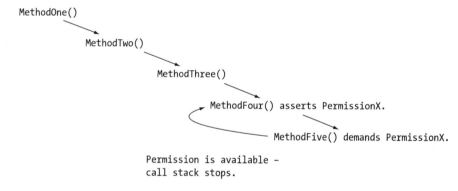

Figure 4-9. Call stack walk

When MethodFive() demands that all callers have the permission PermissionX granted, the runtime will start to examine the call stack to see if any caller has been denied PermissionX. Since MethodFour() asserted PermissionX, the other three methods (MethodOne(), MethodTwo(), and MethodThree()) will not be checked.

Limiting Permissions

There are a couple of ways that you can prevent downstream callers from accessing a resource you currently have permission to. Note that these techniques override a downstream call to `Assert()`, as they effectively remove permission to a resource they think they have. These techniques are useful from a self-protection perspective, as you can ensure that no downstream code will be able to use resources that you don't want them to.

The first method I'll cover is denial. `Deny()` allows you to prevent a class or any downstream code from using a resource it has permission to. This can be done either declaratively or imperatively—I'll demonstrate the imperative syntax here:

```
public void SecurityNeeded()
{
    FileIOPermission fip = new FileIOPermission(FileIOPermissionAccess.Read,
        @"c:\apress\securedirectory");
    fip.Deny();
}
```

If `Deny()` is called within a method, the denial remains in effect until either the method completes or `RevertDeny()` is called on the permission object. Similarly, if the denial is made at the class level, it exists for the lifetime of class instances.

`PermitOnly()` is the opposite of `Deny()`: the permission you call `PermitOnly()` on is the *only* permission that will be allowed downstream. Again, both declarative and imperative syntax is possible with `PermitOnly()`. Since I showed the imperative syntax with `Deny()`, I'll demonstrate the declarative syntax here:

```
[method: FileIOPermissionAttribute(SecurityAction.PermitOnly,
    Read=@"c:\apress\securedirectory")]
public void SecurityNeeded() {}
```

Of course, you need this permission in the first place before you can call `PermitOnly()`; that would be a big security hole if that were possible. As you saw with `Deny()`, there's a method to reverse the effects of `PermitOnly()`—it's called `RevertPermitOnly()`.

Unmanaged Code Access

There's one oddball out of the code access permission bunch—it's
SuppressUnmanagedCodeSecurityAttribute. For one thing, there's no corresponding SuppressUnmanagedCodeSecurity class, so the only way to use its
functionality is with an attribute declaration. Second, this attribute is not a normal security attribute, as it does not descend from SecurityAttribute; it's just
a normal attribute. But its usage has some implications that you should know
about.

Take a look at the following class, which uses an unmanaged method:

```
using System.Security;
using System.Runtime.InteropServices;

public class UnmanagedCode
{
    [DllImport("Kernel32.DLL")]
    private static extern int GetTickCount();

    public int GetUnmanagedTickCount()
    {
        return GetTickCount();
    }
}
```

When GetUnmanagedTickCount() is called, the code will use the unmanaged
exported function GetTickCount() from kernel32.dll. If you call this code, which
has the permission to call unmanaged code, like so:

```
using System;
using System.Security.Permissions;

[assembly:SecurityPermission(SecurityAction.RequestMinimum, UnmanagedCode=true)]
public class UnmanagedCodeTest
{
    static void Main(string[] args)
    {
        UnmanagedCode uc = new UnmanagedCode();
        Console.WriteLine(uc.GetUnmanagedTickCount());
    }
}
```

you should see a number on the command line when you run
`UnmanagedCodeTest`.

Now, if you were to change the security action to `RequestRefuse`, you would
get a `SecurityException` when you tried to call `GetUnmanagedTickCount()`.
However, you can get around this by adding the following line of code just above
the declaration of `GetUnmanagedTickCount()`:

```
[SuppressUnmanagedCodeSecurityAttribute()]
```

After recompilation, you'll see that the number is back on the command line
after `UnmanagedCodeTest` is run.

As you can probably guess, `SuppressUnmanagedCodeSecurityAttribute` prevents a call stack walk to see if all callers have the ability to call unmanaged code.
This does have its advantage. For example, if you're creating a framework that is
quite large and makes calls to unmanaged methods deep within a couple of core
classes, you may want to use this attribute so you eliminate the call stack walk
penalty. However, be very careful if you decide to use this attribute. You should
make sure that the only entities that can use your class are ones that you trust. If
you don't, code that was denied access to unmanaged code can use your class
(directly or indirectly) to call unmanaged code.

SOURCE CODE   *The UnmanagedCodeAccess folder in the
Chapter3 subdirectory contains two C# code files:
UnmanagedCode.cs, which is used to create a DLL that's ref-
erenced by UnmanagedCodeTest.cs.*

Now that you've seen how permissions work in detail, you may be wondering
whether you can create your own permission. That's what the next section is all
about.

Creating Custom Permissions

So far, you've seen how to use permissions to access resources defined in the
.NET Framework. Now I'll cover how .NET allows you to create your own permissions to lock down resources that you define.

Motivation for Creating Custom Permissions

Before I show you how you can create a permission, it's good to spend some time examining the reasons you would want create a custom permission and when you should do it.

Generally, if you ever create an API that isn't managed by the standard permissions, you should create a custom permission if it is important to prevent just anyone from accessing that resource. For example, if you create a grid control, you probably want everybody to use the control for their own purposes. However, if you create a number of classes that perform tax calculations, and people pay you to use these classes, you probably want to ensure that these individuals are the only ones who can access their financial information. Creating a custom permission gives you control over how this information can be obtained.

Defining the Resource

Before you start coding the custom permission, create a resource that you want to protect. Listing 4-11 provides the code for performing this task.

Listing 4-11. Defining a Resource to Protect

```
public class Customer
{
    private string m_firstName = null;
    private string m_lastName = null;
    private long m_id = 0;

    public Customer() : base() {}

    public Customer(string FirstName, string LastName, long ID)
    {
        this.m_firstName = FirstName;
        this.m_lastName = LastName;
        this.m_id = ID;
    }

    public string FirstName
    {
        get { return this.m_firstName; }
        set { this.m_firstName = value; }
    }
```

```
    public string LastName
    {
        get { return this.m_lastName; }
        set { this.m_lastName = value; }
    }

    public long ID
    {
        get { return this.m_id; }
        set { this.m_id = value; }
    }
}
```

This is a class that defines a customer. Again, as you saw with the Book class earlier in this chapter under "Controlling Evidence in Application Domains and Assemblies," it's a simplistic model of the real world, but you want to concentrate on the security aspects of this class.

You want to have two permission levels—one to prevent someone from creating the class and another to stop others from changing the customer's ID. In a moment, you'll see how to accomplish these tasks with one permission.

Implementing the Custom Permission

Now that you know what the custom resource is, begin implementing the custom permission. To start out, you need a class that implements the IUnrestrictedPermission and IPermission interfaces. All custom permissions must implement IPermission; only code access permissions need to implement IUnrestrictedPermission. By inheriting from CodeAccessPermission, you inherit from IPermission.

Now, I'll break down each part of the custom permission implementation into distinct sections so you can see how the process works.

Creating the Custom Constructor

First, you need to create a custom constructor for the custom permission that takes as its only argument a PermissionState value. Listing 4-12 shows what that looks like (along with some other field information for CustomerPermission).

Listing 4-12. Defining the CustomerPermission

```
[Serializable]
public sealed class CustomerPermission :
    CodeAccessPermission, IUnrestrictedPermission
{
    private const string ATTRIBUTE_CLASS = "class";
    private const string ATTRIBUTE_VERSION = "version";
    private const string ELEMENT_FLAGS = "Flags";
    private const string ELEMENT_IPERMISSION = "IPermission";
    private const string ELEMENT_UNRESTRICTED = "Unrestricted";
    private const string ERROR_WRONG_ARGUMENT =
        "The given argument is not the correct type.";
    private const string VERSION = "1";
    private CustomerPermissionFlag m_flags =
        CustomerPermissionFlag.NoAccess;

    public CustomerPermission(PermissionState State) : base()
    {
        SetUnrestricted(State);
    }
```

The Serializable attribute is needed for the attribute you'll create later on in this section. As you can see, all the constructor does is evaluate the value of UnrestrictedState and call SetUnrestricted() appropriately—I'll explain what this method does in the next section. This field will be used a lot in this class, as you'll see when you implement more methods.

Adding Informational Attributes

As you have seen with FileIOPermission, permission classes can have a number of attributes (like Read and Write) that they use to determine what the running assembly can do. For this assembly, you'll create the following enumeration, which allows two levels of access:

```
public enum CustomerPermissionFlag
{
    NoAccess = 0, ObjectCreation = 1, AllAccess = 15
};
```

Code can request to get access to the entire resource, or refuse the capability to create the object. This can be set when `SetUnrestricted()` is called as shown here:

```
private void SetUnrestricted(bool IsUnrestricted)
{
    if(true == IsUnrestricted)
    {
        this.m_flags = CustomerPermissionFlag.AllAccess;
    }
    else
    {
        this.m_flags = CustomerPermissionFlag.NoAccess;
    }
}
```

`SetUnrestricted()` can also be called by passing a `PermissionState` value, like so:

```
private void SetUnrestricted(PermissionState state)
{
    SetUnrestricted(PermissionState.Unrestricted == state ? true : false);
}
```

Implementing IsUnrestricted()

If your custom permission implements `IUnrestrictedPermission`, you need to implement `IsUnrestricted()`, which should return true if the current permission can do whatever it wants. This is pretty easy to do, as you can see here:

```
public bool IsUnrestricted()
{
    bool retVal = false;

    if(CustomerPermissionFlag.AllAccess == this.m_flags)
    {
        retVal = true;
    }

    return retVal;
}
```

Overriding Base Implementations

As CodeAccessPermission is an abstract class that implements IPermission, you must override the following methods to handle your permission's behavior correctly:

- Copy()

- Intersect()

- IsSubsetOf()

- Union()

ISecurityEncodable is implemented by CodeAccessSecurity, so if you want to handle XML encoding and decoding, you must override ToXml() and FromXml(). Take a look at how you implement each method.

Overriding Copy()

By the SDK's definition, this method should return an identical copy of the current object:

```
public override IPermission Copy()
{
    return new CustomerPermission(this.m_flags);
}
```

Simply create a new CustomerPermission instance depending on the current state.

Overriding Intersect()

Intersect() should return an IPermission-based object of the current type that has the highest permission level of the given object and the current object. Therefore, in this case, you use the AND operator (&) on the m_flags fields from the given and current objects to ensure that you don't increase the returned object's permissions. Listing 4-13 provides an example.

Listing 4-13. Implementing the Intersect() Method

```
public override IPermission Intersect(IPermission target)
{
    IPermission retVal = null;
    CustomerPermission customerTarget = null;

    if(null != target)
    {
        customerTarget = target as CustomerPermission;

        if(null != customerTarget)
        {
            if(customerTarget.IsUnrestricted())
            {
                retVal = this.Copy();
            }
            else if(this.IsUnrestricted())
            {
                retVal = customerTarget.Copy();
            }
            else
            {
                retVal = new CustomerPermission(
                    customerTarget.m_flags & this.m_flags);
            }
        }
        else
        {
            throw new ArgumentException(ERROR_WRONG_ARGUMENT, "target");
        }
    }
    return retVal;
}
```

If the given object (customerTarget) is unrestricted, then an intersection will only contain the current object permission level, so you simply call Copy() on the current instance. Conversely, if the instance is restricted, a copy is made of the given object.

Overriding IsSubsetOf()

IsSubsetOf() returns true if the given permission can do everything that the current object can do. Listing 4-14 provides an example.

Listing 4-14. Implementing the IsSubsetOf() Method

```
public override bool IsSubsetOf(IPermission target)
{
    CustomerPermission cp = null;
    bool retVal = false;

    if(null == target)
    {
        if(CustomerPermissionFlag.NoAccess == this.m_flags)
        {
            retVal = true;
        }
    }
    else
    {
        cp = target as CustomerPermission;

        if(null != cp)
        {
            if(true == cp.IsUnrestricted())
            {
                retVal = true;
            }
            else if(true == this.IsUnrestricted())
            {
                retVal = false;
            }
            else
            {
                if(this.m_flags <= cp.m_flags)
                {
                    retVal = true;
                }
            }
        }
```

```
        }
        else
        {
            throw new ArgumentException(ERROR_WRONG_ARGUMENT,
                "target");
        }
    }

    return retVal;
}
```

The first check is to see whether the objects are unrestricted. If the given one is unrestricted, then the current instance is definitely a subset, so it can return true. If the instance is unrestricted, there's no way it can be a subset of the given permission, so IsSubsetOf() returns false. If neither object is unrestricted, then the method returns true if the current access level is equal to or less than the given permission. If the given reference is null, then the method only returns true if the current object can't do anything (that is, m_flags equals NoAccess).

Overriding Union()

Union(), shown in Listing 4-15, should return a CustomerPermission object that is a combination of the given permission and the current instance. This means that the returned CustomerPermission object has the ability to do what the current instance plus the given object can do.

Listing 4-15. Implementing the Union() Method

```
public override IPermission Union(IPermission other)
{
    IPermission retVal = null;
    CustomerPermission cp = null;

    if(null == other)
    {
        retVal = this.Copy();
    }
    else
    {
        cp = other as CustomerPermission;

        if(null != cp)
        {
```

```
            if(true == cp.IsUnrestricted() || true == this.IsUnrestricted())
            {
                retVal = new CustomerPermission(PermissionState.Unrestricted);
            }
            else
            {
                retVal = new CustomerPermission(this.m_flags | cp.m_flags);
            }
        }
        else
        {
            throw new ArgumentException(ERROR_WRONG_ARGUMENT, "other");
        }
    }

    return retVal;
}
```

Essentially, you need to make two checks. First, if either object is unrestricted, the union is automatically an unrestricted `CustomerPermission` instance. Otherwise, you use the OR operator (`|`) on the `m_flags` values to yield the correct combination of the two objects.

Overriding ToXml() and FromXml()

To make your class security-encodable, you need to override these two methods. As you can see in Listing 4-16, the process isn't that hard.

Listing 4-16. Adding XML Serialization to CustomerPermission

```
public override SecurityElement ToXml()
{
    SecurityElement element = new SecurityElement(ELEMENT_IPERMISSION);
    Type type = this.GetType();
    StringBuilder AssemblyName = new
        StringBuilder(type.Assembly.ToString());
    AssemblyName.Replace('\"', '\'');
    element.AddAttribute(ATTRIBUTE_CLASS,
        type.FullName + ", " + AssemblyName);
    element.AddAttribute(ATTRIBUTE_VERSION, VERSION);
```

```
        if(true == this.IsUnrestricted())
        {
            element.AddAttribute(ELEMENT_UNRESTRICTED,
                true.ToString().ToLower());
        }
        else
        {
            element.AddAttribute(ELEMENT_FLAGS,
                this.m_flags.ToString());
        }

        return element;
    }

    public override void FromXml(SecurityElement PassedElement)
    {
        string elementRestrict =
            PassedElement.Attribute(ELEMENT_UNRESTRICTED);

        if(null != elementRestrict)
        {
            this.SetUnrestricted(Convert.ToBoolean(elementRestrict));
        }

        string elementFlags =
            PassedElement.Attribute(ELEMENT_FLAGS);

        if(null != elementFlags)
        {
            this.m_flags = (CustomerPermissionFlag)Enum.Parse
                (typeof(CustomerPermissionFlag), elementFlags);
        }
    }
}
```

ToXml() creates a SecurityElement with the correct elements and attribute values. The version is not the assembly version, but the version of the XML encoding. Therefore, if you add different properties, you should update this value and make sure you handle older encoding correctly.

FromXml() gets the two attributes set in ToXml() and sets the object's values appropriately. Again, any future updates would require you to read the version attribute to make sure the decoding is done properly.

Implementing the Custom Permission Attribute

Although it's not necessary, I'd recommend creating a related permission attribute for your custom permission so code can make declarative statements about your permission. As you did with CustomerPermission earlier in this chapter under "Managing Permissions," you can create an attribute called CustomerPermissionAttribute that descends from CodeAccessSecurityAttribute. When you do this, you need only override CreatePermission() as shown in Listing 4-17.

Listing 4-17. Adding Declarative Security Support for CustomerPermission

```
[AttributeUsageAttribute(AttributeTargets.All, AllowMultiple = true)]
public sealed class CustomerPermissionAttribute :
    CodeAccessSecurityAttribute
{
    private const int OBJECT_CREATION_OFF = -2;
    private CustomerPermissionFlag m_flags =
        CustomerPermissionFlag.NoAccess;
    private bool m_unrestricted = false;

    public CustomerPermissionAttribute(SecurityAction action) :
        base(action) {}

    public override IPermission CreatePermission()
    {
        return new CustomerPermission(this.m_Flags);
    }

    public CustomerPermissionFlag Flags
    {
        get{ return this.m_flags; }
        set{ this.m_flags = value; }
    }
}
```

As you can see, adding declarative support is straightforward. The most interesting method of the bunch is CreatePermission(), which creates a new CustomerPermission object with the access level set to the attribute's m_Flags value.

Testing the Custom Permission

Once the coding is complete, the permission should be tested. I *strongly* suggest that your tests be done on the custom permission type itself; don't try to test the permission after you've made .NET aware of it and you've added the custom attribute to code (which I'll show in the following sections). Your overridden methods will be called very often, and it becomes difficult to keep track of which reference is being passed to which method, much less trying to trace down a bug in the code. I've create a test harness in a console application that goes through each scenario I could think of to ensure the new permission is working correctly. Here's one test that I wrote:

```
int testNum = 0;
bool result = true;


//  Test #1.
//  Create a new unrestricted CP and
//  make sure it's unrestricted.
testNum++;
CustomerPermission unrestrictedCP =
    new CustomerPermission(PermissionState.Unrestricted);
bool retVal = unrestrictedCP.IsUnrestricted();
Console.WriteLine("Is unrestricted (should be true)?  " + retVal);
Console.WriteLine("Test #" + testNum + ":  Passed?  " + retVal);
result &= retVal;
Console.WriteLine();
```

After you're confident that your code works as expected, you can move on to the next step.

Adding the Permission's Assembly to the GAC

Although it's not very explicit in the SDK, you need to add your assembly to the global assembly cache, or GAC. To do this with the .NET Admin tool is pretty simple. Right-click the Assembly Cache node, and select Add from the menu. Find your assembly, and click the OK button. That's all you need to do.[12] If you don't do this, the runtime won't be able to find your assembly, and you'll get an error whenever you try to use the permission.

---

12. Assemblies that are installed in the GAC must be strong-named; the project I've created that contains `CustomerPermission` uses the `AssemblyKeyFile` attribute, so this is all taken care of.

Making Your Assembly Trusted

Now that you have your custom permission implemented, you need to let the runtime make your assembly trusted.[13] Follow these steps to do so:

1. Open up .NET Admin. Right-click the Runtime Security Policy node, and select Trust Assembly. Figure 4-10 shows the dialog box for the wizard that's loaded.

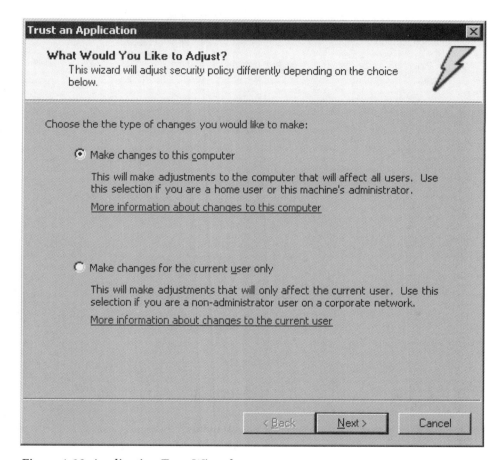

Figure 4-10. Application Trust Wizard

---

13. For further details, please look up the article, "Adding Assemblies to Security Policy," in the .NET SDK. This also explains why assemblies that contain custom permissions need to be in the GAC.

2. For now, just select the option Make changes to this computer.

3. On the next screen, enter the location of the assembly (or click the Browse button to find it). Once the tool is done with whatever it needs to do to verify your assembly, you'll see the dialog box in Figure 4-11.

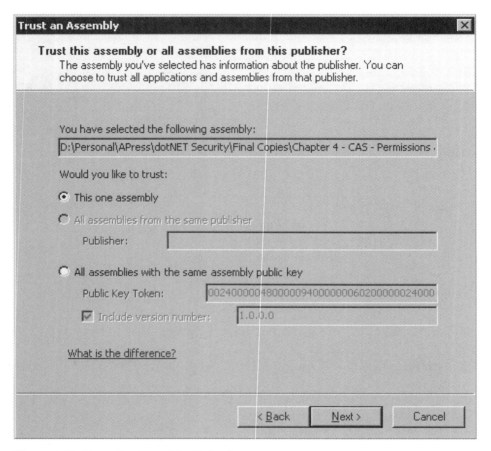

Figure 4-11. Trust An Assembly dialog box

4. You can either choose to trust just this one assembly or all assemblies that have that strong name. For now, just choose the option This one assembly. Once the wizard is done, your assembly will be fully trusted by the runtime.

If you like command-line tools, you can make the assembly trusted with one command via the Code Access Security Policy Tool (caspol.exe):

```
caspol -addfulltrust CustomerPermission.dll
```

There is one caveat to making your assembly fully trusted. It's possible that your permission may be used by code that does not have full trust, although it should be granted access to your permission via policy configuration. If the permission is used by partially trusted callers, these callers won't be able to use your permission because strong-named assemblies require callers to have full trust. To avoid this problem, all you need to do is add this attribute to your assembly:

```
[assembly:AllowPartiallyTrustedCallers]
```

Doing so will allow all callers to access your permission, no matter what their level of trust.

> **NOTE** *You won't find any documentation in the SDK on this attribute, as it was added right before version 1 of .NET was released. If you search MSDN online, you'll find a couple of articles on it. Eventually, it'll make its way into the SDK.*

Adding Your Permission to a Permission Set

Before moving to the final part of this section on custom permissions, you should add the custom permission to a permission set that's associated with a code group.[14] It really doesn't matter which permission set it's in, so long as you know your assembly will be granted the permission from that set.[15] To add the permission, click the Import button when you alter the permission set as shown in Figure 4-12.

---

14. Technically, this isn't a requirement if the calling code already has full trust.

15. An easy one to do is a code group based on a strong name—please refer to the section "Creating Custom Code Groups" earlier in the chapter.

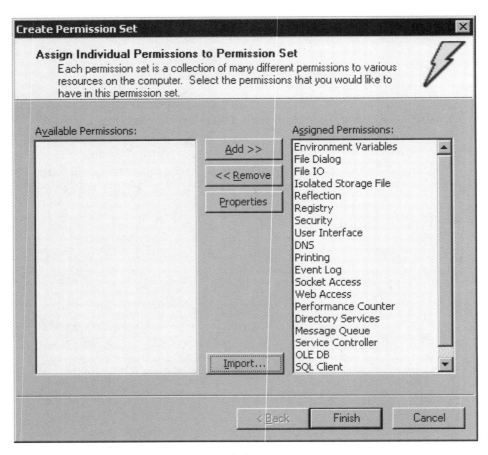

Figure 4-12. Importing a custom permission

To make this XML is actually pretty easy. Simply call ToXml() on your custom permission and save the output to a file as shown here:

```
CustomerPermission perm =
    new CustomerPermission(PermissionState.Unrestricted,
    Flags=CustomerPermissionFlags.All);
StreamWriter file = new StreamWriter("mypermissionset.xml");
file.Write(perm.ToXml());
file.Close();
```

Using the Custom Permission

Now that you have everything set up for your custom permission, use it to see if it works as expected. First, go back into the `Customer` class, and make the following attribute additions (I'll show the line of code that the attribute declaration should go above):

```
[method: CustomerPermissionAttribute(SecurityAction.Demand,
    Flags=CustomerPermissionFlag.ObjectCreation)]
public Customer() : base() {}

[method: CustomerPermissionAttribute(SecurityAction.Demand,
    Flags=CustomerPermissionFlag.ObjectCreation)]
public Customer(string FirstName, string LastName, int ID)

[method: CustomerPermissionAttribute(SecurityAction.Demand,
    Flags=CustomerPermissionFlag.AllAccess)]
set { this.m_ID = value; }
```

As you can see, you now require that the callers in the stack have the ability to create a customer. You also require that the callers must have all levels of access to change the ID. Therefore, depending on the policy you set up, you can allow everyone to create a customer, but not allow everyone to change the ID once it's set.

Now, suppose the client code does something like this:

```
Customer c = new Customer("Jason", "Bock", 123);
c.FirstName = "Pete";
CustomerPermission cp =
    new CustomerPermission(CustomerPermissionFlag.AllAccess);
cp.Deny();
c.ID = 456;
```

An error message like the one you see in Figure 4-13 will appear.

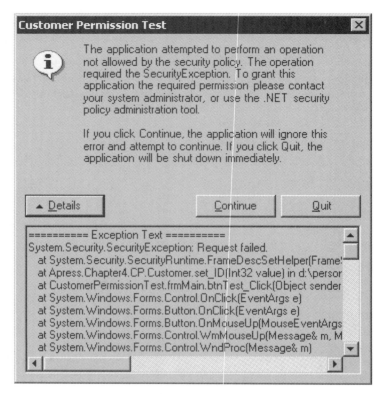

Figure 4-13. Custom permission denial error

You can even make things worse by doing this:

```
[method: CustomerPermissionAttribute(SecurityAction.Deny,
    Flags=CustomerPermissionFlag.ObjectCreation)]
private void SomeMethod()
{
    Customer c = new Customer("Jason", "Bock", 123);
    c.FirstName = "Pete";
    c.ID = 456;
}
```

In this case, your program fails on the customer creation line of code.

As you can see, being able to create custom permissions gives you the ability to lock down your own resources. I encourage you to play with custom permissions—not only will you become intimately familiar with the CAS classes, but you'll also learn how to administer .NET security policies.

SOURCE CODE *The CustomerPermission solution in the Chapter3 subdirectory contains all of the custom permission classes. The Customer solution contains the* Customer *class. To runs tests on the permission to verify that it works as expected, try CustomerPermissionTest. Use the CustomerTest project to experiment with the custom permission.*

Before I end this chapter on CAS, I'd like to cover one issue that I've seen come up quite often when I give a talk on .NET security, and that is the interaction between .NET security and the current configuration of the operating system's security layer.

Examining .NET and Operation System Security

As you've seen, .NET has a lot to offer when it comes to managing what code can and cannot do. However, just as managed code cannot circumvent what the runtime decides, the runtime cannot overcome what the operating system's security policies are. For example, take a look at the method in Listing 4-18.

Listing 4-18. Securing File Access in .NET

```
public class Employee
{
    // Other code goes here...
    [method: FileIOPermission(SecurityAction.Demand,
        Write = IMAGE_DIR)]
    public void SaveImage(string FileName)
    {
        FileName = IMAGE_DIR + FileName;

        if(true == File.Exists(FileName))
        {
            File.Delete(FileName);
        }

        FileStream fs = File.Create(FileName);
        fs.Write(this.m_Image, 0, (int)this.m_Image.Length);
        fs.Close();
    }
}
```

This method takes the name of a file and writes information (m_Image) to the file, which is automatically stored in the directory defined by IMAGE_DIR. If you call this method from a .NET Windows application like so:

```
FileStream fs = File.OpenRead(this.txtImageSourceValue.Text);
byte[] imageData = new Byte[fs.Length];
fs.Read(imageData, 0, (int)fs.Length);
fs.Close();

IEmployee emp = new Employee(
    this.txtFirstNameValue.Text,
    this.txtLastNameValue.Text,
    Guid.NewGuid(), imageData);

emp.SaveImage(this.txtImageDestinationValue.Text);
this.pctImage.SizeMode = PictureBoxSizeMode.StretchImage;
Bitmap empImage = new Bitmap(Employee.IMAGE_DIR +
    this.txtImageDestinationValue.Text);
this.pctImage.Image = (Image)empImage;
```

you would expect the image data to be in a file defined by the text value in the text box control called txtImageDestinationValue.

Of course, that depends on the .NET policy configuration. But since local code by default can do whatever it wants, this code will probably work when you run it. However, just because you can do something in .NET *does not mean* you can do anything on the machine. To prove this point, follow these instructions:

1. Change the directory access of IMAGE_DIR (defined to be c:\assembly\EmployeeImages\) on a Windows machine.

2. Open up an Explorer window, find the correct directory (or create it if it doesn't exist yet), right-click it, and select Properties from the pop-up menu.

3. Select the Security tab, and make sure the Deny check box for the Write permission is checked as shown in Figure 4-14.

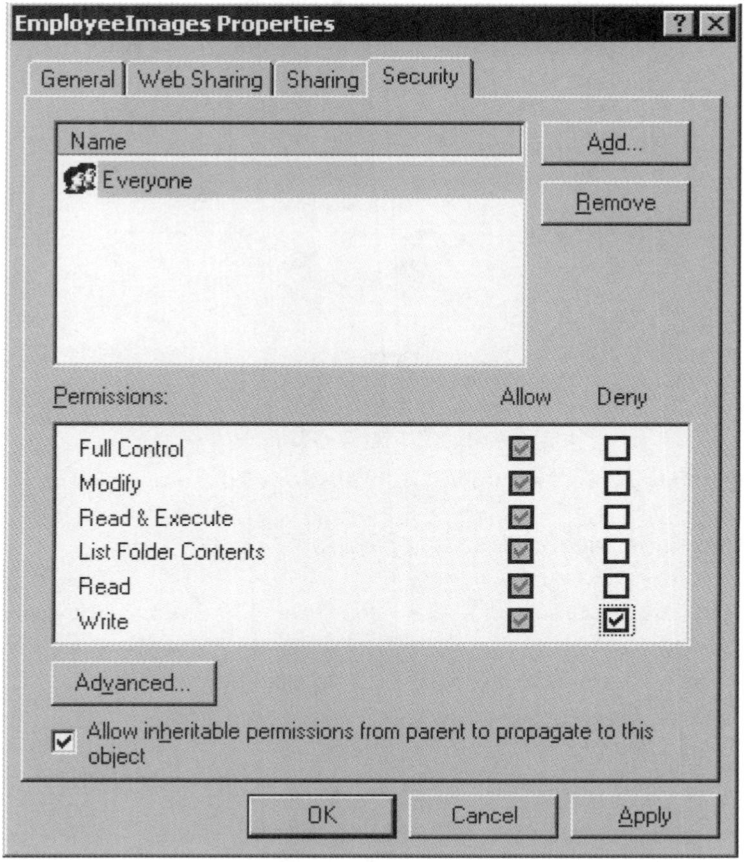

Figure 4-14. Denying write access

4. Rerun the client code.

You should now see that the file write operation can't take place—the runtime throws an `UnauthorizedAccessException`. This is the case with other resources as well, such as the Registry or network access. Remember, .NET sits on top of the operating system—it still needs to make calls to the operating system (OS) to open files or create windows. If these resources are protected by *native* configurations, .NET can't do anything about that via its own security layer. Therefore, if policies have been set up in Windows to prevent certain users from accessing files on a network, .NET will not let them circumvent it.

SOURCE CODE *The EmployeeExample directory in the Chapter3 subdirectory contains two projects: EmployeeLibrary, which will try to write image data to a specified directory, and EmployeeClient, which uses EmployeeLibrary.*

Summary

In this chapter, I covered the following topics:

- Using evidence to determine what code groups a loaded assembly is a member of to get a number of permissions from named permission sets

- Presenting evidence to a new `AppDomain`

- Implementing different kinds of security actions and how they work

- Creating a custom permission to secure a custom resource

In the next chapter, you'll see how role-access security works in .NET.

CHAPTER 5

Role Access Security

IN THIS CHAPTER, you'll investigate how to use Role Access Security (RAS) to protect resources. You'll study the definitions that are found in .NET and how they work. Finally, you'll learn about impersonation and how it works in .NET.

Let's start by looking at the .NET types that are used in RAS from a coding perspective.

Using .NET Class Definitions

All of the .NET class definitions types are in the System.Security.Principal namespace, and all can be found in the mscorlib assembly. Some classes define what identities and principals there are along with their relationship to each other. Other classes exist that help in defining how identities and principals are established for the current thread of execution. In this section, I'll cover the basics of these classes.

Let's start by looking at the definition of an identity in .NET.

IIdentity Interface

The IIdentity interface is used to define information about a user. Typically, that user is running the current code, although there's no requirement that a class that implements this interface has to relate to the underlying OS user. IIdentity defines three read-only properties:

- Name: A string that defines the logical name of the user. This can take on any form—a typical format is "domain\user" (for example, "apress\jbock").

- AuthenticationType: A string that defines the kind of authentication used to verify the user. Examples of common authentication schemes are Kerebos and Passport.

- IsAuthenticated: A Boolean that states whether the current user has been authenticated.

.NET supplies the four following implementations of IIdentity:

- GenericIdentity

- WindowsIdentity

- FormsIdentity

- PassportIdentity

Let's take a quick dive into these implementations.

GenericIdentity

As its name implies, GenericIdentity is not directly tied to any protocol to authenticate the identity in question. Creating a GenericIdentity object is pretty easy, as you can see here:

```
IIdentity genericNameOnly =
    new GenericIdentity("jbock");
IIdentity genericNoNameOnly =
    new GenericIdentity("");
IIdentity genericNameAndTypeK =
    new GenericIdentity("jbock", "Kerebos");
IIdentity genericNameAndTypeNT =
    new GenericIdentity("jbock", "NTLM");
```

You have two options for object construction. You can simply pass in a user name, or you can pass in a user name plus an authentication type.

Although it looks like the last two objects (genericNameAndTypeK and genericNameAndTypeNT) are using some kind of authentication protocol, GenericIdentity doesn't use that last argument value to authenticate the given user. In fact, if you ran this code in a console application and called IsAuthenticated on each object:

```
Console.WriteLine("Name only - is it authenticated?  " +
    genericNameOnly.IsAuthenticated.ToString());
Console.WriteLine("No name only - is it authenticated?  " +
    genericNoNameOnly.IsAuthenticated.ToString());
```

```
Console.WriteLine("Name + Kerebos - is it authenticated?   " +
    genericNameAndTypeK.IsAuthenticated.ToString());
Console.WriteLine("Name + NT - is it authenticated?  " +
    genericNameAndTypeNT.IsAuthenticated.ToString());
```

you'd get the following results:

```
Name only - is it authenticated?  True
No name only - is it authenticated?  False
Name + Kerebos - is it authenticated?  True
Name + NT - is it authenticated?  True
```

GenericIdentity only "authenticates" the identity if a user name is given.

WindowsIdentity

As the name suggests, WindowsIdentity is all about identifying a specific Windows user. The biggest difference between WindowsIdentity and GenericIdentity is in the construction of the object. WindowsIdentity has four constructors, and all of them have as its first arguments an IntPtr type, as you can see here:

```
IntPtr windowsToken /* =...*/;
IIdentity windowsUser =
    new WindowsIdentity(windowsToken, "NTLM",
        WindowsAccountType.Normal, true);
```

This example shows the constructor that takes the most arguments (the other constructors are just simplified versions of this one). The second argument is the authentication type. The third argument is a WindowsAccountType enumeration value that identifies the kind of account the identity is. It has the following four values:

- Anonymous: An anonymous account

- Guest: A guest account

- Normal: A regular Windows account

- System: A system account

The fourth parameter allows the client to specify if the user represented by the first argument is authenticated or not.

As the preceding code snippet suggests, you need to do some extra work to set the identity object to a user. (I'll show you later on in the section "Windows Impersonation" how to set the windowsToken value appropriately.) However, you can get the current Windows user's information by calling the static method GetCurrent(), like this:

```
IIdentity currentWindowsUser = WindowsIdentity.GetCurrent();
```

The Name value will be of the format "domain\user" and the authentication type will be "NTLM". The user should also be authenticated.

If you want to get an anonymous Windows user, you could use the static method called GetAnonymous() as follows:

```
IIdentity anonWindowsUser = WindowsIdentity.GetAnonymous();
```

In this case, there's no user name or authentication type, nor will the anonymous user be authenticated.

FormsIdentity and PassportIdentity

For the sake of completeness, I'll mention that there are two other IIdentity implementations in .NET: FormsIdentity and PassportIdentity. FormsIdentity is primarily used in ASP.NET applications, and PassportIdentity represents the user authenticated from a Passport. I won't delve into their workings here; I'll revisit these types in Chapters 7 and 8.

Now that you have a good understanding of how identities work in .NET, let's move on to the IPrincipal interface.

IPrincipal Interface

This interface is also pretty bare bones—it has two members:

- Identity: A read-only property to get the identity related to the principal

- IsInRole: A method that informs you if the principal is a member of a given role.

.NET provides two implementations of IPrincipal: GenericPrincipal and WindowsPrincipal, and I'll discuss these next.

GenericPrincipal

GenericPrincipal is a simplistic implementation of IPrincipal. To create a GenericPrincipal object, you have to give it an IIdentity-based object along with a list of roles that the identity belongs to. Here's an example:

```
string[] roles = {"administrators", "developers"};
IIdentity genericNameOnly = new GenericIdentity("jbock");
GenericPrincipal genericPrincipal =
    new GenericPrincipal(genericNameOnly, roles);

Console.WriteLine("Is the principal in the developer's role?  " +
    genericPrincipal.IsInRole("developers"));
Console.WriteLine("Is the principal in the accountant's role?  " +
    genericPrincipal.IsInRole("accountants"));
```

In this case, the console results would be as follows:

```
Is the principal in the developer's role?  True
Is the principal in the accountant's role  False
```

WindowsPrincipal

WindowsPrincipal is almost identical in looks to GenericPrincipal, except for its constructor. It will only take a WindowsIdentity instance as shown here:

```
WindowsPrincipal winPrincipal =
    new WindowsPrincipal(WindowsIdentity.GetCurrent());
Console.WriteLine("Is the principal in the administrator's role?  " +
    winPrincipal.IsInRole(@"weinstefaner\Administrators"));
```

Now, given that the box that this code is running on is called weinstefaner and I'm in the Adminstrators group, what do you think the console will show this time? Here's the answer:

```
Is the principal in the administrator's role?  False
```

This surprised me the first time I saw it. After doing some digging, I found out that you have to use the string BUILTIN in place of the machine name:

```
Console.WriteLine("Is the principal in the administrator's role?  " +
    winPrincipal.IsInRole(@"BUILTIN\Administrators"));
```

This will work, but this is also a little unintuitive, especially if you're not very familiar with how Windows security works.[1] Fortunately, WindowsPrincipal overloads IsInRole() to make this check easier to manage. One overload takes a WindowsBuiltInRole enumeration, which defines the following standard Windows roles:

- AccountOperator

- Administrator

- BackupOperator

- Guest

- PowerUser

- PrintOperator

- Replicator

- SystemOperator

- User

Therefore, you can change that last code snippet to the following, which is better from a locale-neutral perspective, as you identify the logical role with a physical number:

```
Console.WriteLine("Is the principal in the administrator's role?  " +
    winPrincipal.IsInRole(WindowsBuiltInRole.Administrator));
```

The other overload takes a relative identifier (RID) as an int as shown here:

```
Console.WriteLine("Is the principal in the administrator's role?  " +
    winPrincipal.IsInRole(0x00000220));
```

---

1.   All BUILTIN represents is a domain that exists on every Windows box.

This value represents the Administrator role.[2]

Now that you know how principals are defined, let's see how you can retrieve the current principal for a given thread.

Principal Policy

As you saw in one of the code snippets in the section "WindowsIdentity," it's possible to determine the current Windows user via GetCurrent() on WindowsIdentity. There's no equivalent GetCurrent() method on WindowsPrincipal, but there is the following static property called CurrentPrincipal on the Thread object to retrieve the current principal:

```
using System.Threading;
IPrincipal currentPrincipal = Thread.CurrentPrincipal;
```

However, if you ran the following code:

```
IPrincipal currentPrincipal = Thread.CurrentPrincipal;
IIdentity currentIdentity = currentPrincipal.Identity;
Console.WriteLine("Current user - is it authenticated?  " +
    currentIdentity.IsAuthenticated.ToString());
Console.WriteLine("Current user - name?  " +
    currentIdentity.Name);
Console.WriteLine("Current user - authentication type?  " +
    currentIdentity.AuthenticationType);
```

you'd get these results:

```
Current user - is it authenticated?  False
Current user - name?
Current user - authentication type?
```

The reason nothing comes up when you do this is due to the AppDomain's default principal policy choice. An enumeration called PrincipalPolicy defines these three policy schemes:

---

2. If you want to find out what RIDs are available, look in the Winnt.h file. The values for the WindowsBuiltInRole members match these RIDs, but there are more RIDs in the header file than what the enumeration defines.

- NoPrincipal

- UnauthenticatedPrincipal

- WindowsPrincipal

UnauthenticatedPrinicipal is the default. Therefore, if you want the identity contained in the principal to be determined via Windows, you need to call SetPrincipalPolicy() on the current AppDomain and pass it the WindowsPrincipal value, like so:

```
AppDomain.CurrentDomain.SetPrincipalPolicy(
    PrincipalPolicy.WindowsPrincipal);
```

Now, when you extract the current principal from Thread and examine the identity values, here's what you get:

```
Current user - is it authenticated?  True
Current user - name?  WEINSTEFANER\Administrator
Current user - authentication type?  NTLM
```

I've covered the essentials of identities and principals. Now, let's put that knowledge to work by securing code based on these values via permission attributes.

Understanding Identity Permission Attributes

So far, you've seen how to use IIdentity- and IPrincipal-based objects in .NET. However, you'll also want to use them for more than simply investigative purposes, like preventing users from executing a piece of code if they don't have the right credentials. .NET has a permission for just such a purpose, PrincipalPermission, with an attribute you can use for declarative security purposes, PrincipalPermissionAttribute.

PrincipalPermission has these three properties that you can set:

- Authenticated

- Name

- Role

For example, this code requires that the caller must be in the `Manager` role:

```
[PrincipalPermission(SecurityAction.Demand, Role="Manager")]
private static void RunManagerCode()
{
    Console.WriteLine("Manager work goes here...");
}
```

However, this code requires that the only one who can run this code is an authenticated manager named `Joe` as shown here:

```
[PrincipalPermission(SecurityAction.Demand,
    Authenticated=true, Role="Manager",
    Name="Joe")]
private static void RunAuthenticatedManagerJoesCode()
{
     Console.WriteLine("Authenticated manager Joe's work goes here...");
}
```

You can also combine these permission checks if you'd like:

```
[PrincipalPermission(SecurityAction.Demand, Role="Cook")]
[PrincipalPermission(SecurityAction.Demand, Role="Manager",
    Name="Joe")]
private static void RunCookOrManagerJoesCode()
{
    Console.WriteLine("Cook or manager Joe's work goes here...");
}
```

Of course, you're not limited to declarative checks with `PrincipalPermission`; you can make imperative checks as well:

```
PrincipalPermission prinPerm =
    new PrincipalPermission(null, "Manager");
prinPerm.Demand();
```

 NOTE *This permission can only work at the method or type level. It cannot be used across an entire assembly.*

CROSS-REFERENCE *Declarative and imperative checks are discussed in Chapter 4 in the section "Permission Requests."*

Now take a look at Listing 5-1 to see what happens when you use these permission checks. Given that you have declared the three preceding RunXXXCode() methods, set up two principals and call these methods.

Listing 5-1. Protecting Code via Role Membership

```
string[] managerRoles = {"Manager", "Cook"};
string[] cookRoles = {"Cook"};
IIdentity managerIdentity = new GenericIdentity("Jane");
IPrincipal managerPrincipal = new GenericPrincipal(managerIdentity, managerRoles);
IIdentity cookIdentity = new GenericIdentity("Joe");
IPrincipal cookPrincipal = new GenericPrincipal(cookIdentity, cookRoles);
Thread.CurrentPrincipal = cookPrincipal;
try
{ RunManagerCode(); }
catch(Exception managerEx)
{
    Console.WriteLine("Could not run the managers's code:  " +
        managerEx.Message);
}

try
{ RunCookOrManagerJoesCode(); }
catch(Exception managerEx)
{
    Console.WriteLine("Could not run cook or manager Joe's code:  " +
        managerEx.Message);
}

try
{ RunAuthenticatedManagerJoesCode(); }
catch(Exception managerEx)
```

```
{
    Console.WriteLine("Could not run authenticated manager " +
        "Joe's code:   " +
        managerEx.Message);
}
```

With the current principal set to a cook, this is the output:

```
Could not run the managers's code:  Request for principal permission failed.
Cook or manager Joe's work goes here...
Could not run authenticated manager Joe's code:
    Request for principal permission failed.
```

Now, set the principal to a manager:

```
Thread.CurrentPrincipal = managerPrincipal;
```

This change gives the new results:

```
Manager work goes here...
Cook or manager Joe's work goes here...
Could not run authenticated manager Joe's code:
    Request for principal permission failed.
```

In both cases, the last method (RunAuthenticatedManagerJoesCode()) could not be called. With cookPrincipal, the identity is not in the "Manager" role—with managerPrincipal, the identity's name is not "Joe". The only way RunAuthenticatedManagerJoesCode() can be invoked is if the identity has the name "Joe" and is in the "Manager" role.

SOURCE CODE   *The IdentityTest application in the Chapter5 subdirectory contains code that looks at how* IIdentity- *and* IPrincipal-*based objects work, as well as using* PrincipalPermission *to restrict access to code.*

Now that you know how to secure methods via identity and role membership, let's investigate how impersonation works.

Exploring Impersonation

As you may know, *impersonation* means taking on the identity of someone else to execute code with his or her credentials. Sometimes, this is a desired feature; other times, malicious code will try to act like another user with elevated permissions to get access to resources.

As you saw in the last section, you can use `PrincipalPermissionAttribute` to limit access to code. However, it's pretty easy to break through this barrier. For example, let's say there are two methods on a type called `SpecificRoleMembershipOnly()` and `SpecificWindowsUserOnly()` as shown here:

```
public class Privileged
{
    [PrincipalPermission(SecurityAction.Demand, Role="BigBucksClub")]
    public void SpecificRoleMembershipOnly()
    {
        Console.WriteLine("A privileged role member has arrived...");
    }

    [PrincipalPermission(SecurityAction.Demand,
        Name=@"WEINSTEFANER\Administrator")]
    public void SpecificWindowsUserOnly()
    {
        Console.WriteLine("A specific Windows user has arrived...");
    }
}
```

Now, if you attempted to call these methods from a .NET application without doing anything with principals and identities on the current thread, you wouldn't be successful, as `CurrentPrincipal` wouldn't contain any principal information. Of course, if you were the administrator on the `WEINSTEFANER` domain, you could alter the call to set the thread's current principal as follows:

```
Thread.CurrentPrincipal = new
    WindowsPrincipal(WindowsIdentity.GetCurrent());
Privileged p = new Privileged();
p.SpecificWindowsUserOnly();
```

But as the following code snippet demonstrates, you don't need to be an adminis-trator to call SpecificWindowsUserOnly():

```
IIdentity fakeWindowsIdentity = new
    GenericIdentity(@"WEINSTEFANER\Administrator");
IPrincipal fakeWindowsPrincipal = new
    GenericPrincipal(fakeWindowsIdentity, null);
Thread.CurrentPrincipal = fakeWindowsPrincipal;
p.SpecificWindowsUserOnly();
```

Don't be fooled by the format of the name! In this case, all PrincipalPermission enforces is that the name matches the current thread's identity name; it doesn't care how it got there.

You can run into the same case with the role-secured method as demon-strated here:

```
String[] fakeRole = {"BigBucksClub"};
IIdentity fakeRoleIdentity =
    new GenericIdentity(@"BigBucksWannabe");
IPrincipal fakeRolePrincipal =
    new GenericPrincipal(fakeRoleIdentity, fakeRole);
Thread.CurrentPrincipal = fakeRolePrincipal;
objRef.SpecificRoleMembershipOnly();
```

In all cases, the problem is that you can change the thread's current principal. To prevent this kind of mischievous activity, you could use the SecurityPermission attribute and deny yourself the ability to change the prin-cipal, like so:

```
[SecurityPermission(SecurityAction.Deny,
    Flags=SecurityPermissionFlag.ControlPrincipal)]
```

At first glance, this may seem kind of odd. After all, you're trying to circumvent all this role-access security junk anyway, so why would you rid yourself of the workaround?

The key is to refuse assemblies the ability to change the principal, which can be done by not granting the permission to assemblies via the .NET Configuration tool. Specifically, if you edit the permission settings for SecurityPermission, you need to leave the Allow principal control option unchecked as Figure 5-1 shows.

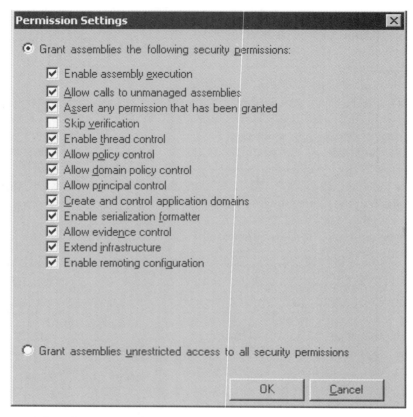

Figure 5-1. Denying principal control

In this case, I'm assuming that the permission is part of a permission set that's used in a code group and that the assembly matched the membership condition of that code group.

You can also prevent the principal from being changed when you create an AppDomain (an object that provides code isolation between unrelated applications):

```
AppDomain newAD = AppDomain.CreateDomain("ApressDomain");
newAD.SetPrincipalPolicy(PrincipalPolicy.WindowsPrincipal);
SecurityPermission sp =
    new SecurityPermission(
    SecurityPermissionFlag.ControlPrincipal);
sp.Deny();
int ret =
    newAD.ExecuteAssembly(@"D:\assembly\PPTester.exe");
```

In this case, you create the AppDomain, and call SetPrincipalPolicy() to make sure the principal is based on the current user. You deny any downstream code the capability to change the principal, and then you run an EXE.

Caveats with Limiting Principal Modification

Now, it may seem like you've done your job to prevent any code in the PPTester assembly from changing the principal. However, you've actually been too aggressive. So, say the following code is the start of its entry point method:

```
static void Main(string[] args)
{
    Console.WriteLine("Main entered.");
    Console.WriteLine("Identity name:  " +
        Thread.CurrentPrincipal.Identity.Name);
    //  More code goes here...
}
```

If you run this code, you may be a bit surprised by the results in the console window:

```
Main entered.
System.Security.SecurityException: Request failed.
```

You're probably thinking, "Hey! All I'm doing is trying to see what the current identity's name is. Why am I getting the exception?" The reason is a little subtle. If you look at the documentation for SetPrincipalPolicy() in the SDK, here's what it says:

> *Specifies how principal and identity objects should be attached to a thread **if** the thread attempts to bind to a principal while executing in this application domain. [Emphasis mine.]*

This means if the principal is never needed, it's never created. Once it's needed, it's cached for future reference. So what you did is state that you wanted to use the current Windows user for the principal's identity. However, no entity tried to use the principal in any way before Deny() was called. Therefore, simply looking at the Name property internally sets the thread's current principal, which you can't do.

You might try to solve this by using the thread's principal object in some way before Deny() is called as shown here:

```
newAD.SetPrincipalPolicy(PrincipalPolicy.WindowsPrincipal);
bool isAuth =
    Thread.CurrentPrincipal.Identity.IsAuthenticated;
SecurityPermission sp =
    new SecurityPermission(
    SecurityPermissionFlag.ControlPrincipal);
sp.Deny();
```

However, that doesn't work as expected either:

```
Main entered.
Identity name:
```

Again, the problem isn't obvious. You've set the new AppDomain's principal policy to WindowsPrincipal, but the current AppDomain's policy has never been touched. Therefore, when you call CurrentPrincipal on Thread, you're going to get the principal for the current AppDomain—in this case, the no-name user you saw earlier in this chapter, at the end of "Understanding Identity Permission Attributes."

You could set the current AppDomain's principal as well, but I think the easiest way to set this up is by specifying the new AppDomain's principal explicitly. Here's an example:

```
newAD.SetThreadPrincipal(
    new WindowsPrincipal(WindowsIdentity.GetCurrent()));
```

Now everything works as planned. Any code in the new AppDomain that tries to set the principal to impersonate another principal will get a SecurityException.

 SOURCE CODE *The PrincipalPermTest folder in the Chapter5 subdirectory contains two projects: PPTester and PPLauncher. PPTester contains the* Privileged *type along with code that you can use to try and set the current principal. PPLauncher will load PPTester—you can change the code here to see what happens when you prevent PPTester from changing the principal. Remember to set the target directory correctly when* ExecuteAssembly() *is called!*

I've covered the essentials of impersonation. Next, I'll show you how Windows-specific impersonation works.

Windows Impersonation

Now it's time to talk about the WindowsIdentity constructor that takes an IntPtr as its only argument. If you've done security programming in Windows, you may have run across the LogonUser()[3] API call. The function in the SDK looks like this:

```
BOOL LogonUser(
   LPTSTR lpszUsername,      // user name
   LPTSTR lpszDomain,        // domain or server
   LPTSTR lpszPassword,      // password
   DWORD dwLogonType,        // type of logon operation
   DWORD dwLogonProvider,    // logon provider
   PHANDLE phToken           // receive tokens handle
);
```

To use this call requires an unmanaged method invocation (or P/Invoke) as shown here:

```
[DllImport("advapi32.dll")]
static extern int LogonUser(String UserName, String Domain,
    String Password, int LogonType,
    int LogonProvider, ref IntPtr WindowToken);
```

The first three parameters are pretty easy to figure out how to use. The UserName is set to the user you want to impersonate (for example, "BobK"). Domain specifies the name of the server or domain that should contain the given user information. (Note that you can set Domain to "." if you want to authenticate against the local database, or "null" if the user name will be in user principal name, or UPN, format—for example, "BobK@SomeDomain".) And Password is the associated password that only the user (or trusted identities that want to impersonate the user) should know.

Now take a look at the last three parameters in detail. LogonType specifies the kind of logon you want to perform. The SDK lists seven different types, but for these purposes, use LOGON32_LOGON_NETWORK.[4] LogonProvider allows you to specify the provider you wish to use to authenticate against. For these tests, you'll use

---

3. There's also LogonUserEx(), but I'm going with LogonUser() here because it's a bit easier to use.

4. You can find the values of the constants LogonUser() uses in WinBase.h.

the default provider, which is LOGON32_PROVIDER_DEFAULT. Finally, if the logon is successful, WindowToken will contain a valid handle to a user token. Therefore, you need to pass in an IntPtr by reference to get this value when the method is done.

If the method is successful, you'll get zero as the return value. Any other value denotes some kind of error. You can find out what the error code is by calling GetLastError() as shown here:

```
[DllImport("kernel32.dll")]
static extern int GetLastError();
```

One error code you may immediately run into when you try to call LogonUser() is ERROR_LOGON_TYPE_NOT_GRANTED.[5] To use LogonUser() requires that the account that the process is running under has the SE_TCB_NAME privilege. You can find out if your account has this by running the Local Security Settings tool, which is found under Administrative Tools. Figure 5-2 shows what the interface for this tool looks like when you run it.

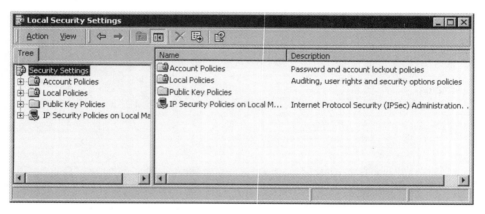

Figure 5-2. Local Security Settings tool

Now open Local Policies ➤ User Rights Assignment, and double-click the list view item Act as part of the operating system. Figure 5-3 shows what the resulting dialog box looks like.

---

5.   To find out all of the return values for LogonUser(), search for the phrase "ERROR_LOGON" in WinError.h.

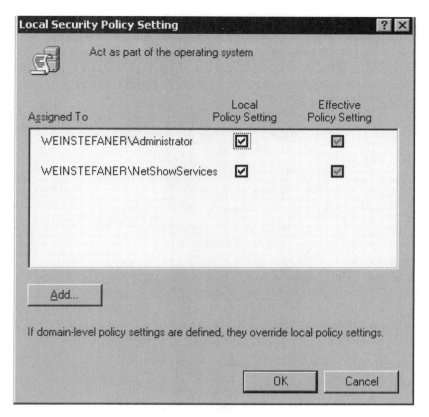

Figure 5-3. Privilege dialog box

To add a specific user, click the Add button at the lower-left corner of the screen, and select the user you want. When the user is added, the Effective Policy Setting option won't be checked, so if that user is currently logged on, he or she must log off to receive the SE_TCB_NAME privilege.

CAUTION *There are a lot of reasons why you do not want to grant this privilege to just any user. Essentially, this privilege gives the account access to anything in the operating system. Even the Administrator account does not receive this privilege by default. The only reason you have to do so in this case is for you to be able to call* LogonUser().

Next, assume that you added this privilege to the account you run under. Now, try to get a user token in a .NET application. To illustrate how you might approach this, I created two accounts on my machine, JaneDoe and JohnSmith. JaneDoe is part of the Administrators and Users group, whereas JohnSmith is only in the Users group.[6] I then added the code you see in Listing 5-2 to a console application.

Listing 5-2. Using LogonUser() in .NET

```
class WIT
{
    private static String t_Domain = null;
    private static String t_Password = null;
    private static String t_UserName = null;
    private const int LOGON32_LOGON_NETWORK = 3;
    private const int LOGON32_PROVIDER_DEFAULT = 0;
    private const int FORMAT_MESSAGE_FROM_SYSTEM = 0x00001000;
    private const int FORMAT_MESSAGE_ALLOCATE_BUFFER = 0x00000100;

    [DllImport("advapi32.dll")]
    static extern int LogonUser(String UserName, String Domain,
        String Password, int LogonType, int LogonProvider,
        ref IntPtr WindowToken);

    [DllImport("kernel32.dll", CharSet=CharSet.Auto)]
    static extern int FormatMessage(int Flags,
        ref IntPtr MessageSource, int MessageID,
        int LanguageID, ref IntPtr Buffer,
        int BufferSize, int Arguments);

    [DllImport("kernel32.dll")]
    static extern bool CloseHandle(IntPtr Handle);

    [DllImport("kernel32.dll")]
    static extern int GetLastError();

    [STAThread]
    static void Main(string[] args)
    {
```

---

6. You can set these accounts on your local machine by traversing to the Local Users and Groups node in the Computer Management tool. I'll leave that as an exercise for you—it's pretty easy to do.

```
        try
        {
            Console.WriteLine("Main entered...");
            GetLogonInformation();

            Console.WriteLine("Attempting logon...");
            IntPtr windowsToken  = IntPtr.Zero;
            int logonRetVal = LogonUser(t_UserName, t_Domain, t_Password,
                LOGON32_LOGON_NETWORK, LOGON32_PROVIDER_DEFAULT,
                ref windowsToken);

            if(0 != logonRetVal)
            {
                Console.WriteLine("Logon successful.");
                WindowsIdentity newWI = new WindowsIdentity(windowsToken);
                Console.WriteLine("Logon name: " + newWI.Name);
                CloseHandle(windowsToken);
            }
            else
            {
                throw new Exception(
                    "Error occurred with LogonUser().  " +
                    "Error number:  " + GetLastError() + ", " +
                    "Error message:  " + CreateLogonUserError(GetLastError()));
            }
        }
        catch(Exception ex)
        {
            Console.WriteLine(ex.ToString());
        }
    }

    private static void GetLogonInformation()
    {
        Console.WriteLine("Please enter the user name.");
        t_UserName = Console.ReadLine();
        Console.WriteLine("Please enter the password.");
        t_Password = Console.ReadLine();
        Console.WriteLine("Please enter the domain.");
        t_Domain = Console.ReadLine();
    }
```

```
private static String CreateLogonUserError(int ErrorCode)
{
    IntPtr bufferPtr = IntPtr.Zero;
    IntPtr messageSource = IntPtr.Zero;

    int retVal = FormatMessage(
        FORMAT_MESSAGE_FROM_SYSTEM | FORMAT_MESSAGE_ALLOCATE_BUFFER,
        ref messageSource, ErrorCode, 0, ref bufferPtr, 1, 0);

        string strRetval =
            Marshal.PtrToStringAuto(bufferPtr, retVal);

    return strRetval;
}
}
```

There's a fair amount of code here, so I'll go through each section in detail.

First, you get the username/password/domain combination from the user via GetLoginInformation(). Once that's done, you call LogonUser(). Note that you initialize the token value to IntPtr.Zero before you make this call. If the call was successful, you create a new WindowsIdentity object with the token value. You also have to call CloseHandle() on the token when you're done with it.

If the call didn't work, you throw an exception. The string that is passed to the new Exception object is built with the error code returned from GetLastError(), and an error message that can be obtained with FormatMessage(). FormatMessage() can be a tricky API to call. However, all you need to do is get a message from the system, so the call declaration can be simplified to what I have in the code snippet. Note that by setting Flags to contain FORMAT_MESSAGE_ALLOCATE_BUFFER, you get a pointer to the string. This is why you're calling PtrToStringAuto() to get the string's contents. Figure 5-4 shows what happens when the credentials are correct, and Figure 5-5 displays the results of a bad authentication.

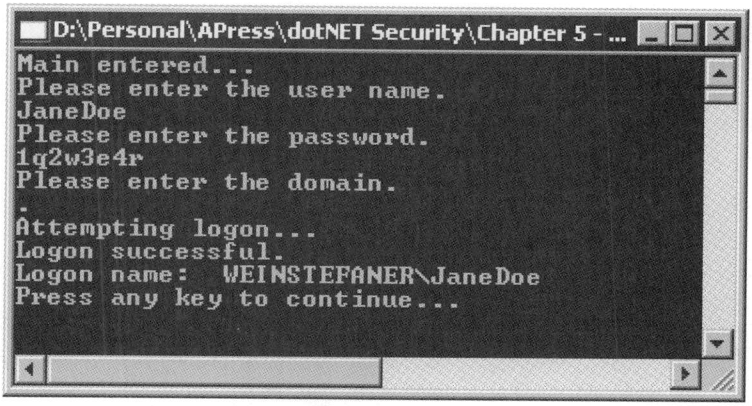

Figure 5-4. Successful LogonUser() call

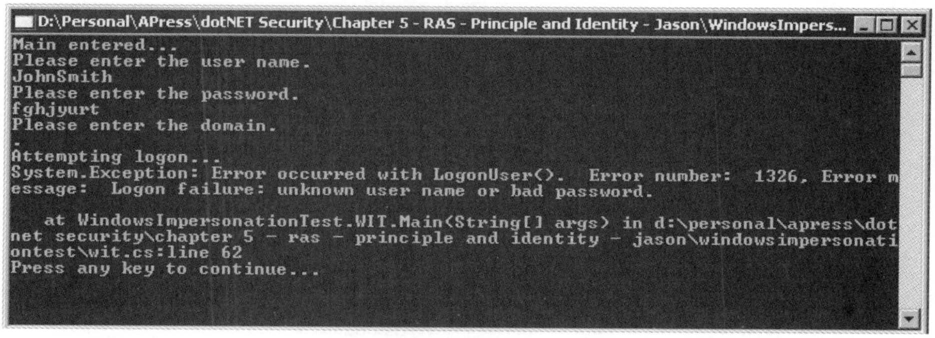

Figure 5-5. Unsuccessful LogonUser() call

Okay, now that you have all of this baseline code in place, you can finally perform Windows impersonation as shown in Listing 5-3. This is actually the easy part.

Listing 5-3. Windows Impersonation in .NET

```
WindowsImpersonationContext wic = newWI.Impersonate();
WindowsIdentity currentWI = WindowsIdentity.GetCurrent();
Console.WriteLine("Current Windows name after impersonation:  " +
    currentWI.Name);
wic.Undo();
currentWI = WindowsIdentity.GetCurrent();
Console.WriteLine("Current Windows name after Undo():  " +
    currentWI.Name);
```

You call `Impersonate()` on a `WindowsIdentity` object, and store the return value in a `WindowsImpersonationContext` object. This is basically a caching mechanism to store the current user's information, as a call to `Undo()` will revert the user to the current Windows user. Figure 5-6 shows what the console application does when you add this code.

```
Main entered...
Please enter the user name.
JohnSmith
Please enter the password.
hm90vbok
Please enter the domain.
.
Attempting logon...
Logon successful.
Logon name: WEINSTEFANER\JohnSmith
Current Windows name after impersonation: WEINSTEFANER\JohnSmith
Current Windows name after Undo(): WEINSTEFANER\Administrator
Press any key to continue...
```

Figure 5-6. Impersonation results

Windows impersonation is still subject to being able to change the thread's user token. If this has been denied, you won't be able to do Windows impersonation. However, if you are able to do Windows impersonation, you need to grab the current Windows user from `WindowsIdentity` and *not* from the `Thread` class (via `CurrentThread.CurrentPrincipal`). Windows impersonation will not automatically set the current principal, as you can see here:

```
IIdentity curIdent = Thread.CurrentPrincipal.Identity;
Console.WriteLine("Current identity from the thread " +
    "before impersonation:  " +
    curIdent.Name);
WindowsImpersonationContext wic = newWI.Impersonate();
WindowsIdentity currentWI = WindowsIdentity.GetCurrent();
Console.WriteLine("Current Windows name after impersonation:  " +
    currentWI.Name);
curIdent = Thread.CurrentPrincipal.Identity;
Console.WriteLine("Current identity from the thread " +
    "after impersonation:  " +
    curIdent.Name);
```

If you run this code, you'll see that the name of the identity from `Thread` is the same before and after impersonation.

SOURCE CODE   *The WindowsImpersonationTest application in the Chapter5 subdirectory contains all of the code that I went through in this section.*

Summary

In this chapter, I covered the following topics:

- Basics of role-based security in .NET

- Interfaces and the concrete types that .NET provides, and how you can use them to discover principal information

- Impersonation of an identity and how you can prevent this in .NET

In the next chapter, I'll start to move beyond the core .NET types and delve onto some real-world scenarios where security is essential to the problem at hand. Specifically, that problem is communicating with distributed objects, or what is known as remoting in .NET. That's what Chapter 6 is all about.

Remoting and Security

Wʜᴇɴ ʏᴏᴜ'ʀᴇ ᴛʜɪɴᴋɪɴɢ ᴀʙᴏᴜᴛ ᴡʀɪᴛɪɴɢ a distributed application in .NET, your options are .NET Remoting and XML Web services. XML Web services are ideal for applications that need to interoperate with other platforms. Its transport protocol is in strict adherence with the Simple Object Access Protocol (SOAP) specification, so any client that can talk SOAP can talk to a .NET XML Web service. However, this adherence limits some of the distributed capabilities of XML Web service objects. Enter .NET Remoting.

Remoting is used for pure .NET object communication and has several benefits over XML Web services, including performance, remote object activation flexibility, and full by-value object serialization across the wire. And like XML Web services, .NET Remoting allows you to programmatically extend many parts of the remoting infrastructure to service your unique requirements.

Remoting is mostly used to allow one machine to communicate with an application on another across a private network or even across a public network like the Internet. In all cases, security is a very real issue. Your application communicates data across a wire while a server listens for client requests. Both of these scenarios introduce numerous security situations that, if left unaddressed, can jeopardize the success of any distributed application (and the enterprise in which the application runs).

This chapter will discuss how to secure applications that use .NET Remoting. First, I'll provide a quick overview of remoting. Then I'll discuss the different kinds of security associated with remoting and how to implement them. Throughout the chapter, I'll show you how to develop a simple remoting application that will demonstrate each security milestone.

Remoting Overview

Before you can tackle the complex security issues around .NET Remoting, it would be helpful to take a moment to dig into the architecture itself. A solid understanding of how remoting works is key to identifying security issues within it.

To understand remoting, it's helpful to review the technologies you've been using up until now, namely the Component Object Model (COM).[1] This will also

---

1. For those readers who have done distributed development outside of the Windows realm, similar analogies can be made for RMI- and CORBA-based systems.

help you compare the security issues in both COM and .NET. In the COM world, basically two kinds of server objects can be used by clients: *in-process* and *out-of-process*. In-process COM objects, like ActiveX dynamic link libraries (DLLs) or ActiveX Controls, are created, used, and destroyed within the same process as the client. The client has direct access to the object since it resides within the same process.

Out-of-process objects, like ActiveX EXEs, are created and run within a separate process from the client. If the out-of-process object is running on a machine other than the client's, then COM uses the Distributed Component Object Model (DCOM) to communicate to it. By the rules of the operating system, a client does not have direct access to an object running in a separate process. Instead, all calls to the object are marshaled via a proxy object.

The .NET architecture is very similar to that of COM with one major difference: AppDomains. Applications in .NET don't necessarily run in separate dedicated processes; they run in an AppDomain, which provides more of a logical application boundary than a physical one. Depending on the application type, you can have multiple AppDomains running in a single process.[2] Therefore, the .NET equivalent of an in-process object is an object that the client uses that runs within the same AppDomain as the client.[3] And like an in-process COM object, the client has direct access to this type of object.

However, if the client uses an object that is running in a different AppDomain, even if that AppDomain is running in the same process, then by the rules of the .NET common language runtime (CLR), the client cannot have direct access to that object. This scenario is functionally equivalent to COM's out-of-process object. In .NET, the only way to communicate with that object is with remoting. Therefore, remoting is technically defined as the mechanism by which one AppDomain accesses objects in another. This means that remoting is not only used for object communication from one machine to another, but also from one process to another within the same *machine*, and even within the same *process*. This is the case because more than one AppDomain can exist in a process.

The type of remoting that requires the most security considerations is machine-to-machine; this is the type I will discuss for the remainder of the chapter. Interprocess and inter-AppDomain remoting is much safer since it involves no network communication.

---

2. This capability is the result of the .NET CLR's type safety, which can manage multiple applications running within a single process, providing the same application isolation of separate processes without the overhead of cross-process communication.

3. An example would be an object within a Class Library DLL assembly.

Remoting, Under the Hood

On the surface, .NET Remoting looks a lot like DCOM because it also uses a proxy object to communicate between applications. Under the hood, the two technologies operate very differently. Figure 6-1 shows the remoting architecture in a nutshell.

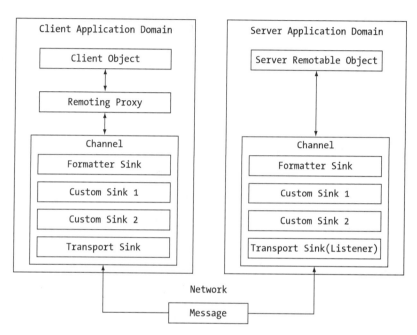

Figure 6-1. Remoting architecture

When a client object wants to communicate to a remoting server object, the following process takes place:

1. The client object in the client AppDomain instantiates a local Proxy object, which has the exact same metadata as the remote server object. This Proxy can be generated using metadata (an assembly) supplied by the remoting server.

2. The client invokes a method on the local Proxy that represents a method on the remote server object.

3. The proxy object sends the method call, called a Message, to the remoting runtime, which in turn dumps it into the remoting channel.

4. The remoting channel is made up of a series of predefined channel sinks that format and send the message to the remote server. The first channel sink formats the message into a stream that can be sent over the wire. Remoting provides a SOAP and a binary formatter, but custom formatters can be developed.

5. Once the message has been formatted, other custom channel sinks can modify the message before it is passed to the final sink, which transmits the message over the wire. Remoting provides a Hypertext Transfer Protocol (HTTP) and Transmission Control Protocol (TCP) transporter, but custom transporters can be developed.

6. The message is sent over the wire and received by the listening server's `AppDomain`.

7. The message gets placed into the server's channel via a receiving transport channel sink.

8. Custom channel sinks can process the message until it finally arrives in the formatter sink, in which it is converted to a method call and invoked against the server object.

9. If the method has a return value or if any of the arguments passed in the method are by-reference objects (and therefore call back to the client), then a server-to-client message is sent back to the client in the same fashion that the client-to-server message was sent to the server.

As you can see, one major difference between .NET Remoting and DCOM is that in the former you have direct access to the actual infrastructure used to communicate calls between objects. You are not forced to use whatever hard-coded networking protocol was chosen by the designers of remoting. You are given a few "out of the box" transport mechanisms, and you have the freedom to create your own.

A Simple Remoting Example

Next, take a look at a very simple remoting example. You'll build on this example throughout the rest of the chapter. The sample application will simulate a public library that allows people to see how many books are available to be checked out for a given International Standard Book Number (ISBN).

LibraryServer Class Library

The remoting server will expose objects in a class library. These objects will live in a class library assembly called LibraryServer. Listing 6-1 shows you how to create the main server object using a class called Library.

Listing 6-1. Creating a Remote Library

```
using System;
namespace LibraryServer
{
    public class Library : MarshalByRefObject
    {
        public Library()
        {
            Console.WriteLine("Library class instantiated.");
        }
        public int GetAvailableCopies(int ISBN)
        {
            switch (ISBN)
            {
                case 1893115593:
                    return 3;
                case 1893115585:
                    return 2;
                case 1893115712:
                    return 0;
                default:
                    return -1;
            }
        }
    }
}
```

Notice that the Library class inherits from the MarshalByRefObject class. This is necessary for the object to be remotable; MarshalByRefObject is a special class used by the remoting infrastructure. By default, objects are serialized and copied between application domains; they are marshaled by value. However, if you want your object to be referenced (not copied) across application domains, then it must be marshaled by reference; to do this, it needs to inherit from the MarshalByRefObject class. A remoting communication must start with a client talking to a marshal-by-reference object. Other objects can then be passed back and forth as arguments or return values that can be either marshal by reference or by value.

Taking a closer look at the logic of the Library class, you'll notice that it is quite simple. It has a constructor that sends feedback to the console when the object is instantiated. It has a single method called GetAvailableCopies(), which returns the number of copies of a given book, specified by an ISBN within a public library, that haven't been checked out. For simplicity's sake, you won't connect to a real database, so the method returns hard-coded results. If the ISBN doesn't exist in your system, the method simply returns the value –1.

LibraryServerHost Console Application

Now you need to make this remoting server object accept client requests. Therefore, you need to place it in some kind of host that will listen for client requests. You'll learn more about the various remoting hosts in a bit, but for now create your own by making a console application as shown here:

```
using System;
using System.Runtime.Remoting;
namespace LibraryServerHost
{
    class Host
    {
        static void Main(string[] args)
        {
            Console.WriteLine("Library server host started.");
            RemotingConfiguration.Configure("LibraryServerHost.exe.config");
            Console.WriteLine("Press enter to shut down.\n");
            Console.ReadLine();
        }
    }
}
```

---

4.   This is a standard .NET application configuration file. It must exist within the same directory as your console application, and its name must be the console application's assembly name, appended with .config (in this case, LibraryServerHost.exe.config).

The server host uses a configuration file[4] to configure the host for remoting and expose the Library class. Here's what the configuration file looks like:

```
<configuration>
    <system.runtime.remoting>
        <application>
            <channels>
                <channel ref="tcp" port="8181" />
            </channels>
            <service>
            <wellknown mode="SingleCall"
                type="LibraryServer.Library, LibraryServer"
                objectUri="LibraryServerURI" />
            </service>
        </application>
    </system.runtime.remoting>
</configuration>
```

This configuration file uses a special remoting section called <system.runtime.remoting>, which registers a TCP remoting channel that listens on port 8181. It then registers the LibraryServer.Library type as a SingleCall server-activated object at the URI "LibraryServerURI".

NOTE   *Remoting objects can use different activation types. The sample object for now uses SingleCall, which means that a separate instance of the server object is created and destroyed for each method call invoked by a client. This type of object is said to be stateless since it doesn't maintain any state between method invocations. More about remoting activation types appears in the section "Remoting Activation Dangers."*

LibraryClientHost Console Application

That finishes the server code. Now you need to create a remoting client that uses the server. In the following example, you'll make the client a console application as well:

```
using System;
using System.Runtime.Remoting;
using LibraryServer;
namespace LibraryClientHost
{
    class Host
    {
        static void Main(string[] args)
        {
            Console.WriteLine("Library client host started.\n");
            RemotingConfiguration.Configure("LibraryClientHost.exe.config");
            Library lib = new Library();

            int intISBN = 1893115585;
            Console.Write("Copies of book (ISBN = " + intISBN.ToString() + "): ");
            Console.WriteLine(lib.GetAvailableCopies(1893115585));
            Console.WriteLine("\nPress enter to shut down.");
            Console.ReadLine();
        }
    }
}
```

Like the server host, the client host also uses a configuration file (LibraryClientHost.exe.config) to specify the remoting type to be used in the client, as shown here:

```
<configuration>
    <system.runtime.remoting>
        <application>
            <client>
                <wellknown url="tcp://shadowfax:8181/LibraryServerURI"
                    type="LibraryServer.Library, LibraryServer"/>
            </client>
        </application>
    </system.runtime.remoting>
</configuration>
```

The `<client>` tag in the configuration file allows the client to instantiate the remoting type by simply using the new keyword. Notice the url attribute in the `<wellknown>` element is pointing to the "shadowfax" host. This is the name of my machine. Please substitute the name of your machine here. If you're keeping in the true spirit of remoting and have your client and server code running on separate machines, then make sure the machine name specified here is your server machine.

The Output

Finally, you can run and test this remoting example. First, start the server console application host. The output should look like this:

```
Library server host started.
Press enter to shut down.
```

Next, start the client console application host. If you've done everything right, the output should look like this:

```
Library client host started.
Copies of book (ISBN = 1893115585): 2
Press enter to shut down.
```

In the server console output window, you should see two new lines added:

```
Library class instantiated.
Library class instantiated.
```

This shows you feedback within the server host when the server object is being instantiated. You will notice that it appears that two instances of the object are being created, when only one was called from the client host. This is because the CLR on the server side must create a local instance of the remoting object the first time it's called by a client as a part of its remoting registration process. All subsequent calls by clients to the object will result in individual instances. You can test this if you run the client host application again; a third feedback line would appear, but not a fourth.

In summary, the client host application is really quite simple. A single line of code activates the remote Library object, and a second calls its only method (GetAvailableCopies()). Figure 6-2 shows a graphical representation of this process.

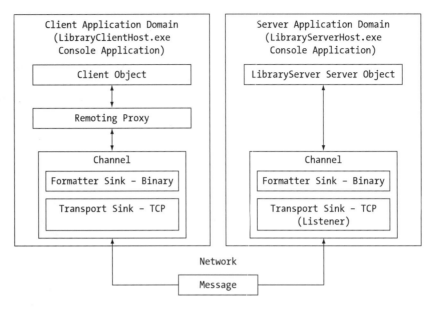

Figure 6-2. The simple remoting example application

The client makes a call to the object on the server via a proxy object on the client side. The request is transformed into a binary format, which is transferred to the server via TCP. The process is reversed on the client side—that is, when a request is received, it is transformed into a method call on the server object.

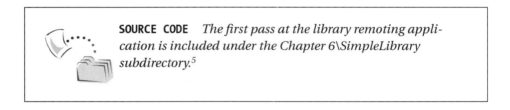

SOURCE CODE   *The first pass at the library remoting application is included under the Chapter 6\SimpleLibrary subdirectory.[5]*

Now that you have some real remoting code to start with, you can finally get down to learning about security as it relates to .NET Remoting.

---

5.   As a point of clarification, the word "Library" in each of the project names refers to the sample code being modeled by a public library. It is not implying that a particular project is a .NET class library.

Network Security Simplified

Remoting gets a little more involved with security than COM did, since DCOM was never really intended to be used across a public network. In fact, if you really want to challenge your networking skills, try configuring a firewall to allow DCOM calls to pass through it and still maintain network integrity for your private network.[6]

Remoting is much simpler from a networking traffic standpoint because it can be configured to operate on a single port, which allows it to jump through firewalls much easier than DCOM. Therefore, remoting security is analogous to the security issues related to any private or public network application. Most network applications have the following security concerns:

- Physical security

- Logical security

- Data security

- Authentication, authorization, and impersonation

Authentication, authorization, and impersonation will be covered in a separate section, "Understanding Authentication, Authorization, and Impersonation," later in this chapter.

Physical Security

Physical security basically refers to any hardware security in place to protect a private network or machine from an outside network. If your remoting application interfaces with the Internet, then having good physical security is your first best defense against malicious clients. The details of implementing physical security for such a scenario are a bit out of the scope of this chapter, but basically it boils down to configuring a firewall device that blocks all traffic not specific to the server applications running on the internal side.

---

6. In case you're interested in how to do this, take a look at the article "Using Distributed COM with Firewalls" on MSDN at http://msdn.microsoft.com/library/default.asp?url=/library/en-us/dndcom/html/msdn_dcomfirewall.asp.

Logical Security

Logical security involves making sure the server resources are safe against malicious clients who are able to authenticate themselves, but wish to perform operations outside of the design of the server resource. There are three questions to consider in this matter:

- How secure is the platform your application is running on?

- How does your application control access to resources (specifically the ones it doesn't use)?

- What are the security risks of the different object activation types?

Framework Security

When it comes to low-level security, your application is ultimately at the mercy of the platform that it's running on. You can write the most secure code in the world, but if your platform has holes, you're still vulnerable. This has always been a stumbling block for many applications in the past, as they were never built upon platforms that handled security well, if at all. One of the benefits of writing on the .NET Framework platform is that your code automatically has a layer of security provided by the CLR. And as you've seen, .NET has a ton of tools for configuring security to the level required by the application.

Below the .NET platform is your operating system (OS). Choosing the right OS with security in mind is also important. .NET can run on several Windows operating systems, but some of them have better intrinsic security (Windows 2000/XP/.NET Servers vs. Windows 9x).

Finally, most of the examples in this chapter host the remoting server in IIS. IIS has its own set of security considerations. For example, through IIS version 5.1, security is pretty much wide open by default. You have to configure IIS to actually lock it down. This is a very good best practice, especially if you're hosting remoting server objects on a public network like the Internet.

Code-Access Security

As you've seen in Chapter 4, .NET has a very effective built-in architecture for managing what code can and cannot do—code-access security (CAS). Given the fact that your remoting server application is only using a few of the many machine resources available to it to do whatever processing it needs to do, it makes sense to constrict your code to only the resources it needs. This is especially true with remoting applications: in the event that a malicious client does compromise your application, it's still limited to accessing the resources that your application is configured to access.

Remoting Activation Dangers

Remoting has three object activation types. There are two types of server activation in which the server controls the lifecycle of the remoting object: SingleCall, which dictates each method invocation uses a separate instantiation of the object on the server;[7] and Singleton, which dictates a single instance of an object is shared by all clients. The third type of remoting object activation is client activation, which specifies the object lives as long as the client keeps a reference to it.

Most of the code in this chapter involves server-activated remoting objects. That's because from a security standpoint, they're much safer than client-activated (or CA) objects. CA objects are dangerous simply because the server has no real control over how many clients are going to instantiate the objects. These object instances take up memory on the server and could be a potential denial-of-service security threat.

 NOTE *CA objects also have the added complexity of managing sponsors, which can represent clients that can't respond in a timely manner when the server wants to refresh the lease on an object instance. The idea of having sponsors that can be independent of the client is in itself a problem in an environment that requires security.*

Not that CA objects don't have their place in the remoting world. They are a good direct replacement for the functionality found in DCOM objects, in which the client also controls the lifecycle of the server object instance. CA has the primary benefit over DCOM of being less chatty and more disconnected since it uses leased-based communication between the client and the server. Regardless, CA objects are better suited within a private network where security is not so much a risk and where there is control over what constitutes a client and the number of clients.

---

7.   SingleCall activation is essentially what XML Web services objects use.

CA objects also have the added complexity of managing sponsors, which can represent clients that can't respond in a timely manner when the server wants to refresh the lease on an object instance. The idea of having sponsors that can be independent of the client is in itself a problem in an environment that requires security.

Data Security

Data security involves protecting sensitive data going across the wire. This usually entails encrypting the data so it cannot be examined by outsiders. Securing the data stream that flows on the channel between the client and server is sometimes a priority, especially if the data contains sensitive information. There are several ways you could implement this with remoting, one of which is very easy. If you're hosting your remoting objects in IIS, then you can take advantage of IIS's built-in Secure Socket Layer (SSL) functionality. SSL will encrypt any data on the wire so malicious stream readers won't be able to decipher the payload of information.

Other out-of-band encryption techniques could be employed. If SSL isn't comprehensive enough, IPSec, which essentially encrypts the entire TCP/IP stream (not just port 443), could be used. Another approach would be to implement your own custom encryption mechanism within the remoting channel sinks. An encryption sink and decryption sink would need to be present on both the client and server so that both method calls and their return values could be processed.

The next section goes into detail about the last security concern—authentication, authorization, and impersonation.

Understanding Authentication, Authorization, and Impersonation

Recall that *authentication* is the process of validating a client identity based on credentials against some kind of authority, like Active Directory, a Passport service, or a custom security database. Authentication basically verifies that users are who they say they are. *Authorization* determines if an authenticated user should have access to the requested resource. An extension of authorization is to group users into roles and specify authorization based on these roles. Finally, *impersonation* involves the server-side code being accessed by an authenticated user to run as a given identity. Many times this is the identity that the client is authenticated as.

CROSS-REFERENCE   *See Chapter 5 for introductory discussions of authentication and impersonation.*

Authentication and Authorization

The first rule of authentication (and authorization) is that it should occur within the server host of the remoting object and not within the remoting object itself. This provides a layer of protection against malicious clients who, if they don't authenticate, won't cause the remoting object to even get instantiated. Having the authentication mechanism within the server host also makes sense since this is where the remoting configuration and initialization itself occurs.

So, if you want authentication for your remoting object, your first task is to choose a proper server host type. Remoting objects can be hosted in IIS, a .NET EXE, Internet Explorer, and even Component Services. However, the only host that has a built-in authentication mechanism is Internet Information Server (IIS). Therefore, it makes for an easy choice for hosting your remoting objects.

NOTE   *Hosting a .NET object in Component Services (COM+) basically involves using COM Interop to wrap the .NET object and host it in a COM+ application. Technically the .NET remoting engine isn't even being used, rather DCOM is; it's a way to remote your .NET object to COM clients on other machines. COM+ also provides its own authentication and role-based security mechanisms, which are outside of the scope of this book. Please refer to* COM and .NET Interoperability *by Andrew Troelsen (Apress, 2002), and* Advanced .NET Remoting *by Ingo Rammer (Apress, 2002) for more information.*

Hosting in IIS does have a limitation. IIS can only host remoting objects using the HTTP channel, not the TCP channel. For performance reasons, a lot of people like to use the TCP channel since it has a fast binary formatter. Luckily, remoting lets you mix and match channels and formatters so you can in fact use the binary formatter in the HTTP channel. And you're going to do just that: host your Library remoting object in IIS using the HTTP channel and the binary formatter, which will give you the power of IIS and the speed of the binary formatter.

In some cases, hosting a secure remoting application in a host other than IIS may make sense—for example, if IIS is not available on the server machine—but these cases are uncommon. For simplicity, from this point on I'll focus on using an IIS host. Unfortunately, the sample application is presently doing just the opposite: it's being hosted in a console application (.NET EXE) using the TCP formatter. So, the first thing you need to do is put the Library object in IIS and tweak the configuration files a bit. Of course, the beautiful thing about remoting is that the changes you need to make to do this are very minor and do not require any modifications to source code.

Hosting the LibraryServer Assembly in IIS

The first thing you can do is eliminate the LibraryServerHost console application that you just wrote because you're now going to host in IIS. For this example, use the IIS default Web site, whose physical root is C:\Inetpub\wwwroot.

Follow these steps to host the LibraryServer assembly in IIS:

1. Create a subdirectory under C:\Inetpub\wwwroot called LibraryServerIISHost.

2. Create a virtual directory within the IIS default Web site called LibraryServerIISHost and point it at the C:\Inetpub\wwwroot\LibraryServerIISHost directory.

3. Create a subdirectory under C:\Inetpub\wwwroot\LibraryServerIISHost called bin and place in it a copy of the LibraryServer.DLL assembly you compiled.

4. Copy the LibraryServerHost.exe.config you created originally into the C:\Inetpub\wwwroot\LibraryServerIISHost directory and rename it to web.config.

5. Modify the web.config file to look like this:

```
<configuration>
    <system.runtime.remoting>
        <application>
            <service>
                <wellknown mode="SingleCall"
                    objectUri="LibraryServer.rem"
                    type="LibraryServer.Library, LibraryServer"/>
            </service>
```

```
            <channels>
                <channel ref="http">
                    <serverProviders>
                        <formatter ref="binary"/>
                    </serverProviders>
                </channel>
            </channels>
        </application>
    </system.runtime.remoting>
</configuration>
```

6. Modify the client host's configuration file (LibraryClientHost.exe.config)
    to look like this:

```
<configuration>
    <system.runtime.remoting>
        <application>
            <channels>
                <channel ref="http">
                    <clientProviders>
                        <formatter ref="binary"/>
                    </clientProviders>
                </channel>
            </channels>
            <client>
                <wellknown
                    url="http://shadowfax/
                    LibraryServerIISHost/LibraryServer.rem"
                    type="LibraryServer.Library, LibraryServer"/>
            </client>
        </application>
    </system.runtime.remoting>
</configuration>
```

Now, run the client host application, and you should get the same results as
before in the section "A Simple Remoting Example." The only difference is that
you can't see the server running as a console window, so you don't get the nice
feedback when a Library object is instantiated.

So what's different under the hood? Hosting in IIS is a snap because all you
need to do is create either a Web site or a virtual directory to place your remoting
assembly in; you don't need to write and compile a hosting application. The only
real change you have to make on the server side is modify the configuration file

(now called web.config) to register the object using the HTTP channel and the binary formatter. The remoting object also needs an IIS-compatible URI (which must either end in .soap or .rem).

All you have to do on the client host is modify the configuration file so it is using the HTTP channel with the binary formatter[8] and an URL that is pointing to the remoting object in IIS. Figure 6-3 shows all of this in a nutshell.

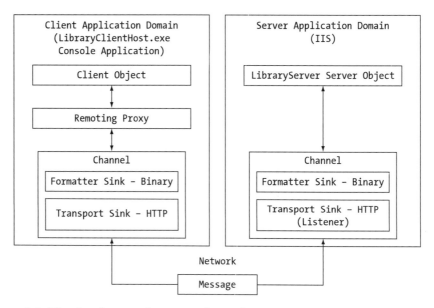

Figure 6-3. The simple remoting example application, hosted in IIS

The only difference between Figures 6-2 and 6-3 is the protocol used. Since you're now using IIS, the protocol has switched from TCP to HTTP.

SOURCE CODE   *The modified source for running this appli-cation under IIS is located in the Chapter 6\ SimpleLibraryInIIS subdirectory.*

---

8.   Notice on the server web.config file you use the <serverProviders> element and on the client config file you use the <clientProviders> element.

Authentication and Authorization Using an IIS Host

You can configure authentication and authorization with ASP.NET resources simply by configuring IIS like you would any other Web application. But there is another benefit to using IIS as a server host for your remoting objects, besides the fact that IIS has built-in authentication mechanisms. IIS, as a .NET host, uses the ASP.NET Internet Server Application Programming Interface (ISAPI) filter, aspnet_isapi.dll, to execute .NET applications.

ASP.NET has its own layer of security that sits on top of IIS, providing more granularity and protection for your Web applications, XML Web services, and remoting objects hosted in IIS. And, of course, these added security settings can be easily configured via your web.config file. This is good and bad because it adds yet another layer of complexity to understanding and configuring security. There are, in fact, three logical layers to this security infrastructure: the operating system, IIS, and ASP.NET. Rather than examine all the permutations of all three of these layers, I will focus on the few that make sense for remoting in IIS.

Authenticated Modes in ASP.NET

Now look at the four authentication modes available on the topmost layer (ASP.NET):

- *None.* No ASP.NET-specific security is used except for the ability (or lack thereof) to impersonate the IIS IUSR account. This setting, which is the default, leaves all authentication up to IIS.

- *Windows.* The authentication method specified in IIS (Anonymous, Basic, Digest, or Integrated Windows) is used and extended by specifying authorization rights to specific users and groups (roles).

- *Passport.* Authentication occurs against the Microsoft Passport service.

- *Forms.* Authentication is performed in a custom fashion against whatever source of data required. However, clients can only provide credentials via an HTML form.

These authentication modes can be specified in the web.config file of the Web application in an <authentication> element in the <system.web> section.

So, which of these options makes sense for remoting? Well, the default None mode will still give you all of the security benefits of IIS and the OS, but it wastes the new features available with ASP.NET. Forms authentication only allows the client to authenticate via an HTML form, which doesn't work for a client who's trying to authenticate programmatically (that is, a remoting client host).

Therefore, Windows and Passport are the two best options for remoting. To keep things simple for now, focus on the Windows authentication mode. Chapters 7 and 8 will cover the forms authentication and Passport modes, respectively.

Authenticated Modes in IIS

When you use Windows (and None), ASP.NET authentication modes, you need to decide what underlying IIS authentication should accompany it. The options are as follows:

- *Anonymous.* No authentication occurs with this setting, which is the default, and the client runs as the IUSR IIS anonymous account. In an ASP.NET application, the ASP.NET worker process (aspnet_wp.exe) always runs as the special ASPNET account unless impersonation is set. I will discuss this more a bit later.

- *Basic.* The client is authenticated, and the username and password are sent as clear text.

- *Digest.* The client is authenticated and the username and password are encoded in a hash digest. The server can then decode the digest and authenticate the client. This mode only works in Active Directory domains with proper configuration. It also works well through firewalls.

- *Integrated Windows.* Otherwise known as NTLM, this predecessor to Digest is useful within a Windows domain. Its main downfall is that it doesn't work well through firewalls.

If you set IIS to Anonymous, all authentication and authorization is out the window, so that pretty much defeats the purpose of an application that requires authentication. Basic is not really secure because the passwords are transmitted over the wire in clear text. So, you're left with Digest and Integrated Windows. Integrated Windows is best when both the client and server are on the same Windows domain (usually behind the same firewall) and Digest is useful when the client is outside the firewall and not within the same Windows domain.

Remoting and Authenticated Modes

So, this discussion has successfully boiled down all of the remoting authentication options to three flavors:

- ASP.NET—Windows/IIS—Basic

- ASP.NET—Windows/IIS—Digest

- ASP.NET—Windows/IIS—Integrated Windows

However, because I can't assume you're able to run the sample code on a machine in an Active Directory domain that has a properly configured Windows Digest infrastructure, I will limit the application to Basic and Integrated Windows. Basic is somewhat insecure, but it will allow you to have some authentication variety as you test the application.

What's left to do at the operating system (OS) layer? I'll talk more about this in the upcoming section "Locking Down Security ACLs".

Turning Off IIS Anonymous Access

Now, I'll show you how hard it is to implement authentication and authorization using an IIS host. The easiest way to start is to simply disable anonymous access in IIS on the LibraryServerIISHost virtual directory you created earlier in this chapter in the section "Hosting the LibraryServer Assembly in IIS." When you do this and run the LibraryClientHost.exe, you should get this exception:

```
Unhandled Exception: System.Net.WebException:
    The remote server returned an error: (401) Unauthorized.
...
```

The server application is secure (at least on an IIS level!). But now you have the challenge of somehow configuring the client host to authenticate against the server application. Before you do that, add a method to the remoting object so you can get some feedback of the identity of the authenticated client and the impersonation account. This will be useful when you play around with different authentication users and modes.

Adding an Authenticated User Feedback Method

At the top of the LibraryServer class library, add the following namespaces:

```
using System.Web;
using System.Security.Principal;
```

Now add the following method to the Library class:

```
public string GetUserInfo()
{
    string authenticatedUser;
    string userName = HttpContext.Current.User.Identity.Name;
    if(userName == null || userName.Equals(string.Empty))
    {
        authenticatedUser = "  {Unavailable}";
    }
    else
    {
        authenticatedUser = "  Username = " + userName + "\n"
            + "  Authentication Type = " +
            HttpContext.Current.User.Identity.AuthenticationType;
    }
    string identityUser = "   " + WindowsIdentity.GetCurrent().Name;
    return "Authenticated User:\n" +
        authenticatedUser + "\n" +
        "Impersonated User:\n" + identityUser;
}
```

In the LibraryClientHost application, you're going to replace the code that executes the GetAvailableCopies() method with code that executes the GetUserInfo() method. The complete source code should look something like Listing 6-2.

Listing 6-2. Obtaining User Information

```
using System;
using System.Runtime.Remoting;
using LibraryServer;
using System.Collections;
using System.Runtime.Remoting.Channels;
using System.Net;
namespace LibraryClientHost
```

```
{
    class Host
    {
        static void Main(string[] args)
        {
            Console.WriteLine("Library client host started.\n");
            RemotingConfiguration.Configure("LibraryClientHost.exe.config");
            Library lib = new Library();
            try
            {
                Console.WriteLine(
                    "Remoting Library object user info:\n\n" + lib.GetUserInfo());
            }
            catch (Exception e)
            {
                Console.WriteLine(
                    "Exception occurred when invoking Library.GetUserInfo:\n");
                Console.WriteLine(e.ToString());
            }
            Console.WriteLine("\nPress enter to shut down.");
            Console.ReadLine();
        }
    }
}
```

Three more namespace includes appear at the top—System.Collections, System.Runtime.Remoting.Channels, and System.Net—that you'll use in the next section, "Configuring the Client Host to Authenticate." I've also incorporated a try-catch block to trap any authentication exceptions and display them without killing the client process.

Now, if you turn authentication back on in the LibraryServerIISHost IIS virtual directory, you should get the following output when you run LibraryClientHost application:

```
Library client host started.
Remoting Library object user info:
Authenticated User:
  {Unavailable}
Impersonated User:
  SHADOWFAX\ASPNET
Press enter to shut down.
```

So, the remoting object is saying that the authenticated user is "{Unavailable}", which in this case means the anonymous IIS user. It's also saying that the impersonated user (the user that the remoting object's process is running as) is the ASP.NET worker process account (ASPNET). The impersonated user is always ASPNET unless you modify the machine.config file or specify impersonation in the web.config. I'll talk more on impersonation later in the chapter.

SOURCE CODE   *The source code for running the* LibraryServer *remoting object with a user feedback method is located in the Chapter 6\UserFeedbackLibrary subdirectory.*

Configuring the Client Host to Authenticate

Now create a local user account that clients can use to access the remoting server when anonymous access is turned off. Create a user that's a member of the local Users NT security group called LibraryUser. Set its password to "password". Add the following code to the LibraryClientHost application, just after the instantiation of the lib variable:

```
IDictionary httpChannelProps = ChannelServices.GetChannelSinkProperties(lib);
NetworkCredential cred = new NetworkCredential(
    "LibraryUser", "password", "SHADOWFAX");
Uri uri = new Uri("http://shadowfax/LibraryServerIISHost");
CredentialCache credCache = new CredentialCache();
credCache.Add(uri, "NTLM", cred);
credCache.Add(uri, "Basic", cred);
httpChannelProps["credentials"] = credCache;
```

Remember to replace the "shadowfax" hostname in the preceding example with the hostname of your computer.

Now, turn off anonymous access once again on the LibraryServerIISHost virtual directory and recompile and run the LibraryClientHost application, and you should get the following output:

```
Library client host started.
Remoting Library object user info:
Authenticated User:
  Username = SHADOWFAX\LibraryUser
  Authentication Type = NTLM
Impersonated User:
  SHADOWFAX\ASPNET
Press enter to shut down.
```

Now, you can see that you've actually authenticated the client with the LibraryUser account. Authorization is automatic because you haven't set any specific authorization rights in web.config. To do this, you could add the following `<system.web>` section to the web.config file (as a child to the `<configuration>` element):

```
<system.web>
    <authentication mode="Windows"/>
    <authorization>
        <allow users="SHADOWFAX\LibraryUser"/>
        <deny users="*"/>
    </authorization>
</system.web>
```

This configuration will authorize LibraryUser to access your remoting application. To test this, try changing the credentials in the LibraryClientHost application to something besides the LibraryUser account (even an administrator account). If you do, you will get the same 401 (Unauthorized) exception you saw when you first turned anonymous access off.

Now take a moment to examine the new chunk of client authentication code you've added to LibraryClientHost. Basically, the challenge is to somehow transmit the client credentials out of band[9] over the channel to the server in a way that the server can discover it. With the HTTP channel, one way is to embed this data in a special channel sink properties dictionary object. This HTTP channel's dictionary object has a special member (with the keyname "credentials"), which contains your credentials, that you can stuff a `CredentialCache` object into.

---

9. *Out of band* refers to passing data via the remoting channel that is outside of the method call itself.

Using the `CredentialCache` object, you can specify multiple credentials for various remoting object URIs[10] and IIS authentication modes. In effect, this code could service several remoting objects residing at several URIs using several different authentication modes. In this case, you just have one remoting object at one URI, but you are able to specify credentials for both Basic and NTLM (Integrated Windows) authentication modes, in case the server had one or the other modes disabled.

SOURCE CODE   *The source code for having your LibraryClientHost authenticate to the IIS host is located in the Chapter 6\HardCodedAuthLibrary subdirectory.*

Configuring Client Host Authentication in the Configuration File

Now, this code works, but all the credentials are hard-coded into the source code, which means you have to recompile each time you want to change the credentials. Ideally, you should be able to specify your credentials outside the source code in a configuration file. All this calls for a recipe to cook up a custom remoting channel sink.[11]

The real goal of the client sink code is to somehow access the same dictionary object you got in the LibraryClientHost application with `GetChannelSinkProperties()` and stuff it with a `CredentialCache` object that you generate from new XML in your configuration file. Normally when you create a custom remoting channel sink, you need to create both a sink provider class and a sink class. But in this case, you can access the credentials dictionary object from within the sink provider. Therefore, you don't need to write a sink class, just a sink provider.

To do this, you're going to code `ClientAuthenticationProvider`, a new class which will read credential information from your configuration file and pass it into the remoting channel, which is in turn passed to IIS during the request. Listing 6-3 provides the code for this example.

---

10. The URIs need only include the host and path to the remoting application, not the full URI ending in .rem.

11. As you will see in the rest of the chapter, implementing a custom channel sink can solve most complex situations like this. It's a great way to extract a lot of out-of-band functionality, which can be plugged in as needed, independent of the logic of your client and server code.

Listing 6-3. Automatically Authenticating the Client

```
using System;
using System.Runtime.Remoting;
using System.Runtime.Remoting.Channels;
using System.Runtime.Remoting.Channels.Http;
using System.Runtime.Remoting.Messaging;
using System.Net;
using System.Collections;
using System.IO;
namespace LibraryClientAuthSink
{
    public class ClientAuthenticationProvider : IClientChannelSinkProvider
    {
        private IClientChannelSinkProvider _nextProvider = null;
        private CredentialCache _creds = new CredentialCache();

        public ClientAuthenticationProvider() { }
        public ClientAuthenticationProvider(
                            IDictionary properties, ICollection providerData)
        {
            foreach (SinkProviderData spdCredentials in providerData)
            {
                string url = (String)spdCredentials.Properties["serverObjectUrl"];
                Uri uri = new Uri(url);
                foreach (SinkProviderData spdCredential in spdCredentials.Children)
                {
                    string userName = (String)spdCredential.Properties["userName"];
                    string password = (String)spdCredential.Properties["password"];
                    string domain = (String)spdCredential.Properties["domain"];
NetworkCredential cred = new NetworkCredential(
                        userName, password, domain);
                    foreach (SinkProviderData spdAuthentication
                        in spdCredential.Children)
                    {
                        string mode = (String)spdAuthentication.Properties[
                            "mode"];
                        _creds.Add(uri, mode, cred);
```

```
                        }
                    }
                }
            }

            public IClientChannelSink CreateSink(IChannelSender channel,
                string url, object remoteChannelData)
            {
                IClientChannelSink nextSink = null;
                if (_nextProvider != null)
                {
                    nextSink = _nextProvider.CreateSink(
                        channel, url, remoteChannelData);
                    if (nextSink == null)
                    {
                        return null;
                    }
                }
                nextSink.Properties["credentials"] = _creds;
                return nextSink;
            }

            public IClientChannelSinkProvider Next
            {
                get { return _nextProvider; }
                set { _nextProvider = value; }
            }
        }
    }
}
```

Add the corresponding configuration data into LibraryClientHost.exe.config to register the new client-side sink provider with the remoting infrastructure. Below the </application> element, insert the following lines:

```
<channelSinkProviders>
    <clientProviders>
        <provider id="client_auth"
            type="LibraryClientAuthSink.ClientAuthenticationProvider,
            LibraryClientAuthSink"/>
    </clientProviders>
</channelSinkProviders>
```

Below the `<formatter ref="binary"/>` element near the top, insert these lines:

```
<provider ref="client_auth">
    <credentials serverObjectUrl="http://shadowfax/LibraryServerIISHost ">
        <credential userName="LibraryUser" password="password"
domain="SHADOWFAX">
            <authentication mode="Basic"/>
            <authentication mode="NTLM"/>
        </credential>
    </credentials>
</provider>
```

This places an instance of the sink provider in the provider chain just after the binary formatter, and it contains the custom authentication data, which is accessed by the client sink provider class.

Finally, in the LibraryClientHost application, comment out the hard-coded client authentication block of code; the configuration file, along with the new client sink provider class, perform the same function. Here's the code:

```
/*
IDictionary httpChannelProps = ChannelServices.GetChannelSinkProperties(lib);
NetworkCredential cred = new NetworkCredential(
    "LibraryUser", "password", "SHADOWFAX");
Uri uri = new Uri("http://shadowfax/LibraryServerIISHost/LibraryServer.rem");
CredentialCache credCache = new CredentialCache();
credCache.Add(uri, "NTLM", cred);
credCache.Add(uri, "Basic", cred);
httpChannelProps["credentials"] = credCache;
*/
```

Run the LibraryClientHost application, and you should see the same results as before, but now all the credentials are contained within the configuration file! You've also made the structure of the credentials in the configuration file quite flexible. You can group credentials by server object URL (which corresponds to the URIs of the previous `CredentialCache` object), and each credential can specify multiple IIS authentication modes.

So, what is the custom sink provider code really doing? In short, it's reading the configuration file using the sink provider data objects that get passed into its constructor. With this data, it is able to construct a `CredentialCache` object, very similar to the one you made when you hard-coded the credentials in the client host.

A sink provider has a special method it needs to implement called CreateSink(). Normally within this method is where your custom sink object is created and passed back to the caller. In this case, you don't need to actually create a custom sink object, so you are able to simply pass back the sink object generated in the next sink provider. And just before that, you stuff your CredentialCache object in the sink properties of that sink. Your sink provider is really nothing more than a "helper" sink provider because it doesn't create a sink of its own, but simply modifies other existing sinks.

Figure 6-4 shows how this new client sink provider class fits into the remoting application thus far.

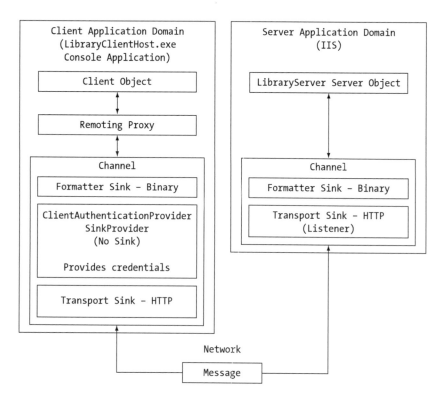

Figure 6-4. Remoting application using a client sink provider to access authentication information from a configuration file

The difference between Figures 6-3 and 6-4 is that in this case the client code does not provide the authentication information. It's handled by the authentication sink that you just created.

SOURCE CODE   *The source code for having your LibraryClientHost authenticate using a configuration file is located in the Chapter 6\ConfigAuthLibrary subdirectory.*

Impersonation Using an IIS Host

Sometimes it's necessary to allow certain users not only to access a given resource, but also to run the resource as a specific identity (as you saw in the section "Exploring Impersonation" in Chapter 5). By default, if you don't turn impersonation on in ASP.NET, the ASP.NET worker process (aspnet_wp.exe) runs as the special ASPNET account, which is a local user account with very limited system access. However, your remoting server object may need to do things that ASPNET doesn't have rights to do. For example, your server object may need to use DCOM (via COM Interop) to talk to a COM+ component on an internal application server. Usually to make this work, the identity accessing the COM+ server object needs to be a domain account so multiple client machines can use it. Therefore, your remoting object would have to impersonate using that domain account instead of the local ASPNET account.

Enabling impersonation in ASP.NET is as easy as adding the following XML to your web.config file under the <system.web> section:

```
<identity impersonate="true"/>
```

This will impersonate using the identity that authenticated to the remoting application. If you want to impersonate using a specific identity, you can do the following, which will force impersonation of SHADOWFAX\LibraryUser no matter what the client authentication credentials are:

```
<identity impersonate="true"
    userName="SHADOWFAX\LibraryUser"
    password="password"/>
```

Finally, the impersonation account needs some minimum Access Control List (ACL)[12] permissions in order to work in ASP.NET. Here they are:

- *Read access to the .NET Framework install root hierarchy.* This is usually C:\WINNT (or C:\Windows if XP) \Microsoft.NET\Framework\v{version}, where {version} is the version of the Framework you're running against.

---

12. This is the list of users and user groups and their permissions (each called an ACE, or Access Control Entry) for a given resource (file, directory, and so on).

- *Read/Write access to the ASP.NET temp files directory.* This is usually a sub-directory under the preceding directory called Temporary ASP.NET Files.

- *Read/Write access to the Windows temp directory.* This directory is C:\WINNT\Temp (C:\Windows\Temp if using Windows XP).

- *Read access to the directory of your application (in this case, the IIS virtual root directory).* This ACL is usually already in place since the Everyone and Users groups are set by default.

If you were to make all these changes and modify the web.config file as specified in the preceding list, the LibraryClientHost application should produce the following output:

```
Library client host started.
Remoting Library object user info:
Authenticated User:
  Username = SHADOWFAX\LibraryUser
  Authentication Type = NTLM
Impersonated User:
  SHADOWFAX\LibraryUser
Press enter to shut down.
```

As expected, the impersonated user has changed from the ASPNET account to the LibraryUser account.

 SOURCE CODE *The source code for having your* `LibraryServer` *remoting object use impersonation is located in the Csubdirectory Chapter 6\ ConfigAuthWithImpersonationLibrary subdirectory.*

Locking Down Security ACLs

That last item on the preceding impersonation ACL checklist may concern you. The fact that, by default, your application directory's ACL allows the Everyone and Users groups full access may be a bit of a security hole. Granted, you still have two layers above the OS layer (IIS and ASP.NET) that protect against unauthorized access, but to be completely thorough, you may wish to lock down the ACLs as well. This is sometimes known as *hard security,* which is pretty much the tightest form of security you can implement on an ASP.NET application (outside of unplugging the server's network cable). Of course, the drawback to doing this is that the ACL settings and the settings in IIS/ASP.NET aren't going to auto-matically stay in sync with each other in the event you change the impersonation account(s). You'll have to manually manage that yourself.

If you want to strip your IIS application directory down to the bare minimum ALC, here's what you need to do:

1. Remove the Everyone, Users, and VS Developers (if it exists) groups.

2. Add the local ASPNET user account with Read access.

3. Include impersonation accounts with Read access if you're going to be doing any impersonation.

Role-Based Security on Object Members

In the COM days, one of the big pluses of COM+ was the capability to specify authorization granularity beyond the server application itself. With COM+ you could define role-based security right down to the object member level (property and method); and you could do all of this outside of the business object itself, within the Component Services MMC snap-in. Up to this point, ASP.NET <web.config> security has allowed you to specify role-based security on the application level. However, there has been no way to specify authorization down to the object member level. This is because .NET doesn't provide an out-of-the-box means of doing this, not even under IIS/ASP.NET. This requires a custom solution that is very similar to what you did earlier in this chapter in the section "Configuring Client Host Authentication in the Configuration File" with the client-side authentication sink provider.

Of course, an easy solution would be to put the authorization logic within the object itself. However, there are two problems with this approach. First, it forces you to add extra logic to the business objects, which in many cases is hard-coded. This limits their implementation flexibility. Second, this means that the object itself (and its assembly) would be accessed before authorization occurs. Therefore this approach violates the security rule of thumb that all authentication and authorization should occur within the hosting process, not within the object itself.

So take a look at how to build a custom server-side remoting sink that enables object and object member authorization. Once again you're using remoting channel sinks to achieve an out-of-band solution to the problem. This solution is going to be a bit more complex than the client-side authentication solution you just provided because you're going to have to create a sink provider class and a sink class.

The sink will be the object that checks each incoming request. It will examine the authenticated user and the method signature embedded in the incoming IMessage object. It will compare that against some custom configuration data you'll place in the web.config file. If the configuration data allows that user to use that method (or property) on the given object type, then the remoting call will be allowed to pass through. Otherwise, an exception will be returned back to the client.

Of course, you have to first configure the application-level authorization in IIS and ASP.NET to allow all the users specified in your custom member-level authorization to have access. Otherwise, placing a user in your custom member-level authorization configuration is meaningless since that user can't even authorize against the application.

Start by creating the server-side channel sink provider and sink. If you end up putting both classes within the same file, then these are the includes and the namespace they will both use:

```
using System;
using System.Runtime.Remoting;
using System.Runtime.Remoting.Channels;
using System.Runtime.Remoting.Channels.Http;
using System.Runtime.Remoting.Messaging;
using System.Net;
using System.Collections;
using System.IO;
using System.Web;
namespace LibraryServerMemberRBSSink
{
```

Now, take a look at the following ServerMemberRBSProvider sink provider class:

```
public class ServerMemberRBSProvider : IServerFormatterSinkProvider,
    IServerChannelSinkProvider
{
    private IServerChannelSinkProvider _nextProvider = null;
    private ICollection _types;
    public ServerMemberRBSProvider() { }
    public ServerMemberRBSProvider(
        IDictionary properties, ICollection providerData)
    {
        _types = providerData;
    }
```

```
public void GetChannelData(IChannelDataStore channelData) { }
public IServerChannelSink CreateSink(IChannelReceiver channel)
{
        IServerChannelSink nextSink = null;
        if (_nextProvider != null)
            nextSink = _nextProvider.CreateSink(channel);
        return new ServerMemberRBSSink(nextSink, _types);
}
public IServerChannelSinkProvider Next
{
    get { return _nextProvider; }
    set { _nextProvider = value; }
}
}
```

The ServerMemberRBSProvider class is actually pretty simple compared to the
client authentication sink provider class coded earlier in this chapter in
the section "Configuring Client Host Authentication in the Configuration File."
It does exactly what a normal sink provider does and that is to provide an
instance of the underlying sink class.

Code that class next (see Listing 6-4). Like the ClientAuthenticationProvider
class you coded earlier in this chapter in the section "Configuring Client Host
Authentication in the Configuration File," it's a bit lengthy, but it has similar functionality. The bulk of the logic is in the ProcessMessage() method, which extracts
the member-level role information from the web.config file and compares that to
the incoming credentials and method signature generated by the client as it
invokes a method.

Listing 6-4. Providing Member-Level Role-Based Access

```
public class ServerMemberRBSSink : BaseChannelObjectWithProperties,
    IServerChannelSink
{
    private IServerChannelSink _nextSink = null;
    private ICollection _types;
    public ServerMemberRBSSink(
        IServerChannelSink nextSink, ICollection types) : base()
    {
        _nextSink = nextSink;
        _types = types;
    }
    public ServerProcessing ProcessMessage(
        IServerChannelSinkStack sinkStack,
        IMessage requestMsg, ITransportHeaders requestHeaders,
```

```
                    Stream requestStream, out IMessage responseMsg,
                    out ITransportHeaders responseHeaders,
                    out Stream responseStream)
            {
                string requestTypeName =
                    (String)requestMsg.Properties["__TypeName"];
                string requestMethodName =
                    (String)requestMsg.Properties["__MethodName"];
                string userName = HttpContext.Current.User.Identity.Name;
                bool accept = true;
                foreach (SinkProviderData spdType in _types)
                {
                    string typeName = (String)spdType.Properties["type"];
                    string requestTypeNameSub =
                        requestTypeName.Substring(0, typeName.Length);
                    if (typeName == requestTypeNameSub)
                    {
                        foreach (SinkProviderData spdMember
                            in spdType.Children)
                        {
                            string memberType = spdMember.Name;
                            string memberName = (String)spdMember.Properties["name"];
                            string allowUser = (String)spdMember.Properties["allowUser"];
                            bool memberMatch = false;
                            switch(memberType)
                            {
                                case "method":
                                    if (memberName == requestMethodName)
                                        memberMatch = true;
                                        break;
                                case "property":
                                    if (("get_" + memberName == requestMethodName) ||
                                        ("set_" + memberName == requestMethodName))
                                        memberMatch = true;
                                        break;
                            }
```

```
                    if (memberMatch)
                    {
                            if(allowUser.ToLower() == userName.ToLower())
                                accept = true;
                            else
                                accept = false;
                            break;
                    }
                }
                break;
            }
        }
        if (accept)
        {
            return _nextSink.ProcessMessage(sinkStack, requestMsg,
                requestHeaders, null, out responseMsg,
                out responseHeaders, out responseStream);
        }
        else
        {
            responseHeaders = new TransportHeaders();
            responseHeaders["__HttpStatusCode"] = "401";
            responseMsg = null;
            responseStream = null;
            return ServerProcessing.Complete;
        }
    }
    public void AsyncProcessResponse(
        IServerResponseChannelSinkStack sinkStack,
        Object state, IMessage msg,
        ITransportHeaders headers, Stream stream) {}
    public Stream GetResponseStream(
        IServerResponseChannelSinkStack sinkStack,
        Object state, IMessage msg, ITransportHeaders headers)
    { return null; }
    public IServerChannelSink NextChannelSink
    {
        get { return _nextSink; }
    }
  }
}
```

Now, you need to add the corresponding configuration data to web.config, which registers the new server sink provider. Below the </application> element, insert this code:

```
<channelSinkProviders>
    <serverProviders>
        <provider id="member_rbs"
            type="LibraryServerMemberRBSSink.ServerMemberRBSProvider,
            LibraryServerMemberRBSSink"/>
    </serverProviders>
</channelSinkProviders>
```

Below the <formatter ref="binary"/> element near the top, insert these lines:

```
<provider ref="member_rbs">
    <type type="LibraryServer.Library, LibraryServer">
        <method name="GetUserInfo" allowUser="SHADOWFAX\LibraryUser"/>
        <property name="TotalBooks" allowUser="SHADOWFAX\LibraryUser"/>
    </type>
</provider>
```

This custom configuration data specifies authorization for the GetUserInfo() method and a new property called TotalBooks. You need to create this property in the LibraryServer.Library and then call it from the client host. Add the following property definition code to the Library class:

```
public int TotalBooks
{
    get { return 7643; }
}
```

Finally, call this property from the client host. In the LibraryClientHost application, just below the Console.WriteLine() that calls the lib.GetUserInfo() method, add this code:

```
Console.WriteLine("\nTotal books = {0}", lib.TotalBooks);
```

If you run LibraryClientHost now, it should still work fine because the LibraryUser is set to have access to both the GetUserInfo() method and

`TotalBooks` property. However, if you edit web.config and change the `allowUser` attribute on one of the members to something else, you should see an exception when you run the client.

The logic in the sink class to make this all work is somewhat simplified. It does allow you to specify multiple object types (if your server host serves up multiple remoting objects). However, within each type, you can only specify authorization on methods and properties. You could easily extend this to include other member types like constructors (for client-activated objects), simply by knowing how to parse the data within the `IMessage` object.

This example also has a limited authorization scheme. The `allowUser` attribute of the `<method>` or `<property>` element only allows for a single user. You also cannot specify a role or user group. Once again, you could easily extend this with your own logic. Ideally, you could make it behave similarly to the ASP.NET's `<authorization>` element in the `<web.config>` section.

Finally, you may have noticed that you placed the new server-side sink provider *after* the server-side formatter sink provider in the web.config file.[13] This is necessary because the type and member information (method or property name) is inside the `IMessage` object. Before the formatter sink is used, `IMessage` is still a binary serialization and you can't read it! So, you have to place the custom sink after the formatter sink. Normally, this isn't possible, because on the server-side the formatter is supposed to be the last sink in the chain before the message gets passed to the dispatch sink. So, the server sink provider class is actually a formatter sink provider itself (it inherits from the `IServerFormatterSinkProvider` interface).

Next, a few tricks make the remoting engine accept two formatter sinks. The main trick is in the `ProcessMessage()` method of the `ServerMemberRBSSink` class. Normally you call `ProcessMessage()` of the next sink and return that result. You do this when the user is authorized to call the method, but you call the next sink's `ProcessMessage()` method a little differently than usual. Because the `IMessage` has already been authorized by the preceding formatter sink, you need to pass `null` for the `requestStream` argument.

At this point, you've completed the evolution of the sample application. Figure 6-5 shows you the final product. You have a secure IIS host with anonymous access disabled. You've configured the client host to programmatically authenticate. Finally, you've configured the server host to authorize client requests on an object member level.

---

13. The order that sink providers are specified in the configuration file is important because it is the order that the corresponding sink objects will be created and used in the channel when processing the passed `IMessage` object.

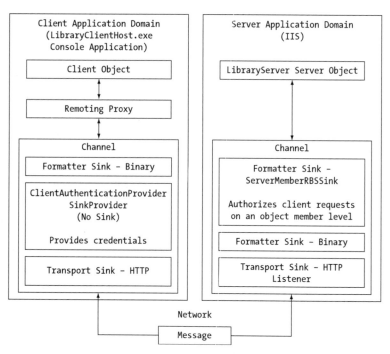

Figure 6-5. Remoting application final product: client authentication via configuration file and server authorization at an object member level

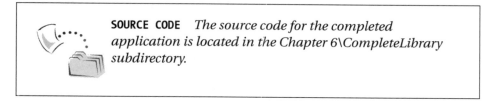

SOURCE CODE *The source code for the completed application is located in the Chapter 6\CompleteLibrary subdirectory.*

Summary

In this chapter I covered the following topics:

- Security issues related to .NET Remoting

- Built-in features of IIS and ASP.NET that tackle most of the security implementations necessary to secure the example application

- Solutions using remoting's extensible channel sink infrastructure

In the next chapter you'll see how to secure traditional Web applications by learning more about ASP.NET security.

CHAPTER 7

ASP.NET Web Application Security

THIS CHAPTER IS ALL ABOUT security as it relates to Web applications. I'll begin by explaining the relationship between Internet Information Server (IIS) and Active Server Pages for .NET (ASP.NET), including information on how to configure your machines more securely for Internet access. I will then discuss how Microsoft eased coding security with a few new technologies and toys.

ASP.NET and IIS Considerations

Securing your Web server starts with recognizing a fact that may be overlooked. As far as Windows is concerned, ASP.NET is just another Internet Server API (ISAPI) application that runs on IIS. The dynamic link library (DLL) in question, aspnet_isapi.dll, behaves like any other ISAPI application. It consumes ASP.NET-specific URL requests. When a user requests a Web page, IIS notices that the file with an .aspx extension belongs to ASP.NET and forwards the request to aspnet_isapi.dll.

You can see which ISAPI application handles which extension by viewing a Web site's App Mappings property sheet, which appears in the Application Configuration properties dialog box. Figure 7-1 is a snapshot of my computer's mappings.

Any file extension assigned to the aspnet_isapi.dll becomes an ASP.NET managed resource.[1]

Before leaving mappings and returning to setting up your machine, consider the following question. When playing with the application file extension mappings, what would happen if you assigned an .htm or .gif extension to aspnet_isapi.dll? The answer may surprise you. ASP.NET now secures these files as well.

Of course, nothing is free. Your site pays a performance penalty for processing these files. Whether or not you want to pay the fee is your call. If you elect

---

1. The good news about all these mappings is that the .NET Framework installation routine sets them; you probably won't have to add a mapping to make a resource an ASP.NET resource, at least not very often.

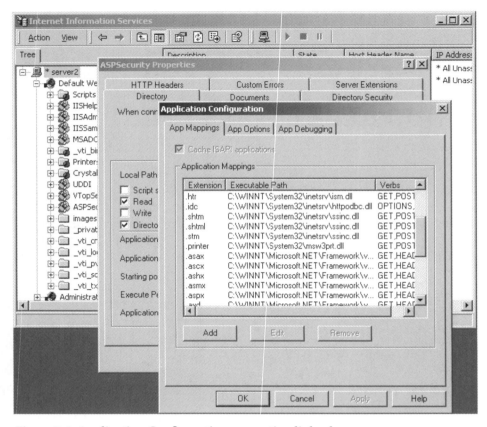

Figure 7-1. Application Configuration properties dialog box

not to, remember that a user will be able to grab a non-ASP.NET resource from an unauthorized location. (See the section "<authentication>" in "Configuring Security," later in this chapter, for an example.) Keeping these files safe without .NET will require either applying NTFS permissions or moving them elsewhere.

Since ASP.NET really is just another ISAPI application, you also need to configure your Web's application protection level. You accomplish this task within your site's Virtual Directory property sheet as shown in Figure 7-2.

You have the following three choices for protection:

- Low

- Medium

- High

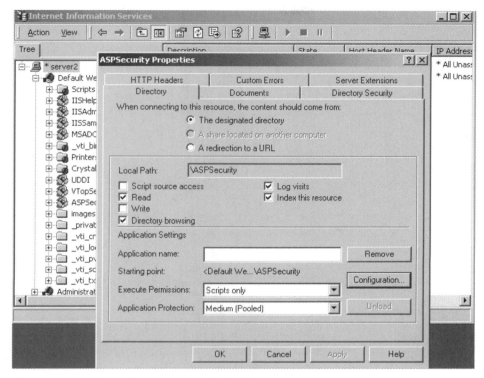

Figure 7-2. ASPSecurity Properties dialog box

They each have their own pros and cons, but whichever you select, I'd suggest avoiding Low (IIS Process), as this setting's security hole is rather large.[2] Web applications with Low protection run within the IIS Server process, inetinfo.exe. The IIS Server process runs with the security credentials of SYSTEM. Essentially, a process running under SYSTEM can do pretty much anything it wants to on the computer. If the site is hacked, the hacker now has tremendous resources at his or her control.

Medium or High protection Web applications run under the auspices of COM+ Services with all the rights and privileges of IWAM_MACHINE.[3] By the way, the IWAM (where WAM stands for Web Application Manager) account doesn't have too

---

2. Because this application's code would run under the same process memory space as IIS, any unhandled exception would bring down IIS along with it, which is usually something to avoid!

3. Actually, your machine's name is appended to IWAM, for example, IWAM_SERVER2.

many rights and privileges. In fact, it has very few rights and privileges. If you select either Medium or High protection, your box now executes *unmanaged code* securely.

A little more work may be incurred to run *.NET code* securely with more than minimal rights. To accomplish this feat, you will need to change the default account with which worker threads operate. Open up your .NET computer's machine.config file and search for <processModel>. Then look for the attributes entitled userName and password as the following XML fragment shows:

```
<processModel
    enable="true" timeout="Infinite" idleTimeout="Infinite"
    shutdownTimeout="0:00:05"  requestLimit="Infinite"
    requestQueueLimit="5000" restartQueueLimit="10"
    memoryLimit="60"  webGarden="false"
    cpuMask="0xffffffff" userName="MACHINE"
    password="AutoGenerate" logLevel="Errors"
    clientConnectedCheck="0:00:05" comAuthenticationLevel="Connect"
    comImpersonationLevel="Impersonate"
/>
```

When userName equals MACHINE, worker threads run under the credentials of a special, minimally privileged account called aspnet_wp. However, therein lies a potential problem. This account may not possess adequate rights for your application to operate properly. Fortunately, changing userName to SYSTEM takes immediate care of this problem. Unfortunately, this step creates a new problem; this account is the same account that you "turned off" to plug potential security leaks when running managed code.

One solution may lie with a third option—changing userName to a custom Windows account that possesses the minimal, required permissions. Be advised though, if you choose this option, that you are walking off well-worn paths when bypassing the SYSTEM or MACHINE accounts. For example, when creating the custom account, consider the ramifications of giving it the required "act as part of the operating system" privilege. As I mentioned in the section "Windows Impersonation" in Chapter 5, this has many potential risks, as the account now has the ability to do pretty much whatever it wants.

If all this talk of another potential security hole concerns you, consider the positive side of all this complexity. What makes it all somewhat complex is ASP.NET's newfound ability to decide which identity to assume. Put another way, ASP.NET gives you the ability to decide the identity your code assumes. You've seen what impersonation was like in Chapter 5—later on in this chapter you'll see how this works in ASP.NET applications.

NOTE *As a historical note, before the final release of ASP.NET, the specific account under which* MACHINE *was assigned changed several times. In fact,* ASPNET *was an unknown entity until the release candidate 4 of VS .NET. Moreover, rumor has it that* MACHINE*'s assigned account may change with IIS 6. I suspect we will all be experimenting with this feature when deploying and fine-tuning Web applications in the near future.*

Now that I've covered some of the high-level architecture pieces to ASP.NET security, I'll show you what you need to do to configure your Web applications.

Configuring Security

The heart of the ASP.NET security model lies within two configuration files—machine.config and web.config. You've seen configuration files before (for example, see the section "CryptoConfig and machine.config" in Chapter 2), now take a look at how they work for ASP.NET. These two files contain the XML fragments that control almost every aspect of security.[4] The next few sections might interest the security minded, as they discuss the following elements:

- <appsettings>

- <authentication>

- <authorization>

- <securityPolicy>

<appSettings>

This element can be set almost anywhere. You may find it a useful cul-de-sac for information once placed in the global.asa file. For example, the following code snippet creates and sets the DSN for your Web application:

---

4.   Before forgetting about the IIS management console or admin scripts, someone still needs to tell IIS which folders are Web applications and how to map files to aspnet_isapi.dll. After that, the configuration files set the ASP.NET application properties. This even applies to the protection level that you fiddled with earlier.

```
<configuration>
    <appSettings>
        <add key="DSN"
             value="server=mySQLServer;uid=myUser;pwd=myPassword;
             database=myDB"/>
    ...
```

Before you decide against placing such critical information in a plain XML file, remember that configuration files possess a special status in ASP.NET. By default, these files are not available to users.[5]

<authentication>

While I will discuss this element later on in the section "Form-based Authentication," there are few things worth mentioning here. First, authenti-cation can only be set at the machine and application level. Despite the apparent limitations this constraint imposes, developers can still create holes. One example revolves around the relationship between virtual directories and their underlying physical directories.

Figure 7-3 provides a snapshot of the physical directory structure of the sample Web application for this chapter, ASPSecurity.

Note the relationship between the folders ASPSecurity and TopSecret. Figure 7-4 illustrates the associated virtual directories and Web applications.

SOURCE CODE   *This chapter's sample code (the Chapter7 folder) contains the folders and files that you'll find in ASPSecurity and TopSecret.*

Now assume the following XML fragment resides with the ASPSecurity web.config file:

```
<configuration>
    <location path="TopSecret">
        <system.web>
            <authorization>
```

---

5.   Before deploying configuration files, check whether you installed ASP.NET on the Web server. Otherwise, your configuration files look like any other XML file to IIS. This means that browsers may easily view your confidential configuration information.

```
            <deny users="*">
          </authorization>
        </system.web>
    </location>
</configuration>
```

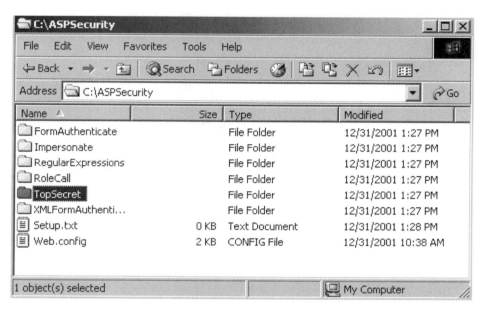

Figure 7-3. ASPSecurity's physical Web structure

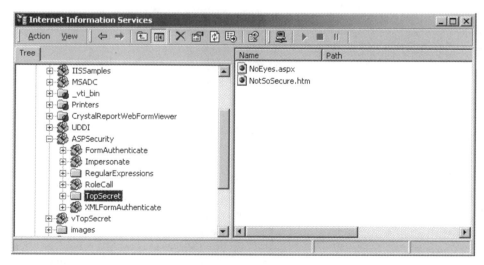

Figure 7-4. ASPSecurity and TopSecret Web structure

Based on all of the preceding information, you might correctly assume that the resource, NoEyes.aspx, is safe from prying authenticated users making the following request:

```
http://localhost/ASPSecurity/TopSecret/NoEyes.aspx
```

Change the request to TopSecret's virtual directory, as shown here, and NoEyes.aspx just acquired eyes:

```
http://localhost/VTopSecret/NoEyes.aspx
```

What is and is not secured by <authentication> constitutes another interesting security aspect alluded to earlier. ASP.NET protects ASP.NET resources. Other resources rely on the same security mechanism as they did before .NET. If you visit the following URLs in the sample Web site you can build for this chapter, you will notice that the plain HTML document, NotSoSecure.htm, is *not* protected by ASP.NET.

```
http://localhost/ASPSecurity/TopSecret/NotSoSecure.htm
http://localhost/VTopSecret/NotSoSecure.htm
```

<authorization>

Controlling HTTP verb permissions adds a new security dimension to an application. You can now decide whether users and roles can GET, HEAD, POST, and DEBUG, as shown here:

```
<authorization>
    <allow verb="GET" users="*">
    <allow verb="POST" roles="Accountants">
    <deny verb="POST" users="*">
</authorization>
```

If the preceding fragment appeared in a directory containing some accounting resources, then only the company's accountants could post them while other authenticated users could view them.

The order of the <allow> and <deny> tags is not accidental. The authorization checking mechanism runs down all these rules in their listed order. The process stops with the first match. In this example, as soon as ASP.NET encounters a user in the Accountants role, it grants that user posting privileges and moves on to something else. Note that when the system encounters several levels of rules, the lower ones take precedence. The system builds a list of all the rules for a URL, with those lowest in the hierarchy placed at the top. Then, it is first come, first serve within each level.

ASP.NET grants any request without a matching rule. Loosely translated, all requests are permitted by default. Given this behavior, it shouldn't be surprising if a company's security policy includes `<deny users="?">` in all machine.config files.

`<securityPolicy>`

Like `<authentication>` and `<authorization>` elements, `<securityPolicy>` works at the machine, site, and application levels. The pertinent information of this section resides in its only subtag, `<trustLevel>`, as shown here:

```
<securityPolicy>
    <trustLevel name="Full" policyFile="internal"/>
    <trustLevel name="High" policyFile="web_hightrust.config"/>
    <trustLevel name="Low" policyLevel="web_lowtrust.config"/>
    <trustLevel name="None" policyLevel="web_notrust.config"/>
</securityPolicy>
```

The `policyFile` attribute specifies the configuration file containing the detailed security policy settings associated with the level specified in the `name` attribute.[6] For example, the preceding `<trustLevel>` subtag with the `name` attribute set to "High" means that this level is explicitly defined in the file "web_hightrust.config".

Although this topic receives a more detailed treatment elsewhere, there are a few ASP.NET-specific issues worth noting here. ASP.NET host does not add any application domain-level policies to an application. The `Full` trust level is always mapped to an internal handler, and the `policyFile` attribute is ignored.

Of course, ASP.NET security configuration is done when you start adding Web applications to your Web servers—the next section covers this interaction.

Exploring ASP.NET

Now that I've covered the basics, I'll discuss ASP.NET in greater detail and show you how security policies and configurations come into play.

---

6. You will find the .Net Framework's default policy files residing at \winnt\Microsoft.NET\Framework\[version]\CONFIG.

Events to Remember

Before delving into the code, let me briefly mention a few security-related events heretofore unexposed by ASP. Prior to .NET, only C++ developers building ISAPI applications handled them. All of these new events reside in the global.asax file. The chapter's sample code demonstrates a common use of application events.

Application_OnBeginRequest()

This event gets raised on every request ASP.NET handles. Whatever the resource, even a Web service, it provides a nice place to execute code before any other HTTP handler sees it.[7]

Application_OnAuthenticateRequest()

Windows, Form-based, and Passport authentication utilize this event. In fact, it fires after any security module establishes the user's identity, including custom components. This event allows you to inspect every request and determine whether to authenticate it.

Application_OnAuthorizeRequest()

Like OnAuthenticateRequest(), custom components, Windows, Form-based, and Passport authentication utilize this event, too, except in this case you inspect privileges. But whatever the security module, it only fires if it verified user authorization.

Impersonation

Before ASP.NET came along, developers were pretty much stuck with the limited rights and privileges of IUSR_MACHINE. With Integrated Windows authentication enabled, you could get some NT LAN Manager (NTLM) information about authenticated users (see Figure 7-5).

---

7. Technically, Visual Basic 6's WebClass exposed a BeginRequest() event, so my previous statement about C++ developers isn't totally correct. Unfortunately, the WebClass's BeginRequest(), EndRequest(), and Terminate() events were about all you had to work with.

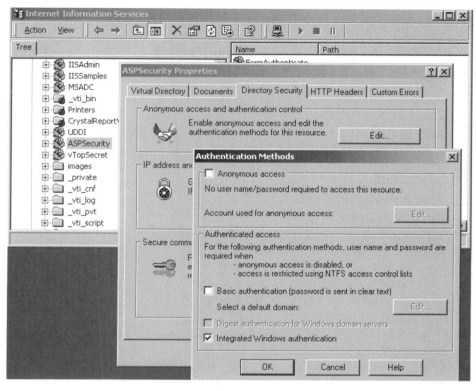

Figure 7-5. IIS Authentication Methods properties dialog box

However, developers were still stuck with `IUSR_MACHINE`'s security tokens. This limitation forced some tough either-or decisions upon a developer when designing a site. ASP.NET's impersonation feature changed all that.

> **NOTE** *To be honest, ASP programmers familiar with the Windows API could build a component that facilitates impersonation without .NET. Check out Microsoft's knowledge base article "HOWTO: Impersonate a User from Active Server Pages." Before you put this trick into production, be mindful that it has its own security problems, too. Make sure you read the last note in the article.*

There are basically three impersonation options with ASP.NET—disabled, enabled, and configurable. Disabled is the default setting. If you go to an application's web.config file you may see the following XML fragment:

```
<identity impersonate="false"/>
```

As result of this setting, IIS operates with the same worker thread accounts discussed earlier in this chapter under "ASP.NET and IIS Considerations." Before dismissing the disabled option, it may be worthwhile to note it possesses an advantage over the other two. The other forms of impersonation consume additional computing resources.

Enabling impersonation, as shown here, is the second choice:

```
<identity impersonate="true"/>
```

Now the worker threads can ply the credentials of any valid Windows account. And since a specific Widows account is not specified, the access token passed to IIS, either that of an authenticated or anonymous user, will be impersonated.

The last option, configurable, lets you be considerably more deterministic about the impersonated account. Implementing it requires a valid Windows account to be set within the identity tag as follows:

```
<identity impersonate="true"
    name="myDomain\myUser" password="myPassword"/>
```

There is one curve ball worth mentioning before moving on. When the Web application is sitting on a Universal Naming Convention (UNC) share, ASP.NET will usually keep the IIS token that accesses that share. This condition does not apply when a specific Windows account is set in the `<identity>` tag.

The next step after obtaining the ability to impersonate a user is to do so. You've seen similar code in Chapter 5 in the section "Windows Impersonation"— the ASP code is just as straightforward:

```
...
<%@ Import Namespace = "System.Security.Principal %>
...
WindowsImpersonationContext impersonatedContext;
impersonatedContext = ((WindowsIdentity)User.Identity).Impersonate();
// Run code with the security context of User.
...
// Back to IUSER_MACHINE?
impersonatedContext.Undo();
```

When a Windows-based `User` object is unavailable, you are not out of it. With impersonation turned on, you can swipe any Windows account's security token for operations. Here's an example of this:

```
<% Import Namespace = "System.Web" %>
<% Import Namespace = "System.Web.Security" %>
```

```
<% Import Namespace = "System.Security.Principal" %>
<% Import Namespace = "System.Runtime.InteropServices" %>
```

Since you will be exercising the Windows API calls, LogonUser() and DuplicateToken(), you will need help from System.Runtime.InteropServices as provided by Listing 7-1.

Listing 7-1. Windows Impersonation in ASP.NET

```
<script language="c#" runat="server">

public const int LOGON32_LOGON_INTERACTIVE = 2;
public const int LOGON32_PROVIDER_DEFAULT = 0;


[DllImport("advapi32.dll", CharSet=CharSet.Auto)]
public static extern int LogonUser(
    String lpszUserName, String lpszDomain, String lpszPassword,
    Int dwLogonType, int dwLogonProvider, ref IntPtr phToken);
[DllImport("advapi32.dll", CharSet=System.Runtime.InteropServices.CharSet.Auto,
    SetLastError=true)]
public static extern int DuplicateToken(
    IntPtr hToken, int impersonationLevel, ref IntPtr hNewToken);

WindowsImpersonationContext impersonatedContext;

public void Page_Load(Object obj, EventArgs args)
{
    if( impersonateUser("myUserName", "myUserDomain",  "myUserPassword") )
    {
        // Run code with the security context of myUserName.
        . . .
        // Cleanup
        undoImpersonation();
    }
}


private bool impersonateUser(
   String userName, String userDomain, String userPassword)
{
    WindowsIdentity tempIndentity;
    IntPtr token = IntPtr.Zero;
    IntPtr tokenDup = IntPtr.Zero;
    If(LogonUser(userName, userDomain, userPassword,
        LOGON32_LOGON_INTERACTIVE, LOGON32_PROVIDER_DEFAULT,
        Ref token) != 0 )
```

```
    {
        tempIdentity = new WindowsIdentity(tokenDup);
        impersonatedContext = tmpIdentity.Impersonate();
        if(impersonatedContext != null)
            return true;
        else
            return false;
    }
    else
        return false;
    }
}

private void undoImpersonation()
{
    impersonatedContext.Undo();
}
</script>
```

The code in Listing 7-1 capably manages security problems associated with letting an impersonated user token live too long by "un-impersonating" it with the call to undoImpersonate(). Nonetheless, there are some potential dangers in using this code. Although the context of myUserName looks innocuous enough, what if it has administrative privileges and the code you call with it is not too safe? Moral of the story: be vigilant about the rights you give to any piece of code in your ASP code.

ViewState

The magic behind any server control's ability to maintain state is a new technology known as ViewState. ViewState performs its trickery with the assistance of the hidden INPUT element. Once spawned by an ASP.NET page, this element gets its value property automatically stuffed with state data. Figure 7-6 shows how a typical Web form might look in Internet Explorer, and Figure 7-7 is a snippet of the downloaded HTML for this same page.

If you are a seasoned Web developer, after digesting ViewState mechanics you will see a new tool for enhancing your work. It is a great way of discreetly passing nonvisual data between requests. Take a look at an example.

Say there is some customer-specific purchase data required on many of your site's pages. The information is not too valuable, so security needs are minimal. Nevertheless, you really do not want to place it on every page for the user to see. It's also visually unappealing sitting at the tail end of every URL query string.

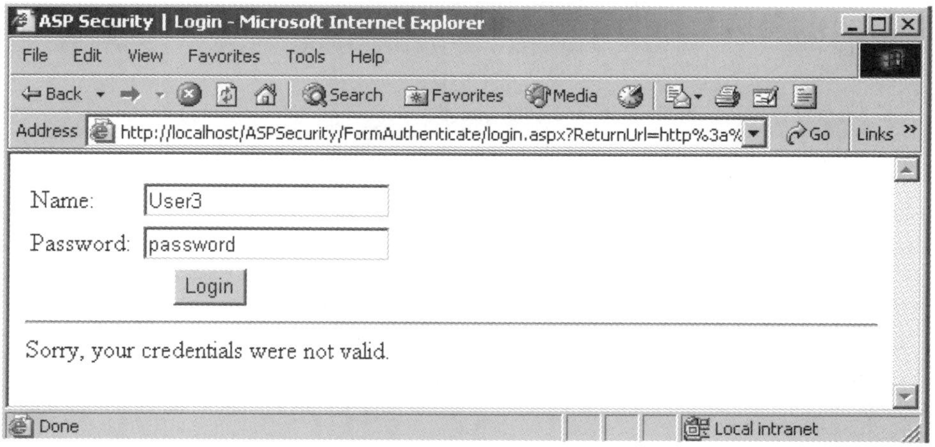

Figure 7-6. Sample Web form with data

Figure 7-7. Sample Web form's source HTML

How might you handle this requirement without too much hassle and without ASP.NET?

You might put the data in the same element that ViewState hired. This same HTML element provides a safe harbor. The following HTML snippet demonstrates how to place the customer's last purchase date out of the customer's view:

```
<INPUT TYPE="hidden" ID="txtLastPurchase" value="04/03/2001">
```

There's a problem with this technique though. Determined users can easily see this information by looking at the underlying HTML.

The ViewState mechanism now offers a better solution. You may store the date discreetly away into the ViewState property as shown here:

```
ViewState["strLastPurchase"] = "04/03/2001"
```

Looking at how ViewState scrambles data (Figure 7-7) might lead you to start placing confidential data inside it as well. The scrambled data stuck in the hidden element, VIEWSTATE, could not mean anything to anyone. Or could it?

Your average user may not be able to decrypt a rendered ViewState control, but the average hacker will. ViewState information is just base64-encoded characters.[8] It is far from being either private or tamper-proof. Not surprisingly, ASP.NET offers solutions transforming ViewState into a more secure data bucket.

The first solution generates a hash code for the ViewState data. You start the ball rolling by setting the EnableViewStateMAC attribute to true. You can do this either at the application or page level with the following directive:

```
<%@Page EnableViewStateMAC=true %>
```

If someone now tries to corrupt the data, the server will not process any data from that page. However, it remains viewable. That person just cannot change the data unnoticed and post it back to the server.

NOTE *Here's a relevant situation I saw on a project. One resourceful fellow figured out that a retail Web site placed a customer discount percentage in a "hidden" field on the order page. He figured 90 percent off the price was a much better discount than the intended 10 percent. He changed the discount, posted the order, and bought the widget for 10 percent of the regular price.*

If you need a more tamperproof hash code, change the machine.config <machineKey> validation attribute from the default SHA1 to the MD5 algorithm. Here's an example:

```
<machineKey validation="MD5"/>
```

---

8. Why use base64 encoding? Doing so lowers the chance of accidentally corrupting information during the roundtrip journeys between browser and server.

Going one step further, encrypting the ViewState data is equally simple. Instead of changing the validation property to MD5, set it to the 3DES encryption algorithm, as shown here:

```
<machineKey validation="3DES" />
```

There is a downside to this protection. First, _VIEWSTATE may easily become quite large, thereby slowing download and upload speeds. Second, computing hash codes and encrypting data consumes processing resources. Lastly, if your site runs on a Web farm, you will need to augment <machineKey> with a common key attribute. For example, one box's <machineKey> is set to MD5 and another to 3DES. The problem is that each computer won't be able to decrypt each other's Form-based authentication cookies. More frustrating may be troubleshooting why the computers are generating different types of cookies!

Form-based Authentication

I was impressed after first hearing about ASP.NET's four authentication models. You now have the following to choose from:

- None (the old standby)

- Windows

- Forms

- Passport

Then I realized something—these options are already available without .NET! After playing with some ASP.NET code, another aspect became clear. Implementing any of these authentication models with .NET just became very simple. Nowhere is this fact more evident than with Form-based authentication.

Installing Forms authentication into your application involves three inter-related steps:

1. Set the authentication model in the appropriate web.config file.

2. Build a login form.

3. Check authentication whenever necessary.

Once these steps are completed, ASP.NET does all the dirty work. With the help of a cookie, the user's credentials are checked. Should the user navigate to a new page and his or her authentication expires, your custom-built login form pops up. After successfully authenticating, the user is allowed to continue on.

Recall that configuring the authentication model starts by editing and placing a web.config file in the desired spot. I say "desired" because you can place web.config files that set the authentication model in both an application directory and a virtual root. This ability has some interesting design implications, as you can potentially install several different authentication models within a Web site.

The following fragment is the first half of a Form-based example:

```
<configuration>
    ...
    <system.web>
        <authenication mode="Forms">
            <forms name="TheCookieName"
                loginUrl="login.aspx" protection="All"
                timeout="60" >
            </forms>
        </authenication>
    </system.web>
    ...
</configuration>
```

In the preceding snippet, you set the following authentication properties:

- Users will discover somewhere in their computer a cookie file entitled, "TheCookieName".

- login.aspx, the workhorse login form, resides in the application root's virtual directory.

- By setting protection to All, the cookie will be both encrypted and hashed. You have four choices: None, Encryption, Validation, or All (the default). As you might have guessed from these options, encryption does not necessarily validate cookies.

- Users reauthenticate after 60 minutes—that is, 60 minutes since a user's last request.[9]

---

9. Cookies may not always expire as expected. Updates occur whenever the time remaining is less than half of the set value. The documentation states that this behavior helps performance and avoids multiple browser warnings for users with the cookies warnings turned on.

You could have also set several other options. One of the more interesting options is the ability to load users and their passwords. By including the optional <credentials> element inside of <forms>, you can load all of the site users' credentials. You can also set the how the passwords are encrypted, as shown in the following snippet:

```
<credentials passwordFormat="Clear">
    <user name="User1" password="password"/>
    <user name="User2" password=""/>
    ...
</credentials>
```

The other encryption choices provide greater security. Instead of allowing anyone with access to the site's code to see passwords, set passwordFormat to either MD5 or SHA1. Now, the fragment becomes something a little less informative to curious onlookers, as you can see here:

```
<credentials passwordFormat="SHA1">
    <user name="User1" password="B081DBE85E1EC3FFC3D4E7D0227400CD"/>
    <user name="User2" password="D41D8CD98F00B204E9800998ECF8427E"/>
    ...
</credentials>
```

Some of you may wonder how I obtained the encoded passwords. It is a surprisingly easy chore. .NET exposes the following very useful method for performing these computations:[10]

```
strHash = FormsAuthentication.HashPasswordForStoringInConfigFile(
    strPassword, encryptionformat);
```

The other half of effectively configuring authentication has nothing to do with authenticating users (at least, technically speaking). You also need to set some authorization properties. Once again returning to web.config, you can do just that, as follows:

```
<authorization>
    <deny users="?"/>
    <allow users="*"/>
</authorization>
```

---

10. I've found HashPasswordForStoringInConfigFile() comes in handy for tasks other than loading a configuration file. It is a great tool for hashing a new user's password before sticking it in a database.

Based on the preceding fragment, you have effectively prevented anonymous (unauthenticated) users from visiting. If you wanted things a little tighter, you could deny all users except for sample users from visiting. And you can go even further by preventing User1 from posting anything. Here's how to do so:

```
<authorization>
    <deny users="*"/>
    <allow users="User1,User2"/>
    <deny VERB="post" users="User1"/>
</authorization>
```

I would suggest that you take the time to play with these different options before making any architectural decisions. For example, unnecessarily encrypting cookies for every user every 30 minutes squanders a Web server's processing power, thereby adversely impacting site scalability and performance.

You are now ready to tackle the login form itself. All you need to do is ask the user for a name and password. If the credentials check out, you will return the user to the page that he or she initially requested. Otherwise, the user gets another chance, as illustrated in Listing 7-2.

Listing 7-2. Authenticating a User in ASP.NET

```
...
<form runat="server" ID="Form1">
Name:<input type="text" id="txtUserName" runat="server">
Password:<input type="text" id="txtUserPassword" runat="server">
<input type="submit" id="btnUserLogin" value="Login" runat="server"
    onserverclick="LoginUser">
<asp:Label id="lblNotifyUser" runat="server"></asp:Label>
</form>
...
public void LoginUser(object s, EventArgs e)
{
    if(FormsAuthentication.Authenticate(txtUserName.Value,
txtUserPassword.Value))
    {
        FormsAuthentication.RedirectFromLoginPage(txtUserName.Value, false);
        NotifyUser.Text = "Welcome " + User.Identity.Name;
    }
    else
        NotifyUser.Text = "Sorry, your credentials were not valid.";
}
...
```

Note that the `false` argument value in `RedirectFromLoginPage()` instructs ASP.NET not to persist user credentials with a cookie when the session expires.

CAUTION *Don't always assume that users will want to persist their credentials after a successful* `FormsAuthentication.Authenticate()`. *Unless you construct a custom cookie of specified duration, the default version will work for future browser sessions! That might pose a security risk when users visit your site from a public computer. In view of such a possibility, you should always let users decide whether their cookie will last "forever."*

Form-based authentication shows its power in all of your other Web pages. You see this in the next few lines code. All it takes is a simple call to the `User` object.

```
    ...
public void Page_Load(Object s, EventArgs e)
{
    If User.Identity.IsAuthenticated Then
        Greeting.Text = "Welcome" + User.Identity.Name + "!";
    ...
```

`User` objects belong to an `HttpContext` object, and `HttpContext` objects belong to the current page. Therefore, the `IIdentity` properties and methods are available on any Web page request. There are other properties, too. The authentication models each generate their own type of `User` object. For example, Windows creates a `WindowsIdentity` object that gives you a `User.IsSystem` property.

As the Form-based authentication application stands, it is not too secure. All you've built is a credential management facility. Since name and password information is transmitted across the Internet unencrypted, anyone could pick them up.[11] The missing magic for a secure solution with Form-base authentication is Secure Sockets Layer (SSL). Serving the login page via HTTPS fixes the problem. Nonetheless, Form-based authentication may still have a life without SSL. For example, a site might employ it to support personalization. It may not be important if someone discovers that a visitor prefers a light blue background and no sound.

---

11. Just like unencrypted ViewState data, plain text passwords get base64-encoded for transmission—making password information ugly, but not secure.

Before moving on, it is worth noting that Form-based authentication does not have to rely on a web.config file to house user credentials. You can validate users against a wide variety of data stores—SQL Server, Exchange, Excel files, and so on. For example, the XMLFormAuthentication Web application contained in this chapter's sample code uses an XML file to store credentials. Instead of calling the built-in `FormsAuthentication.Authenticate` method, it utilizes a "custom" authentication method shown here:

```
public void LoginUser(object s, EventArgs e)
{
    if(ValidateUser(txtUserName.Value, txtUserPassword.Value))
        FormsAuthentication.RedirectFromLoginPage(txtUserName.Value, false);
    else
        Response.Redirect("NewUser.aspx");
}


private bool ValidateUser(String userName, String userPassword)
{
    string xmlPath = Request.PhysicalApplicationPath + "Users.xml";
    XmlDocument xmlUsers = new XmlDocument();
    xmlUsers.Load(xmlPath);
    string userXPath = "User[@Name=\"" + userName +
        "\" and @Password=\"" + userPassword + "\"]";
    XmlElement usersRoot = xmlUsers.DocumentElement;
    XmlNode userNode = usersRoot.SelectSingleNode(userXPath);
    if(userNode != null)
        return true;
    else
        return false;
}
```

Role Call

Did you think something was missing from the role Accountants that you used earlier in this chapter in the section "<authorization>?" Was it a domain or machine name? Developers familiar with Windows's implementation of roles and groups know they need one. ASP.NET removed that requirement. You no longer have to set the Form authorization property to `Windows` to exploit the role/group functionality; things will work just as well with Form-based authentication. This raises the obvious question—without Windows, how do you create and access your custom roles?

One quick answer lies with adding a little code to the Global.asax file as shown in Listing 7-3.

Listing 7-3. Checking for Role Membership in ASP.NET

```
<%@ Import Namespace = "System.Security.Principal" %>
 ...
public void Application_AuthenticateRequest(Object sender, EventArgs e)
{
    if( !(HttpContext.Current.User.Identity == null))
    {
        if(HttpContext.Current.User.Identity.AuthorizationType == "Forms")
        {
            FormsIdentity id;
             id = (FormsIdentity)HttpContext.CurrentUser.Identity;
            String[] myRoles = new String[2];
            myRoles[0] = "Everyone";
            myRoles[1] = "Accountants";

            HttpContext.Current.User = new GenericPrincipal(id, myRoles);
        }
    }
}
```

Now you can check an authenticated user's role in the same way you checked a Windows group or role—like this:

```
if(User.IsInRole("Accountants"))
```

Final Notes

Here are some final notes on using roles in ASP.NET:

- You can build your own class when working with non-Windows roles. You only need to implement the IPrincipal interface.

- The preceding concepts apply to Passport as well as Form-based authentication.

- Remember, ASP.NET automatically handles role mechanics with Windows authentication.

You will find code implementing a sample Accountants-based solution in the ASPSecurity\RoleCall\Global.asax file.

Using Sessions

There once was a time when session objects made ASP professionals cringe. Loaded session objects not only consumed scare memory resources on the server, they failed on some Web farm configurations, and always required cookies.[12] ASP.NET changed that. Another tool is now available for securely maintaining state that meets some tough design requirements.

Although several combinations exist for handling sessions, I will explore one specific configuration that makes for a cookieless, scalable, and secure solution. As expected though, before coding comes editing the web.config file as follows:

```
<configuration>
    <sessionState mode="SqlServer"
        cookieless="true"
        sqlconnectionstring="data source=127.0.0.1;user id=sa;password=""/>
</configuration>
```

The first attribute, mode, determines how the ASP.NET solution persists session data. These are the three choices:

- InProc. Stores data in the memory of the ASP.NET worker process. While the best performing option, it behaves much like the original version of the Session object.

- StateServer. Maintains all state data on any server by means of one Windows service—ASP.NET State. Great for load-balanced solutions; bad if the server crashed, as the session state would be lost.

- SQLServer. Behaves much like the StateServer mode with the added advantage of reliability, as the session state would survive a server crash.

The attribute cookieless is the next most interesting property within <sessionState>. By setting it to true, you link session state to the user via an ID automatically embedded in every URL.[13] For the loss of cookies, users need only live with URLs that look like this:

```
http://localhost/ASPSecurity/(e3rtvv45crnapc45x5wvtc55)/Login.aspx
```

---

12. Even worse was the situation when a VB developer stuck a COM object into the Session object.

13. As some of you may already know, there is a way to create a "cookieless" session without .NET. Microsoft's IIS 4 Resource Kit contains an ISAPI filter that does the trick.

Next, ASP.NET requires a SQL Server database when `<sessionState>` mode equals SQLServer. The .NET Framework contains a special script that creates this dedicated database, cleverly called ASPState.[14]

You are finally ready to put your session object to work.[15] Imagine an XML fragment containing a user's confidential order information, like the following:

```
<Order>
    <LineItem Number="1">
        <ProductID>12345</ProductID>
        <Quantity>2</Quantity>
    </LineItem>
    ...
```

You can drop this XML-based information into the user's session object using one of several techniques. Here's the code:

```
Session["CurrentOrder"] = objXMLDOMNode.text;
// Or maybe the whole XML node...
Session["CurrentOrder"] = objXMLDOMNode;
```

ASP.NET `Session` objects do not require a string data type. You may place any object into a `Session` object. Nonetheless, I would recommend testing if you plan to store reference type objects in any configuration of a session object.

Legal, but Lethal Input

It's still common that developers will let any data through, even data from a valid user. Just because the text that a user entered is legal is not enough; it could be quite lethal. And I am not talking about bogus user and password information passing through a SQL query. I mean the stuff that is so scary that Microsoft actually produced an acronym for it, CSSI—Cross-Site Scripting Security Issues.

---

14. The script that creates the ASPState database, state.sql, resides in the \winnt\Microsoft.NET\Framework\[version]\ folder.

15. You may discover that "out-of-process Session State" is unavailable when the "ASP.NET State" service is not running. Start the service with either the MMC or NET START command.

Punching Through an Exposed SQL Query

There are many ways to punch through an exposed SQL query. This example assumes that a site validates credentials via a simple COUNT query:

```
SELECT COUNT(*) FROM tblUser WHERE name='" &
    Request("User") & "' AND password='" & Request("Password") & "'"
```

What happens when a user posts the following information?

```
Request("User") = "x' or 'a'='a"
Request("Password") = "x' or 'a'='a"
```

This translates into the following query, which will most likely return a positive integer!

```
SELECT COUNT(*) FROM tblUser
    WHERE name= 'x' or 'a'='a' AND password=' x' or 'a'='a'
```

CSSI works with surprising simplicity. Malicious script from an INPUT element becomes just another piece of code interpreted by the targeted ASP page.[16] Preventing CSSI normally involves two steps. First, you encode HTML user input. For example, a function like HTMLEncode() converts a string like "<A" into "&ltA". Second, inspect input for any offending characters. Here is a simple example of this checking process:

```
' Get the password
strPassword = Server.HTMLEncode(Request("txtUserPassword"))
' Start checking
if instr(strPassword, ".") > 0 then
    blnInvalid = true
if instr(strPassword, "-) > 0 then
    blnInvalid = true
...
```

There's a better way to handle string parser than using Instr(), though. The .NET Framework now exposes an entire class that makes it significantly easier to

---

16. For more information, please read one of Microsoft's several knowledge base articles on the subject to learn more about CSSI. "HOWTO: Prevent Cross-Site Scripting Security Issues" is a good place to start.

rid yourself of them. RegEx, which is the short name for Regular Expressions, exposes several sophisticated string manipulation and inspection methods.

 NOTE *Regular Expressions is far from being a new Microsoft technology. It arrived onstage with VBScript version 5, and UNIX folks have fiddled with RegEx long before that. Unlike so many other existing technologies .NET made easy to use, this one remains a bit elusive. If you need to dig deeper, try Jeffrey Friedl's book,* Mastering Regular Expressions *(O'Reilly & Associates, 1997).*

Imagine that your site's user login names equal users' e-mail addresses. Unfortunately this requirement provides more than enough "wiggle room" for the clever hacker. E-mail addresses allow for a bunch of characters! Here is where the power of RegEx shines. It is more than able to ensure that an e-mail address and nothing but an email address gets inside your ASP.NET code.

Now try checking for a valid e-mail address sans those funky CSSI characters like <, >, ', and so on:

```
Regex emailPattern = new Regex("^[a-z][a-z_0-9\.]+@[a-z0-9\.]+\.[a-z]{3}$");
Match emailMatch = emailPattern.Match(txtUserEmail.Text);
if( emailMatch.Success )
    ...
```

Pay close attention to the pattern—it's the brains of any RegEx. The effectiveness of a regular expression hinges on a well-defined pattern. The acceptable characters listed in `emailPattern` only includes letters, numbers, periods, and the @ character.

`RegularExpressionValidator` controls provide another way to harness the power of RegEx. The following example uses the control to ensure an acceptable e-mail address:

```
<INPUT TYPE="text" ID="txtUserEmail" SIZE="50" RUNAT="server"/>
<asp:RegularExpressionValidator ID="ctlValidEmail" RUNAT="server"
    ControlToValidate="txtUserEmail"
    ValidationExpresson = .*@.*
    ErrorMessage = "Please enter a legal email address. "
    Display= "dynamic">*
</asp:RegularExpressionValidator>
```

Before quitting, be warned. Writing effective patterns requires patience and practice. I encourage you to give your own e-mail checking version a spin via the sample code in ASPSecurity\RegularExpression\RegExTest.asp. For example, if you used the pattern employed earlier within the `RegularExpressionValidator`, a user could not only enter BigBob@OuterSpace, but almost any control characters that support a CSSI attack.[17]

Summary

In this chapter, I covered the following topics:

- Securing an ASP.NET application

- Editing the appropriate configuration files to change authentication rules

- Using ASP.NET to change how state is stored in Web applications and the ramifications of using ViewState relative to security

In the next chapter, you'll see how one of the newest authentication protocols, Passport, works.

---

17. In fact, I have seen an e-mail pattern run a few pages long that the developer claimed was still not 100 percent effective.

Passport

Tʜɪs ᴄʜᴀᴘᴛᴇʀ ᴄᴏᴠᴇʀs one of the more controversial topics related to .NET—
Passport. Passport is a single sign-in (SSI) service introduced by Microsoft with
the intent of making a user's Internet experience more friendly. In addition to
providing one set of credentials that work across multiple sites, Passport stores
basic user information such as a user's name, address, e-mail address, and phone
number.

Passport is the keystone to Microsoft's MyServices initiative—a collection of
services that bind useful data to a user's Passport ID. In addition, it's the authentication method for the Microsoft Wallet service. Although the aim of the service is
to provide convenience, Passport has raised the eyebrows of numerous security
and privacy groups. This is due in part to the very nature of Passport—centraliz-
ing and controlling information by a single entity. It may not mean much for you
in the end as a developer, but for product designers, it becomes a significant
political decision.

Passport Fundamentals

In this section, I'll cover the fundamental elements of Passport and how to get it
running successfully on your machine.

Architectural Overview

Before getting too far into the actual login process, I'll discuss the main elements
behind Passport. From the user's perspective, there are only two things to be concerned with: the Passport sign-in and his or her profile. The sign-in is typically an
e-mail address in the passport.com or hotmail.com domains, although a user can
register with an address from any domain. While it doesn't have to necessarily be
a valid e-mail address, sites can check to see if a user's address is valid through
the profile, and he or she may be denied service accordingly.

Quite frankly, this verification process is rather weak, and in reality is left to
a client site to validate, although Passport is capable of validating it. The preferred implementation of this is to send an e-mail to the user's registered e-mail
address with a link pointing to some form of a script file that registers the
e-mail address as being valid. For example, you could store a user identifier and

have the page process the validation based on the ID passed to it. In any case, after verifying the address, you can alter the `Flags` property in the user's profile to indicate that user has been verified. Of course, you can just as easily do this without verifying the address.

The user's profile is really nothing more than a remote repository for user information on the Passport servers. It can contain things such as the user's name, preferred e-mail address, city, and so on, but this may or may not be available to you depending on whether a user chooses to share the information with other sites. The only item you can ever be guaranteed to receive is a Passport User ID (PPUID), which uniquely identifies the user within the Passport system and should serve as your key to identifying him or her within your own data storage systems.

Just as users have IDs, so do member sites, and they're appropriately called Site IDs. Linked to this Site ID is information Passport needs to function with your site and most importantly a key to encrypt data moving from the Passport servers to your site. So, when a user clicks the Sign In logo on your site (referred to as the "Passport scarab" from here on), that user is sent to the Passport servers where he or she actually engages in the sign-in process.

On this journey, the user takes information about who sent him or her, namely your Site ID and domain name. From this point, Passport checks to see if you're valid by comparing the Site ID to the domain and making sure they match up with what's stored in the Passport servers. If these items don't match, the user is given a message indicating that the site isn't a valid Passport site. If the items do match, the user is presented with the Passport Login UI where he or she enters a sign-in and password. If the combination isn't valid, the user is asked to try again. If it is, the user is sent back to your site to a URL specified during the site configuration process called the return URL. When the user comes back, that user brings along any information he or she has actively chosen to share with other sites.

NOTE *Due to the validation by Site ID and domain, you will need to provide fully qualified DNS names. You'll need one for the domain you belong to, and additional ones corresponding to the machine(s) you plan on hosting the service with. If you're following along from a home computer, you're in luck—you just need to find the domain name your computer belongs to as well as your machine name. This is easiest with broadband connections, because your IP address (and your external DNS name) won't be jumping around as frequently as with a dial-up connection.*

Now, it wouldn't do a great deal of good if all of the user information came across in plaintext—that would sufficiently defeat one of the main design goals of keeping the user's information private. To keep this goal, the information is encrypted using the key (168 bits) that's stored on the Passport servers via Triple DES and presented to your site as query string information that the API (namely the Passport Manager class) decrypts and makes available for your use. In order to do this, you need the key installed on the server(s) you're planning on having use Passport as well as the appropriate Site ID configuration; otherwise you won't be able to use the data.

Taking a step back, the Passport service does one more thing before sending the user back to your site, which is related to the process after the user returns. Passport uses cookies to store a ticket (MSPAuth) that contains the PPUID and timestamp information. One cookie is written in the member site's domain and one within the Passport.com domain. This ticket information can be used to determine if a user is still considered valid by examining the age of the ticket, and if not, that user can be refreshed silently or forced through the UI again.

As a user goes through sites, a cookie (MSPVis) is modified in the Passport.com domain, which contains a list of sites the user has visited. When a user indicates that he or she wants to sign out of Passport, each site in this list initiates a sign-out process for the user through a URL specified in the configuration manager. Upon a successful sign-out (defined by each site deleting all Passport-related cookies), each site returns an image file indicating the success of the operation. If anything other than an image is returned, Passport assumes failure.

This overview of Passport is illustrated in Figure 8-1.

On top of the authentication and storage aspects, Passport provides a reasonable amount of customization through co-branding information. This allows a member site to provide its branding information or semicustomized interface for the user to more appropriately conform to the site's look and feel. This is covered further in the section "Co-branding Your Site" later in this chapter.

In summary, Passport is a third-party authentication and storage system that relies on a lot of trust. As you go through the rest of the chapter and the SDK documentation itself, you'll most likely be left with the impression that if you choose to ignore the licensing agreement, you can pretty much do what you want in terms of interfering with the authentication mechanism itself or storing user information. Of course, Microsoft can certainly revoke your site membership, but how many sites would admit to inappropriately storing or sharing user's information?

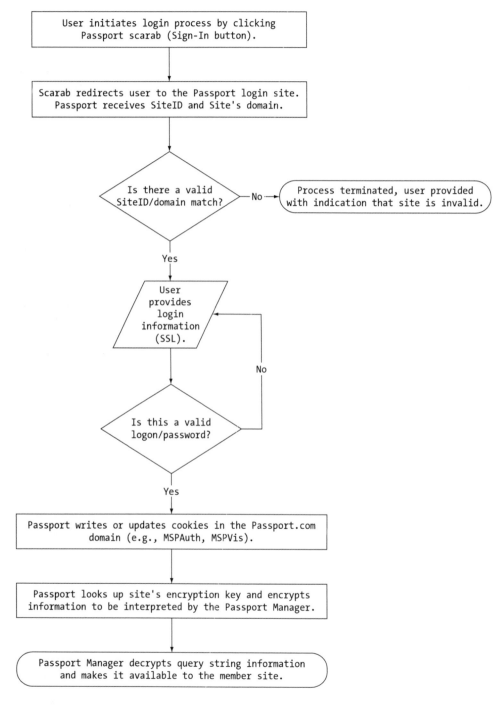

Figure 8-1. Passport workflow

Installation

To install Passport, you'll need to download the necessary components, as they're not shipped with Visual Studio; this can be done at the Passport site (http://www.passport.com). First, you should download the SDK documentation—this will prove useful, as it provides you with a list of everything you need and the processes required to make your site function successfully. These elements are available in the SDK in the section entitled "Registering Your .NET Passport Site." Because some of the elements pertain to URLs, having them in place prior to requesting a Pre-Production ID makes things easier to manage. Of note are the following:

- *Domain name.* You must provide the DNS domain name to which the machine you're installing the SDK on belongs.

- *Customer support URL.* This is a URL that points to a page presenting customer service data to a user.

- *Privacy policy URL.* The URL for your site's privacy policy. This should include information about your user data capture policies and how you plan on using that data. For example, if you share information with business partners or sell user information, state that clearly in this document.

- *Co-brand image URL.* The URL for the 468×60 GIF image used when displaying the Passport UI elements.

- *Co-brand image2 URL.* The URL for the 102×80 GIF image to be used when displaying additional Passport UI elements (such as on Windows XP).

- *Co-brand URL.* The URL that points to a .js file containing your co-branding variables. These variables control how the Passport UI is rendered, if specified. This URL is used if you don't specify another when generating Passport URLs.

- *Co-brand CSS URL.* The URL for the CSS file that will be included when rendering the Passport UI. For example, if you reference specific CSS styles in your co-branding variable file, you'll need to include this so that the browser can render them.

- *Co-brand image HREF.* The URL your image will redirect users to if it's clicked. Basically, it's used to construct an A tag around the IMG tag containing your co-branded image.

- *Terms of use URL.* The URL of any terms of service (TOS) agreement for your site.

- *Default return URL (a.k.a. registration URL).* The URL a user returns to after completing a login or registration action, if no other is specified.

- *Expire cookie URL.* The URL that points to the file where you delete all Passport and Passport-derived cookies from a user's machine and return a status to indicate the success of the operation.

- *Logout URL.* The URL the user is redirected to once that user has logged out of Passport.

Some of these resources are optional or have specific formatting requirements. For example, the file referenced by the co-brand image must be a 468×60 GIF or JPEG file, so consult the documentation prior to committing yourself to a particular file format or content of the file in general. Once you've reviewed and implemented the required items, download the Passport 2.x SDK.[1] The

Next, install the Passport 2.x SDK by executing the file you downloaded. The installation is straightforward, and the only configuration parameter you need to specify is given on the first screen. When presented with the option of how to install the SDK, select Development/Test. This will set up the service on your machine so that it runs within the proper environment (Pre-Production mode).

To utilize Passport, you'll need to provide some basic information about your site. The majority of the information doesn't require any effort other than typing names, addresses, phone numbers and so on. As you progress through the application, you'll be asked for URLs of specific files. As I stated, not all of the files are mandatory, so you can leave certain fields blank; unfortunately, you can't receive a Pre-Production ID until you've provided information for the mandatory fields. This is why I suggest having things in place prior to registering; it will make the process much smoother. At the very least, make a note of the values you enter so that you know where to place files when you go to implement your test site.

To access the site configuration and registration tool, go to http://www.netmyservicesmanager.com. When you've set everything up, you'll be given a Site ID. This will be used to configure the Passport Manager on your local server as shown in Figure 8-2.

Having the correct Site ID is critical to the system functioning properly as it tells the Passport service which key to use when encrypting information. If your key and Site ID don't match, you won't be able to retrieve any information about the user.

---

1. The Passport SDK and documentation are available at http://msdn.microsoft.com/ downloads/default.asp?URL=/downloads/sample.asp?url=/MSDN-FILES/027/001/644/ msdncompositedoc.xml.

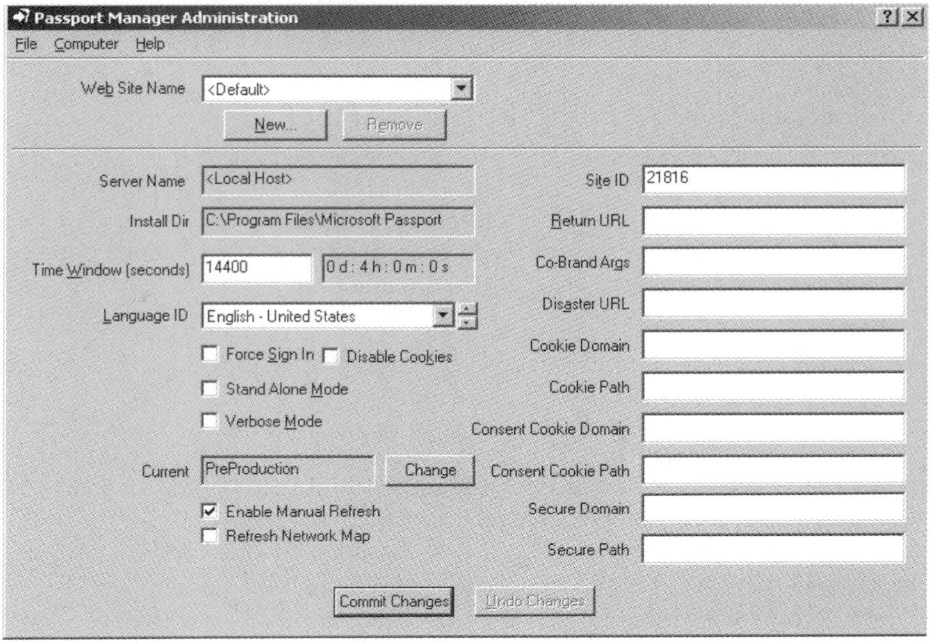

Figure 8-2. Passport Manager Administration utility

The final phase of configuring Passport involves setting up the Passport Manager. This consists of two steps: setting the Site ID and installing the encryption key. To get the encryption key, go to the Service Manager and do the following:

1. Select Manage My Applications.

2. Select the application you want to manage from the drop-down list.

3. Select the Download Key option.

4. Download the EXE and store it in your C root.

Now, configure the local manager by running the Passport Administration Utility.[2] Once it's loaded, enter the Site ID recorded earlier in the Site ID field

---

2. The Passport Administration Utility is accessed from the Start menu by selecting Start ➤ Program Files ➤ Microsoft Passport ➤ Passport Administration Utility.

(refer back to Figure 8-2) and close the administration tool. Finally, using a command prompt, execute the following commands:

```
partnerNNNN_A.exe /addkey
partnerNNNN_A.exe /makecurrent /t 0
```

where partnerNNNN_A.exe is the key installation program you downloaded.

In summary, I recommend setting up your development environment in the following order:

1. Install the operating system.

2. Install Visual Studio .NET.

3. Read SDK section "Registering Your .NET Passport Site."

4. Create sample project.

5. Make graphics.

6. Add necessary files.

7. Install Passport SDK.

8. Register your site with Passport.

9. Install the Passport encryption key and update the Passport Manager.

If you're running Windows XP, you'll find that no matter how often you repeat the previous instructions, they simply won't work. This is due to the way that XP handles Passport authentication. The manner in which XP works with Passport is discussed later along with the changes required to get XP to function in the Pre-Production environment.

Now that you have Passport set up on a machine, start looking at Passport from the developer's perspective.

Implementing Passport in Your Web Applications

In this section, I'll cover how you use Passport in your .NET applications starting with user authentication.

Authenticating a User

Thankfully, the installation and configuration of the software is the most difficult aspect of using Passport—the process of simply authenticating a user can be as simple as a few lines of code. Since this book is concerned with .NET, I'll be covering this from the perspective of the .NET platform; however, this process can be done in a similar matter using the COM components that the SDK provides.

The first thing to do is to familiarize yourself with what you'll be working with—the PassportIdentity class. I briefly mentioned this class in Chapter 5; now it's time to see how it works. The members you'll be using the most are listed in Table 8-1.

Table 8-1. Frequently Used Members of the PassportIdentity *Class*

MEMBER	DESCRIPTION
Compress	Compresses information to save bytes being transmitted over the Internet.
Decompress	Decompresses information compressed by the Compress method.
Decrypt	Decrypts information based on the key of the current Site ID.
Encrypt	Encrypts information based on the key of the current Site ID.
GetProfileObject*	Returns a value from the user's profile. The profile elements are available in the SDK. In C#, this property serves as the indexer.
HexPUID	The Passport User ID. This is a 64-bit unsigned integer returned via this property as a hexadecimal string. Use System.Convert to coerce this into an UInt64 or any other numeric format that suits your needs.
IsAuthenticated or GetIsAuthenticated	IsAuthenticated is a property that simply returns a bool value indicating if the user is signed in or not. GetIsAuthenticated is a function that allows you to specify additional parameters such as the time window since they last signed in.
LogoTag2	Generates an HTML string containing an IMG tag that is based on the user's status with Passport (signed-in or signed-out), embedded within a hyperlink to sign in or out as appropriate.

* Some profile attributes are keys into index files. These are located in <PassportInstallDirectory>\ dictionaries\<LangID (US English is 1033)>. The COM interfaces provide a PassportLookupTable class that allows you to load these files and retrieve the values from them. The .NET implementation does not currently provide this; however, you can add a reference to the existing COM component.

If you've used the COM interfaces to the Passport objects, you should find these familiar—they've been consolidated into the single `PassportIdentity` class. To put these members to use, create a new C# Web project called MyPassportDemo. When the application core has been created, open the web.config file so you can tell IIS to authenticate resources in this Web application using Passport.

More than likely the file should scream "change me here" to you, but in the event it doesn't, navigate to the authentication element in the document. The legal values for the mode attribute are "Windows", "Forms", "Passport", and "None". Since you're using Passport in this chapter, stick with the "Passport" value. At this point, you've told the framework to authenticate using Passport and could get by with this alone.

For the sake of thoroughness, there are two more configuration changes you can make to alter the Passport behavior. Start by considering a situation when you want to deny anonymous users access to your Web site. This is a pretty simple change, and requires adding the following snippet to your web.config file:

```
<authorization>
    <deny users="?"/>
</authorization>
```

This denies all anonymous requests to your site and will force the user to authenticate.

 NOTE *While I'm on the subject, the behavior of the authorization list differs from what you'd find in the operating system. For example, John Q is a member of two groups, GroupA and GroupB. GroupA is granted read/write access to a file, and GroupB is denied write access. For the pending MCSEs among you—John Q is only allowed to read the file— the most restrictive permissions are taken by the operating system. To get to the point, pay attention to what order you put things in, as the global.asa file processes whatever it comes across first.*

The other Passport-related option in the web.config file is that of specifying the `redirectURL`. By specifying `redirectURL`, you'll provide a page of your own to handle any steps you may want to take prior to having a user sign in. A good use for this might be a terms of use screen, although it would most likely frustrate users to have to see that screen repeatedly. That aside, you can specify the option by modifying the "authentication" element as follows:

```
<authorization mode="Passport">
    <passport redirectURL="http://www.mydomain.com/MyPassportDemo/tos.aspx"/>
</authorization>
```

To proceed with the example, undo any changes you made to the web.config file, with the exception of setting the mode attribute of the passport element (passport/@mode='Passport'). Next, create a new Web Form called "mainpage.aspx" in the root of the new project.

Right-click the newly created file and select View Code. To work with the appropriate classes, you'll need to reference the namespace by adding the following code to the top of the .cs file:

```
using System.Web.Security;
```

Now, open the file in the design view and add a table similar to this:

```
<table border=0 cellpadding=3 cellspacing=0>
    <tr>
        <td><img src="/support/images/ourLogo.jpg"></td>
        <td runat=server id=scarabCell name=scarabCell></td>
    </tr>
</table>
```

To take this process even further, switch back to the code view of the file and see if it added the reference to the scarabCell. If not, alter the file so that it reads as follows:

```
public class mainpage : System.Web.UI.Page
{
    ... other declares ...
    protected HtmlTableCell scarabCell;
    ... rest of code ...
}
```

Finally, here's what you've been waiting for—alter the Page_Load() event so that it reads like so:

```
private void Page_Load(object sender, System.EventArgs e)
{
    Passportdentity myIdentity=(PassportIdentity)Context.User;
    if (myIdentity.IsAuthenticated)
    {
```

```
        scarabCell.InnerHtml="Welcome <b>" + myIdentity.HexPUID + "</b>";
    }
    else
    {
        scarabCell.InnerHtml=myIdentity.LogoTag2(
            "http://mydomain.com/mainpage.aspx",1800,1,"",1033,0,"",10,0);
    }
}
```

Right-click the "mainpage.aspx" file, make it the start page, and run the application. If all goes well (and you didn't run any other tests that have inadvertent side effects), you should see the Sign In logo on your page. In reality, you should see it either way—the question is whether it will work or not. So, click the logo, and you should be redirected to the Passport login screen. Once you've logged in, you should see a message along the lines of "Welcome FFCA12A . . . ".

You may be surprised to see that the name you have registered in your Passport account has become "FFCA . . . ", but in fact it hasn't. The Name property represents your PUID—a 64-bit unsigned integer.

Signing Out of Passport

Part of the Passport protocol depends on cookies being set on the client. For someone to successfully be signed out and to fulfill the licensing agreement, you must delete these cookies and any private cookies that are Passport related. For instance, if you store the user's first name, retrieved from the Passport Manager, in a cookie, it has to be deleted during the sign-out process. In addition, you'll need to return an image that appropriately indicates the status of the checkout operation. Microsoft provides examples of these cookie deletion files with the SDK. For the sample application, use Listing 8-1 to implement a sign out.

Listing 8-1. Signing Out of Passport

```
private void Page_Load(object sender, System.EventArgs e)
{
    Response.AddHeader("pragma","no-cache");
    Response.AddHeader("cache-control","no-cache");
    Response.AddHeader("P3P","P3PURL");

    Response.ContentType="image/gif";

    signoutPassport();
```

```
      Response.WriteFile(
          @"c:\inetpub\wwwroot\ExplorePassport\support\img\signout.gif");
}
private void signoutPassport()
{
    clearCookie(Response.Cookies["MSPAuth"]);
    clearCookie(Response.Cookies["MSPProf"]);
    clearCookie(Response.Cookies["userNameLast"]);
    clearCookie(Response.Cookies["userNameFirst"]);
    clearCookie(Response.Cookies["userID"]);
}
private void clearCookie(System.Web.HttpCookie cookieToDelete)
{
    if (cookieToDelete==null) return;

    cookieToDelete.Expires=DateTime.Now.AddYears(-1);
    cookieToDelete.Value="";
    cookieToDelete.Path="/";
}
```

SOURCE CODE *You'll find these functions implemented in the ExploringPassport project in the \signout.aspx file.*

These procedures implement the necessary steps to sign out of Passport: they clear the Passport cookies (MSPAuth and MSPProf), clear cookies that are derived from Passport (userNameLast, userNameFirst, and userID), and write the Sign Out logo to the response stream. Note the use of the Response.WriteFile() function. This was chosen for demonstration purposes only, as it's simpler to show a single function than to show the function and the implementation in an aspx file. The appropriate way to accomplish this is to #include the GIF file in your aspx page. Doing this will make your sign-out page (and any others) easier to manage.

Securing Passport Data

In the event you plan on writing sensitive data or data retrieved from the Passport service to a cookie, you should encrypt it using the appropriate static methods on the PassportIdentity class, which provides four methods related to this: Encrypt(), Decrypt(), Compress(), and Decompress(). Although Encrypt()

and Decrypt() are required in order to manipulate secured data, the Compress() and Decompress() functions allow you to save storage in the cookie file as well as any parameters you plan on passing to other pages via query string, form posts, and so on.

You can certainly use any algorithm you choose to encrypt or decrypt the data, but the functions implemented by the API are primarily for manageability and convenience—you don't have to wander out of the namespace or write your own encryption software, and you can swap keys out without modifying anything by simply going to the .NET My Services manager and requesting and installing a new key.

Start with two functions, setSecureCookie() and readSecureCookie(), that show how to implement data encryption in Listing 8-2.

Listing 8-2. Securing Data with Passport

```
private void setSecureCookie(string cookieName, string cookieValue)
{
    string secureValue;
    secureValue=PassportIdentity.Encrypt(PassportIdentity.Compress(cookieValue));

    if (Response.Cookies[cookieName]==null)
    {
        Response.Cookies.Add(new HttpCookie(cookieName,secureValue));
    }
    else
    {
        Response.Cookies[cookieName].Value=secureValue;
    }
}
private string readSecureCookie(HttpCookie cookieToRead)
{
    string unsecureVal;

    unsecureVal=cookieToRead.Value;
    unsecureVal =PassportIdentity.Decompress(
        PassportIdentity.Decrypt(unsecureVal));
    return unsecureVal;
}
```

The purpose of these functions should be pretty self-evident; they save and read encrypted cookies (based on the site's encryption key), respectively.

Co-branding Your Site

Co-branding allows you to provide a consistent appearance to your users. For example, when they visit the Passport login screen, they can see your logos and color scheme rather than the Passport default. There are two elements involved in the co-branding process that I'll discuss in this section: co-branding templates and co-branding images. Each of these is applied to the two Passport UI elements—the Login screen and Registration screen. For each of these elements, you can implement flexible or fixed co-branding.

I'll start by looking at co-branding templates, which are nothing more than JavaScript files containing variables to be used by the Passport servers.[3] Depending on the type of co-branding you're implementing, the variables available to you will differ. Tables 8-2 through 8-5 indicate the variables available by the co-branding type.

Table 8-2. Login Server Flexible Co-branding Variables

VARIABLE NAME	PURPOSE
CBLoginHead	Contains the content of the HEAD tag on rendered pages.
CBLoginBody	Contains the content of the BODY tag on rendered pages. This does not contain the BODY tag itself.
CBLoginOnLoad	Expression to be evaluated in the onLoad() event of the document body.

Table 8-3. Login Server Fixed Co-branding Variables

VARIABLE NAME	PURPOSE
CBLogo	A URL of a 468×60 GIF file to be displayed at the top of the page when it's rendered.
CBSigninTxt1	Text to be displayed above the Passport UI.
CBSigninTxt2	Text to be displayed to the right of the Passport UI.

---

3. The co-branding files are configured through the .NET My Services manager where you provide the URL to the appropriate files. In general, Passport uses the co-branding files to render the UI to the browser, performing token substitution where appropriate.

Table 8-4. Registration Server Flexible Co-branding Variables

VARIABLE NAME	PURPOSE
CBRegistrationHead	Contains the content of the HEAD tag on rendered pages.
CBRegistrationBody	Contains the content of the BODY tag on rendered pages. This does not contain the BODY tag itself.
CBRegistrationOnLoad	Expression to be evaluated in the onLoad() event of the document body.

Table 8-5. Registration Server Fixed Co-branding Variables

VARIABLE NAME	PURPOSE
CBLogo	A URL of a 468×60 GIF file to be displayed at the top of the page when it's rendered.
CBRegTxt1	Text to be displayed above the Passport UI.
CBRegTxt2	Text to be displayed to the right of the Passport UI.

As you can see, the variables are similar in both instances, and corresponding variables serve the same function in each. Of course, you'll need to place the appropriate Passport interface somewhere. This is accomplished by embedding the text string "PASSPORT_UI" in your document. For the sample application, use the co-branding scripts in Listing 8-3.

Listing 8-3. Co-branding a Web Page

```
var CBLoginHead="<link type=text/css rel=stylesheet href=
    http://apress.sfnphxdelivery.net/support/css/passport_cobranding.css";

var CBLoginBody=
    "<table border=0 cellpadding=0 cellspacing=0 align=center width=450>";

CBLoginBody+="<tr><td><img src=\
    "http://apress.sfnphxdelivery.net/ExplorePassport/support/img/
        passport_explore_468_60.gif\"></td></tr>";

CBLoginBody+="<tr><td class=itemText><br><b>Welcome to the Exploring Passport
    sample application</b>.<br><br>Please use your .Net Passport to sign in.";
```

```
CBLoginBody+="<tr><td>PASSPORT_UI</td></tr>";

CBLoginBody+="</table>";

var CBLoginOnLoad="";
```

> **SOURCE CODE** *This code is located in the ExploringPassport project in the \support\script\passport_cobranding.js file.*

You can see the effects of applying co-branding by comparing Figure 8-3 to Figure 8-4—before and after examples of co-branding.

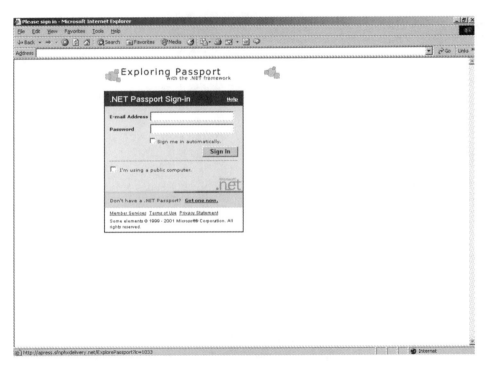

Figure 8-3. Passport Login UI prior to applying co-branding

You're free to put whatever you want in a co-branding template with a few limitations on HTML tags—for example, you can't put a BODY tag in your template variables. These restrictions are documented in the SDK reference, of course.

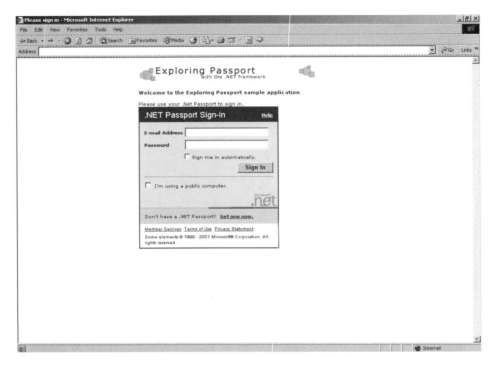

Figure 8-4. The result of applying co-branding variables

Integrating Passport

The effort required to integrate Passport into your existing application environment can't be quantified without a thorough analysis of not only your code, but also your business practices. This can be as simple as altering the way the key field on a fictitious "users" table behaves, or reengineering the way you handle cookies, what information you pass to other sites, how you communicate with pages in your own site, and so on.

When beginning the integration process, the first issue you're likely to encounter is that of keying users. Simply put, how are you going to migrate your current implementation for identifying a user to one that works with Passport? The PassportIdentity class provides a way of doing this via the HexPUID property. The HexPUID property returns the user's PUID in hexadecimal format (hence the name). Given this, your task is to find a way to make this function with your current database design. A few examples of what you could do follow:

```
public Guid PPUIDtoGUID(string passportID)
{
    string ppGUID;
```

```
ppGUID="00000000-0000-0000-" + passportID.Substring(0,4) + "-" +
    passportID.Substring(4);

    return new System.Guid(ppGUID);
}
function Int64 PPUIDtoInt64(string passportID)
{
    return System.Convert.ToInt64(passportID,16);
}
```

SOURCE CODE   *Functions similar to this can be found within the* PassportUtilities *class in the \global.asax file in the sample application.*

These functions can integrate a Passport ID with SQL Server using either the uniqueidentifier or bigint type. In terms of storage, using the bigint type would be the most efficient as you won't be wasting bits—using the uniqueidentifier type will result in a storage efficiency of 50 percent (64 wasted bits). Thankfully, 64-bit numbers are native to .NET; however, if you're using VB 6, you'll be better off sticking with the GUID.

Now that the first hurdle is behind you, you should spend time looking over your application for any items that can cause violations of the license agreement. When you go through this process, pay particular attention to the following items:

- Cookie storage

- Variables passed via query string

- Exchange with external entities

Cookie Storage and Query Strings

The cookie issue is covered previously in the chapter in the section "Architectural Overview," so it doesn't warrant discussion here. You can apply the same concepts used with cookies to take care of the query string issue as well. Keep in mind that this may greatly increase the overhead on your servers. Consider the following noncompliant ASP code fragment:

```
function submitForm()
{
    var uid=<% = Request["userID"] %>;
    var firstName = <% = Request["userFirstName"] %>;
    window.open('http://their.com/login.aspx?uid='+uid+'&firstName='+firstName);
}
```

By doing something similar to this, you're passing Passport-based information in plaintext—which you're supposed to guard against. To correct this, you can use a fictitious encryptString() function that can implement some form of encryption on the data.[4] Here's the compliant code:

```
function submitForm()
{
    var uid=<% = encryptString(Request["userID"]) %>;
    var firstName=<% = encryptString(Request["userFirstName"]) %>;
    window.open('http://their.com/login.aspx?uid='+uid+'&firstName='+firstName);
}
```

So, instead of simply writing a value out to the page, you've had to perform two operations to get it there (Compress() and Encrypt()), and you'll need to perform another two operations (Decrypt() and Decompress()) to get the information back for each variable. I can't say that this policy is really of any use other than to make the user feel "safe" when browsing your site. The simple fact is, unless you're utilizing SSL in all of your transactions involving Passport data, a "man in the middle" can read the data from the form posts going across the wire just as easily as reading the URL.

Exchange with External Entities

By accepting the license agreement, you're agreeing not to share information with business partners that are outside of the Passport network. Furthermore, it's not encouraged to share Passport information with anyone within the Passport service either. If a part of your business process requires that you exchange information with business partners, you'll need to gather the user's consent prior to storing the information in your database. Upon receiving consent, you're free to do what you want with the information.

---

4. Note that you can't use the Encrypt() and Decrypt() functions to share data with other sites as the Site ID and Site Key are utilized in these functions. The easiest way to share data with external entities is to use a shared key and algorithm or simply SSL when doing transactions.

Passport doesn't mandate how you treat the data once you've obtained consent to store it, but as with any information you may store, make a reasonable attempt to protect it. This may mean encrypting Passport IDs in the database, mandating SSL connections with business partners, physically delivering data, and so on.

Although not required, adding features to interact with the Passport service can make a user's experience easier. For example, instead of having the user exit your site to change password or profile information, you can provide links directly to the Passport site that will return the user to your site. By doing this, you'll maintain visibility to the user and won't alienate him or her. Arguably, the best way to accomplish this is by including a header in your pages (which saves quite a bit of typing) that includes the Passport scarab, your site logo, and interfaces to the various Passport features. In the sample project, you'll find a page containing the code in Listing 8-4.

Listing 8-4. Adding Passport Functionality to a Web Page

```
<%

    string scarabHTML;
    string returnURL;
    string passportReturnInfo;
    PassportIdentity currentUser;

    returnURL="http://" + Request.ServerVariables["SERVER_NAME"] +
        Request.ServerVariables["SCRIPT_NAME"];
    passportReturnInfo="&ru=" + Server.UrlEncode(returnURL) + "&id=21816";
    currentUser=(PassportIdentity)User.Identity;
    scarabHTML= currentUser.LogoTag2(returnURL, 1800, 0,
        Server.UrlEncode("http://yourURL"),1033,0,"",0,0);
%>
<script language=javascript>
function showPassportWindow()
{
    var targetElement=document.all['passportManipulationWindow'];
    targetElement.style.left=_passportGetWindowLeft(event.srcElement)-20;
    targetElement.style.display='';
}
function closePassportWindow()
{
    var targetElement=document.all['passportManipulationWindow'];
    targetElement.style.display='none';
}
```

```
function _passportGetWindowLeft(eventSource)
{
    var _xPos=0;
    var _currentElement=eventSource;

    while (_currentElement.parentElement.tagName!='BODY')
    {
        _xPos+=_currentElement.offsetLeft;
        _currentElement=_currentElement.parentElement;
    }

    return _xPos;
}
function _passportGetWindowTop(eventSource)
{
    var _yPos = 0;
    var _currentElement = eventSource;
    while (_currentElement.parentElement.tagName!='BODY')
    {
        _yPos += _currentElement.offsetLeft;
        _currentElement = _currentElement.parentElement;
    }
    return _yPos;
}
</script>
<table border=0 cellpadding=0 align=center width=450 >
    <tr>
        <td><img
            src="/ExplorePassport/support/img/passport_explore_468_60.gif"></td>
        <td valign=bottom><% = scarabHTML %></td>
    </tr>
<%
if (currentUser.IsAuthenticated)
{
%>
    <tr>
        <td colspan=2 align=right class="bodyText">
            <a href="javascript:void(0)" onclick="showPassportWindow();">
            Manage My Passport</a></td>
        </tr>
<%}%>
    <tr>
        <td style="border-top:1px solid #3C96FF" colspan=2> </td>
    </tr>
</table>
```

```
<table border=0 cellpadding=3 width=151
    cellspacing=0 name=passportManipulationWindow id=passportManipulationWindow
    style="position:absolute;display:none;z-index:99">
    <tr>
    <td class="bodyText" background="/ExplorePassport/support/img/passport
        _menu_top.gif" height="21px"
        align=center style="border-bottom:1px solid #3C96FF">
        Passport Management</td>
    </tr>
    <tr>
        <td class=bodyText background="/ExplorePassport/support/img/
            passport_menu_slice.gif"> </td>
    </tr>
    <tr>
        <td class=bodyText background="/ExplorePassport/support/img/
            passport_menu_slice.gif">
        <a href="<% = currentUser.GetDomainAttribute("EDITPROFILE",1033,null)
        + passportReturnInfo %>">Edit Profile</a></td>
    </tr>
    <tr>
        <td class=bodyText background="/ExplorePassport/support/img/
            passport_menu_slice.gif"><a href="<% = currentUser.GetDomainAttribute(
            "CHANGEPASSWORD",1033,null) + passportReturnInfo %>">
            Change Password</a></td>
    </tr>
    <tr>
        <td class=bodyText background="/ExplorePassport/support/img/
            passport_menu_slice.gif"><a href="<% =
            currentUser.GetDomainAttribute(
            "PASSWORDRESET",1033,null) + passportReturnInfo %>">
            Reset Password</a></td>
    </tr>
    <tr>
        <td class=bodyText background="/ExplorePassport/support/img/
            passport_menu_slice.gif"> </td>
    </tr>
    <tr>
        <td class=bodyText background="/ExplorePassport/support/img/
            passport_menu_bottom.gif" style="border-top:1px solid #3C96FF"
            height="22px" align=right>
            <a href="javascript:closePassportWindow()">Close
        </a> </td>
    </tr>
</table>
```

SOURCE CODE   *This code is located in the* ExploringPassport *project in the* \support\include\header.aspx *file*

In this example, I'm providing the user with the ability to edit his or her profile, change the password, and reset the password. As you can see, this is accomplished using GetDomainAttribute() on the PassportIdentity class. You can link to other Passport features by using one of the values listed in Table 8-6 for the first argument of the function.

Table 8-6. Valid Values for GetDomainAttribute()

PROFILE VARIABLE	PURPOSE
EDITPROFILE or ACCOUNTINFO	Provides a URL to allow the user to edit his or her profile
AUTH	Gets a URL for the login server for the domain authority
CHANGEPASSWORD	Provides a URL to allow a user to change his or her password
CHANGESECRETQ	Provides a URL to allow a user to modify his or her secret question and answer
CUSTOMERSERVICE	Provides a link to Passport customer service
KIDSPASSPORT	Provides a link to account information and services for Kids Passport
LOGOUT	Provides the logout URL for the domain authority
MPP	Provides a link to the Members Profile Pages
PASSPORTHOME	Represents the home page for the domain authority
PASSPORTINFORMATIONCENTER	Represents the home page for documentation for the domain authority

(continued)

Table 8-6. Valid Values for GetDomainAttribute() *(continued)*

PASSWORDOPTIONS	Allows a user to change or reset his or her password
PASSWORDRESET	Allows a user to reset his or her password
REGISTRATION	Allows a user to register for Passport
REVALIDATEEMAILURL	Represents e-mail address verification interface
WALLET	Provides wallet information manipulation (not covered in this book)
WALLETGET	Represents purchase URL for Wallet users (not covered in this book)

This list is not exhaustive—there are additional parameters you can provide to get links to help pages. As these are all covered in the SDK documentation (in "Reference\Linking to .NET Passport Services"), there's no need to go over them. If you read the functionality provided by the parameter values, you may have noticed that two of them seem redundant—in fact, they are. The AUTH and LOGOUT values are of little use and can be accomplished using the single call to LogoTag2() on the PassportIdentity class. To maintain your site's visibility after the interaction with Passport, you'll need to add ru and id parameters to GetDomainAttribute() to tell Passport where to send the user once the user has completed the task he or she was sent to do. In the header file I included the following snippet, which provides this functionality:

```
passportReturnInfo="&ru=" + Server.UrlEncode(returnURL) + "&id=21816";
```

Note the use of the UrlEncode() function—if you have special characters in the URL, Passport may not be able to route the user back to your site if you don't encode it properly.

Privacy and Use Restrictions

Being a participant in the Passport service comes with heavy restrictions on how you can use data. Not that I disagree with any of them, but you may need to adjust business practices, particularly where sharing is involved. Even with these restrictions in place, you may still encounter resistance by your consumer base when implementing Passport.

Implementing Basic Procedures

According to the SDK, you must at least implement the following procedures (paraphrased and not in a particular order):

- Limit server access to a restricted group of employees and protect servers from intrusion.

- Destroy or secure the encryption key you went to the trouble of downloading.

- Try your best to install patches as they come out.

- Protect any information sent via the Internet pertaining to Passport using whatever cryptography you can feasibly implement.

- Delete any Passport-related information in cookies.

- Do not cache pages containing information that can identify someone.

- Ask for explicit permission to use Passport data from the user's profile.

- Ask for explicit permission to store Passport data from the user's profile.

Even with these "precautions" in place, servers continue to be invaded and in many instances information held hostage. There have been several known cases of intruders acquiring credit card lists and forcing companies to pay a finder's fee to get the information back. Granted, in these situations the companies have yet to relent, as the act is in the public eye, but one must question what goes on out of plain sight.

Another issue to consider is the value of the data to spammers, telemarketers, and other undesirable miscreants. To this point, I can't think of a highly publicized case where one company physically infiltrates another's to retrieve personal information about its customer base (although that doesn't mean it never happens). If it happens, what would make a more logical target—an entity containing a few hundred users or an entity containing a few million? If you thought you were being pestered now, wait until the spammers have your home address, phone number, and e-mail address without your consent.

Meeting Requirements in the Licensing Agreement

The following sections show you how to meet the requirements in the licensing agreement.

Restricting Access to Passport Resources

Implement NTFS security on files and data sources involved in your Web application for only the users that need to access them. In particular, ensure that the encryption key and Passport software is physically secured. Permit physical access only to users who require it, such as network administrators and a relevant developer group. In reality, these practices should be followed for any application you develop.

Keeping Your Servers Patched

Be vigilant about keeping your client and server operating systems patched. Many IT shops border on downright negligence when it comes to this aspect of security, but something that takes relatively little time to do can save you (and possibly your job) in the future.

Securing Transactions Involving Passport Data

Anytime you're going to present Passport data to a client or perhaps to a business partner, enforce some form of encryption across the wire. A simple way to do this is to install an SSL certificate on your server. If you're using your own data, then you're welcome to do with it as you wish.

Cleaning Your Cookies

When a user abandons his or her session or signs out of Passport, or you just don't need the cookies that contain information based on the user's profile anymore, delete those cookies. In a previous section, I covered how to delete the Passport-specific cookies, but as a general rule only keep information as long as you need it.

Preventing Caching of Passport Data

The easiest way to prevent caching of Passport data is to configure the Web server to instruct a client's browser to not cache page information. This is done by adding the "cache-control" HTTP header and assigning it the "no-cache" value. You can modify HTTP headers in the IIS console on the page shown in Figure 8-5. A good practice is to group the pages that present Passport data in a single directory and prevent caching only on that directory. The net result of this practice is that your application will consume less bandwidth.

When was the last time you saw a Passport site asking for your consent to store information derived from Passport? The odds are that you haven't—at least not in a manner that you'd expect. According to Microsoft, simply displaying the

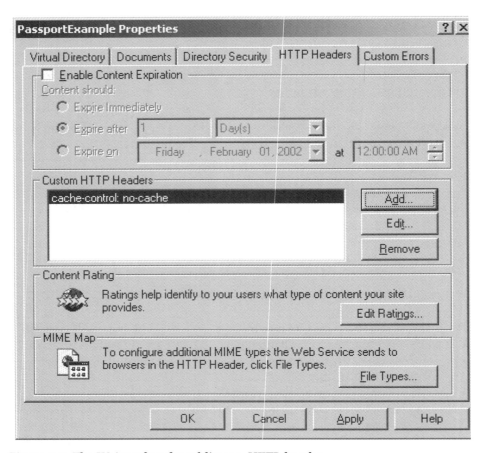

Figure 8-5. The IIS interface for adding an HTTP header

Passport scarab is enough and implies consent. Since I'm not a lawyer, I won't comment on the legal aspects of this, but to me it at least seems questionable. That aside, the only time this should come up is if you choose to use the LoginUser() method on the PassportIdentity class. LoginUser() allows you to perform a silent refresh of a user's credentials and potentially bypass the login mechanism. Using this method, you wouldn't necessarily have to inform users that you're working with Passport—in which case, their consent is not given. As I said, if you display the Sign In logo, or something that drives them to the login servers, their consent is implied and you're safe in terms of the licensing agreement.

Getting consent to utilize information does not imply consent to store the information. To store a user's information, you'll need to present a new interface that gathers the information required for your database. You can use the values attained from the profile[5] to fill in the values on your form and present a device that implies consent to store. This "device" can be as simple as a submit button.[6]

Using P3P Privacy Policies

To support these requirements and to provide your users with some degree of security concerning how their data will be used, consider placing a *P3P* privacy policy in your site. A P3P policy is an XML document that relays your intent for information storage and sharing to a browser and to a user. These are simple to make using a tool such as IBM's P3P Policy Editor[7]—a free tool that creates the policy and allows you to save an HTML version of it so that you can display it to users. To implement it on your site, you can add an HTTP header called P3P with the value "policyref="yourdomain.com/privacy.xml" or you can add the following code to your pages:

```
<link rel="P3Pv1" href="yourpolicy.xml">
```

Tools like the P3P Editor are nice in that they can provide you with instant feedback as to how a browser will interpret and act upon your policy. If you plan on writing cookies, maintaining them forever, sharing them with the world, and not providing an opt-in/out option, you're out of luck. For example, Internet Explorer 6.0 may convert persistent cookies to session cookies or simply not allow you to write them based on the user's privacy settings. Keep these things in mind when developing your policy.

Passport on WindowsXP

XP is an entirely different beast when it comes to Passport. I made the mistake of using it as my initial development platform when creating the samples for this chapter. A quick word of advice—don't do this yourself! Passport works quite differently on XP. Basically, XP has an option set so that WinInet.dll handles authentication challenges issued by the Passport servers. This is why you get a dialog box similar to a network logon when you try to access Passport-protected resources under XP. Unfortunately, this stores configuration

---

5. You must pass the test for gathering consent for use to fill in the values on your form from the Passport profile.

6. See the SDK section entitled "Data Collection" for details. I would at least add a disclaimer to let them know that you're planning on storing the information.

7. Available at http://www.alphaworks.ibm.com/tech/p3peditor/

information it requires in the Registry to implement the protocol and as a result won't let you use Passport authentication in Pre-Production mode.

If you plan on developing on XP, you'll need to follow these steps:

1. Open Notepad and enter the following lines:

```
[HKEY_LOCAL_MACHINE\SOFTWARE\Microsoft\Windows\
CurrentVersion\Internet Settings\Passport]
"NexusHost"="nexus.passporttest.com"
"NexusObj"="rdr/pprdr.asp"
```

2. Save this code as PassportXP.reg.

3. Open the Registry Editor.

4. Back up the Registry Keys: HKLM\Software . . . , HKCU\Software. . . .

5. Delete the key HKLM\Software\Microsoft\Windows\CurrentVersion\Internet Settings\Passport\.

6. Delete the key HKCU\Software\Microsoft\Windows\CurrentVersion\Internet Settings\Passport.

7. Double-click the PassportXP.reg file you created and allow the Registry to be updated.

CAUTION *Executing these steps may render your existing Passport invalid! If you're going to use XP, consider executing these steps first, signing up for a new Passport, and then creating your site on NetMyServiceManager—things will be much simpler this way.*

Once you've put your site into production mode, you can switch back to your old Registry settings, and everything should be working as before.

The following sample application provided for this chapter is a simple demonstration of the functionality Passport provides and gives some guidelines and code you may find useful in your own Passport-based applications.

Sample Application—Exploring Passport

The sample application I provide gives you examples of how to implement the major aspects of Passport—these include authenticating a user, signing out a user, displaying profile information, gathering consent to store data, and implementing simple co-branding. Some of the code you can more or less copy and paste into your application to get you started with Passport.

First things first—it will probably be helpful if you know how to install and configure the application; otherwise, you're going to be left blaming me for something that doesn't work, no matter how many bruised toes you get kicking your computer. The installation goes the same as that of any other Web application really—there's no registration involved. Just copy the files to your Web root, open the ExplorePassport.csproj file, and compile the application. From this point on, the discussion's all Passport related.

The application will fail miserably if you don't have the Passport SDK installed, so install that per the directions in the section "Installing Passport." Once that's done, you'll need to go to Passport and acquire a Pre-Production Site ID.[8] Finally, as you're going through the application, provide the service manager[9] with the values[10] in Table 8-7.

Table 8-7. Passport Configuration Values for Sample Web Application

MANAGER FIELD	VALUE
Default Return URL	`http://yourdomain/ExplorePassport/default.aspx`
Privacy Policy URL	`http://yourdomain/ExplorePassport/privacy.aspx`
Co-branding URL	`http://yourdomain/ExplorePassport/support/script/` `passport_cobranding.js`
Co-branding CSS	`http://yourdomain/ExplorePassport/support/css/` `passport_cobranding.css`
Co-branding Image	`http://yourdomain/ExplorePassport/support/img/` `passport_explore_468_60.gif`
Co-branding Image2	`http://yourdomain/ExplorePassport/support/img/` `passport_explore_102_80.gif`

(continued)

---

8. You will need to perform the additional steps of installing the site encryption key and configuring the Passport Administration Utility as well.

9. For more information, see `http://www.netmyservicesmanager.com`.

10. Remember, you will need fully qualified external DNS names for your machine as well as the domain you belong to. Contact your ISP or LAN administrator for these. Unfortunately, if you're on a corporate LAN, you may be out of luck because this information isn't typically given out or internal machines are masked from the external world.

Table 8-7. Passport Configuration Values for Sample Web Application (continued)

Co-brand Image HREF	`http://yourdomain/ExplorePassport/default.aspx`
Registration Return URL	`http://yourdomain/ExplorePassport/default.aspx`
Terms of Service URL	`http://yourdomain/ExplorePassport/tos.aspx`
Expire Cookie URL	`http://yourdomain/ExplorePassport/signout.aspx`
Logout URL	`http://yourdomain/ExplorePassport/default.aspx`

Site Functionality and Concepts Demonstrated

The header.aspx file, located in the \support\include directory, is the crux of the application. Granted, the code it contains isn't complex, but it serves to provide the scarab to all pages and give the user an interface for manipulating his or her passport information. The critical portion of the file is represented in Listing 8-5.

Listing 8-5. Code Fragment to Present the Sign In Logo to a User

```
<%
    string scarabHTML;
    string returnURL;
    string passportReturnInfo;
    PassportIdentity currentUser;

    returnURL="http://" + Request.ServerVariables["SERVER_NAME"] +
        Request.ServerVariables["SCRIPT_NAME"];
    passportReturnInfo="&ru=" + Server.UrlEncode(returnURL) +
        "&id=yoursiteidgoeshere";
    currentUser=(PassportIdentity)User.Identity;
    scarabHTML=currentUser.LogoTag2(returnURL, 1800, 0,
        Server.UrlEncode(
        "http://YOURDOMAIN.COM/ExplorePassport/" +
        "support/script/passport_cobranding.js"),
        1033, 0, "", 0, 0);
%>
```

SOURCE CODE   *This code is located in the ExploringPassport project in the \support\include\header.aspx file.*

The most important thing the header file provides is reusability. Instead of having to write the code to call LogoTag2() on various pages, you can just write it once and use an #include directive to employ that code throughout the application. Furthermore, by including the page, you'll already have a context for the current user. In other words, you won't have to create a new PassportIdentity and go through the casting process, as the user's information is already stored in the currentUser variable.

The PassportUtilities Class

The pages listed in the upcoming section "Beyond the Basics" serve as implementations for topics discussed in this chapter. For example, get_storage_consent.aspx is a self-posting form that gathers the user's infor-mation from Passport and writes a persistent cookie indicating that the user has given consent to store his or her information outside of the session. This page makes use of the PassportUtilities class (located in global.asax) to write a per-sistent cookie to the browser indicating the user's consent. All you need to do is set the HasStorageConsent property to the desired value, and the cookie will have an expiration time 20 years in the future.

The PassportUtilities class implements support functions found in this chapter and provides a convenient way for you to integrate these into your appli-cation. An instance of this class uses the current HTTP context to access appropriate ASP.NET objects such as Session and Response instances. To accom-plish this, the instance assigns a private member, _currentContext, the value of HttpContext.Current. This means you don't need to do anything like pass Response objects to method calls. The class contains the five following public members:

- SignoutPassport. Deletes the appropriate Passport-generated cookies from the user's machine.

- SetSecureCookie. Sets an encrypted cookie on the user's machine.

- ReadSecureCookie. Decrypts and decompresses a compressed and encrypted cookie.

- GetPassportID. Returns the current user's Passport ID in Int64, UInt64, or Guid formats, depending on the format enumeration value passed.

- HasStorageConsent. A property that returns and sets the user's storage con-sent indicator. This value is stored as a cookie on the client machine.

Static members consist of the following:

- `ReadSecureCookie`. Performs the same function as the nonstatic member, but accepts an HttpCookie as the argument.

- `ClearCookie`. Empties the value and expires an `HttpCookie`.

- `PPUIDtoGUID`. Returns the value of a Passport User ID as a `Guid`.

- `PPUIDtoInt64`. Returns the value of a Passport User ID as an `Int64`.

- `PPUIDtoUInt64`. Returns the value of a Passport User ID as a `UInt64`.

Although the functionality provided by the `PassportUtility` class isn't complex in any regard, hopefully it will serve to show how to work with various aspects of Passport and at the very least furnish some convenience.

Beyond the Basics

The remaining pages take you beyond signing in to Passport. Following is a list of the pages and their relevance to the application:

- *data_protection.aspx*. Demonstrates how to use the security features of Passport such as compression, decompression, encryption, and decryption. A simple interface is provided that allows you to perform one of the four operations on data and see the results.

- *default.aspx*. Represents nothing more than a simple welcome page. It serves as the default return URL for the site.

- *get_storage_consent.aspx*. Provides an example of how you can gather a user's consent to store his or her information in your database. It displays a message based on the user's preference—whether the user does or doesn't want you to store it—which is determined by the `PassportUtilities` class.

- *global.asax*. Functions the same as every other global.asax file, although this contains the implementation for the `PassportUtilities` class.

- *privacy.aspx*. Displays a site security policy; this was just the HTML output (slightly modified) from the IBM P3P Editor.

- *privacy.xml.* Represents the site privacy policy. You can have browsers utilize this by adding a `LINK` tag in your pages or by adding the P3P header with the appropriate value to your server configuration.

- *profile.aspx.* Does nothing more than display a few items from the user's core profile.

- *signout.aspx.* Clears Passport-related cookies and returns a GIF image so that Passport can determine if the user has successfully signed out.

Summary

In this chapter, I covered the following aspects of the Passport architecture:

- Installing and configuring Passport

- Authenticating Passport in ASP.NET

- Securing Passport data on the client

- Co-branding

- Meeting the requirements of the Passport licensing agreement

In the final chapter of this book, I'll discuss how you can protect your investment (that is, your assemblies) from decompilers and reverse-engineering tools.

CHAPTER 9

Protecting Code

To END THIS BOOK, I'd like to reverse the course that I've followed throughout earlier chapters and show you how to protect your investment by securing your .NET code. I'll start by briefly covering the basics of the Common Intermediate Language (CIL). Then I'll explain how you can use this knowledge to reverse-engineer your components. Finally, I'll discuss techniques that you can use to protect your investments.

Decompiling Assemblies

I hope that if there's one thing you've been able to glean from this book, it's this: users now have more choices to determine what runs on a particular machine, and developers now have more choices to specify what their code needs to do at the client side.

As a client, you can prevent either an entire assembly or just one method in one type from running. As a developer, you can demand to write to a file, but you may not get that permission. However, you've probably adopted the perspective most developers have—that it's not the consumer's fault. That is, you're either trying to protect yourself from malicious assemblies or you're taking steps to foil someone from sniffing the network wire to listen to your object communications. But you've pretty much neglected the users, and if they're not your casual users, they can take a lot away from you as a .NET component vender. For example, say you sold a component that had a method with the following code:

```
private int InternalAI(int Weight)
{
    int output = 3;
    return output / Weight;
}
```

Now, you would never release code like this to the general public for fear of ridicule. But that's not really the point here. In the real world, `InternalAI()` (where AI stands for Artificial Intelligence) would contain a genetic algorithm that exceeds the intelligence of mythical machines seen in some Hollywood science-fiction movies. For now, assume that you have something like that here.

And it's probably a safe assumption that you or some other entity has spent a significant amount of time and money creating such an algorithm.

So you shouldn't be surprised when your algorithm is duplicated by other organizations once you release your assembly to the general public. Why? The issue with .NET assemblies lies in one of its greatest assets: the ability for multiple languages to create and consume .NET code. To do this, all .NET languages must compile down to a language called the Common Intermediate Language, or CIL. I don't want to give a full explanation of CIL here,[1] but essentially you can think of CIL as a high-level, object-oriented assembly language designed to support the constructs of many languages. Here's what InternalAI() looks like in CIL:

```
.method private hidebysig instance int32
        InternalAI(int32 Weight) cil managed
{
  // Code size        6 (0x6)
  .maxstack   2
  .locals init (int32 V_0)
  IL_0000:  ldc.i4.3
  IL_0001:  stloc.0
  IL_0002:  ldloc.0
  IL_0003:  ldarg.1
  IL_0004:  div
  IL_0005:  ret
} // end of method AI::InternalAI
```

I'll go through the CIL so you can see how it works. The first two lines define the InternalAI() method, which takes one argument of type int32 (which is what int maps to in C#). Within the method, you declare one local variable of type int32 with a name of V_0.[2] Then, load a value of 3 onto the stack via ldc.i4.3. This value is stored into V_0 with stloc.0. To divide V_0 by Weight, you need to push V_0 and Weight onto the stack first—hence the ldloc.0 and ldarg.1 opcodes. Next, div is called, which leaves the result on the stack. When ret is called, the calling method can read the value on the stack and do what it wants with that value.

Now, you may wonder how I was able to get the CIL. There's a tool that can do this quite easily with any .NET assembly. It's called ILDasm (which stands for IL Disassembler), and it comes with any installation of the .NET Framework. ILDasm is pretty easy to use to get the underlying CIL in an assembly. Simply

---

1.   If you are interested in learning CIL, check out the book, *CIL Programming: Under the Hood of .NET* (Apress, 2002).

2.   The reason it doesn't have the name output is due to its coming from a release build, which replaces friendly variable names with generic ones.

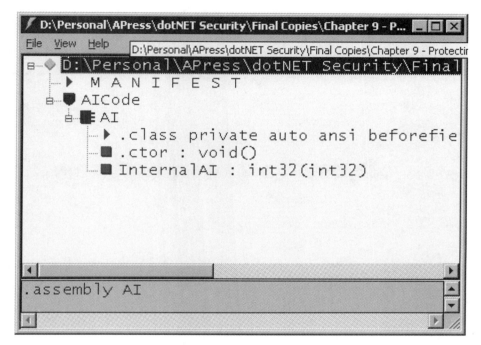

Figure 9-1. Viewing an assembly in ILDasm

enter **ildasm** at the command line, and then load the assembly by selecting File ➤ Open. You should see the screen displayed in Figure 9-1.

Once that's done, it's just a matter of drilling down to the correct method and double-clicking it, as demonstrated in Figure 9-2.

Although this is a great tool for seeing how .NET works at a level underneath the .NET language of your choice, it's also is a bit scary. Once you start to read CIL, it's not that hard to figure out what an assembly is doing. And ILDasm can create a text file that contains all of the CIL from a given assembly. All you need to do is tweak the sections you want, run the ILasm tool (a compiler for CIL code), and now you have a new assembly. Furthermore, there are tools that are freely available for .NET developers to translate the CIL to a higher-level language.[3]

So how can you protect yourself from malicious folk who will simply reassemble your code and try to sell it somewhere else? The next section discusses some options.

---

3. See http://www.saurik.net for more details.

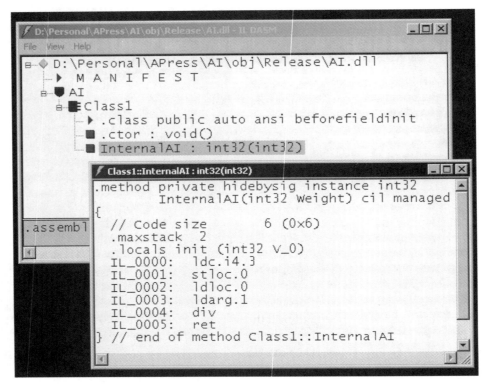

Figure 9-2. Viewing methods in CIL

Preventing Decompilation

There are a couple of options you may try to prevent a user from reverse-engineering your assembly. In this section, I'll cover the following techniques:

- Native image generation

- Strong-naming the assembly

- Hiding the implementation via a Web service

- Obfuscation

Native Image Generation

One technique you may try is to create a native image of your assembly. This is done via the ngen tool that comes with .NET. This tool doesn't work with CIL source files; rather, it takes a .NET assembly and transforms it into a native assembly. For example, you can create a native image of AI.dll as follows:

```
ngen AI.dll
```

The tool creates a native image of the assembly, but it puts the result into the Native Image Cache (NIC). You can see what's in the cache by using the /show argument of ngen:

```
ngen /show
```

Unfortunately, the results aren't what you might expect. The problem is that you still need the original assembly for the client code to run properly. ngen essentially creates implementations of your methods, but the metadata is contained in the original assembly. If you try to run an assembly that uses AI.dll after you employed ngen on it and deleted (or renamed) the source AI.dll, the client will throw a FileNotFoundException.

The runtime will always load the CIL-based assembly, but it's smart enough to use the native implementations if they exist in the NIC. Therefore, you can't distribute a native image without the regular assembly. Someone will always be able to reengineer the code like I did before, and if you rename the resulting assembly and target the client to use this new assembly, you can prevent the runtime from using the native implementations.

Strong-Naming the Assembly

Another possible diversion is using a technique I've discussed before: strong-naming your assembly. Unfortunately, the best you can do with strong-naming your assembly is that you can prevent others from reverse-engineering your code and putting your brand on it. It doesn't prevent others from at least being able to see the underlying code.

Hiding the Implementation as a Web Service

If your clients have high-speed Internet access, another option available is to make them Web services. Clients can access the assembly's functionality, but they can't get the physical assembly itself. Also, if a bug did occur in your assembly, fixing the offending code means that all clients get the fix at one time.

Of course, there may be situations where this is not feasible. For example, if you were writing a high-performance graphics engine to compete with DirectX, you probably don't want the method invocations to occur over HTTP. However, if you know that you must protect your resources, then keeping them off the client's machine may the safest way to do so.

Obfuscation

There's one last option on your plate, and it's called *obfuscation*. This is basically a technique in which a tool will take input, like source code or a PE file, and create output that makes it very difficult for reverse-engineering tools to discover what the executable is doing. However, it will not change the expected behavior of the code, and it may make loading times quicker.

Out of all the options available, this one covers all of the bases, and I think it's the best measure you can take to protecting your investment. Remember, though, that obfuscation is not a guarantee. Someone with enough perseverance may figure out ways to get around an obfuscator in the future.

There are third-party tools that you can purchase to perform this function for you. However, take a look at what an obfuscator will do in more detail so you have a better understanding of how they work.[4]

 NOTE *Check out the following sites for obfuscators that were available at the time of this book's writing:* http://www.wiseowl.com *(Demeanor for .NET),* http://preemptive.com/dotfuscator *(Dotfuscator for Microsoft .NET),* http://www.remotesoft.com/salamander/obfuscator.html *(Salamander .NET Obfuscator), and* http://www.lesser-software.com *(LSW DotNet-IL-Obfuscator). Dan Appleman also has an eBook on obfuscators entitled* Obfuscating .NET: Protecting Your Code from Prying Eyes—*you can find more information (along with a link to his open-source QND-Obfuscator) at* http://www.desaware.com/EBook4L2.htm.

Symbol Obfuscation

Using the InternalAI() example I introduced at the beginning of this chapter, I'll show the class definition as well:

---

4. Full coverage of how obfuscators work is beyond the scope of one chapter. I strongly suggest downloading the paper "Java Control Flow Obfuscation" (available at http://www.cs.auckland.ac.nz/research/theses/1998/low_douglas_thesis1998.pdf) for detailed coverage on this topic.

```
internal class AI
{
    private int InternalAI(int Weight)
    {
        int output = 3;
        return output / Weight;
    }
}
```

As this class is internal, it can only be accessed by code within the assembly that AI is a part of. Therefore, if someone referenced the assembly, that person couldn't use AI. Of course, via ILDasm he or she would still see it, and given its name along with its method name, a reverse-engineer may decide to focus his or her efforts upon this class. That's because the class name has some semantic meaning. If you saw a class in AI's assembly called StringHelper, you probably wouldn't give it much thought, as it's probably used to do some string manipulations that don't have much to do with cognitive science.

Now, to my knowledge there aren't any obfuscators that could change method names to make them "semantically unappealing," but they can do something like this:

```
internal class 29700584-AA62-4a12-A93A-DDFA90936E75
{
    private int 722982AF-32F0-47cd-BFE7-66007C435768(int Weight)
    {
        int output = 3;
        return output / Weight;
    }
}
```

These are invalid C# class and method names, so don't try to mimic this code. I'm only illustrating the point that the semantic meaning behind the class is completely gone. Furthermore, the class and method names are invalid, so a reverse-engineering tool could not blindly take a discovered name and insert it into a generated C# code stream, as this wouldn't work. But the names in Listing 9-1 are perfectly valid from a CIL perspective.

Listing 9-1. Obfuscated Type Names in CIL

```
.namespace AICode
{
  .class private auto ansi beforefieldinit
        '29700584-AA62-4a12-A93A-DDFA90936E75'
        extends [mscorlib]System.Object
```

```
  {
    .method public hidebysig specialname rtspecialname
            instance void .ctor() cil managed
    {
      .maxstack  1
      IL_0000:  ldarg.0
      IL_0001:  call        instance void [mscorlib]System.Object::.ctor()
      IL_0006:  ret
    }
    .method private hidebysig instance int32
            '722982AF-32F0-47cd-BFE7-66007C435768'
            (int32 Weight) cil managed
    {
      .maxstack  2
      .locals init (int32 V_0)
      IL_0000:  ldc.i4.3
      IL_0001:  stloc.0
      IL_0002:  ldloc.0
      IL_0003:  ldarg.1
      IL_0004:  div
      IL_0005:  ret
    }
  }
}
```

An obfuscator will only perform name mangling on features that are not accessible outside of the assembly. And it will also use mangled names smaller than GUIDs; in fact, a good obfuscator will create names that are invalid in most .NET languages and are smaller than the original names, improving load times.[5]

Code Obfuscation

Symbol obfuscation by itself is not enough. Most decompilers will simply keep an internal list of discovered names and emit their own generic yet valid names (like local1 or class1). Although these names aren't very helpful, they are valid and can be used in most any .NET language. However, the real key for any obfuscator is to alter the implementation such that it trips up a reverse-engineering tool without affecting the intended goals of the implementation.

---

5.   Some obfuscators will use language keyword names, like class or If, to confuse decompilers. And one obfuscator, Demeanor for .NET, will name virtually all of the classes and their methods' local variables with the *same* name. Due to the way metadata is handled, this is perfectly valid, and makes the job for a reverse-engineering tool much harder.

There are a number of techniques that obfuscators can use to confuse a decompiler, such as moving implementations into separate threads or adding dead code. One approach, called *opaque predicates*, is particularly effective because it adds code that requires dynamic analysis of the code, which is computationally expensive.

For example, adding opaque predicates to the `InternalAI` method may look something like this:[6]

```
private int InternalAI(int Weight)
{
    Node c = new Node();
    Node d = c.Create();
    if(c == d)
    {
      int output = 3;
      return output / Weight;
    }
    else
    {
      return 8;
    }
}
```

Don't worry what Node looks like. The point is that the inserted code has affected the "look" of the overall code, but it will not affect the intent of the code. That's because it's clear that the c and d variables will always be equal, so the original code will run. However, someone who is reverse-engineering the code now has to worry about the two Node variables and what they are doing.[7]

Unfortunately, a drawback with code obfuscation is that it will bloat the original code base. The degree of the bloat will vary depending on the techniques used, so a good obfuscation tool should allow you to determine which methods should be targeted for obfuscation due to their implementation-sensitive nature. Although decompilers may be able to decompile some methods, they will have a much harder time with the methods you've obfuscated.

---

6.   Note that an obfuscator can work at either the source-code or assembly level. I'm only showing the example in C#, as it's easier to follow than CIL.

7.   And, chances are, Node's name would've been obfuscated as well, which makes the job of reading the reverse-engineered code much more difficult.

Summary

In this chapter, I covered the following topics:

- Decompiling assemblies using the ILDasm tool

- Using obfuscation to make reverse-engineering harder for users

Security is a tricky beast. There are so many perspectives that you as a developer must have to ensure that not only is your investment protected, but your client's investment in your code is also worthwhile. So long as there's money to be made in stealing credit card numbers or satisfaction is gained by destroying files on users' machines, security will remain an issue. With .NET, Microsoft has given you a number of tools to help you in making such breaches much more difficult. I encourage you to apply them to your designs to ensure safe and reliable code becomes more and more commonplace in the .NET world. Good luck!

Index

Apress Titles

ISBN	PRICE	AUTHOR	TITLE
1-893115-73-9	$34.95	Abbott	Voice Enabling Web Applications: VoiceXML and Beyond
1-893115-01-1	$39.95	Appleman	Dan Appleman's Win32 API Puzzle Book and Tutorial for Visual Basic Programmers
1-893115-23-2	$29.95	Appleman	How Computer Programming Works
1-893115-97-6	$39.95	Appleman	Moving to VB .NET: Strategies, Concepts, and Code
1-59059-023-6	$39.95	Baker	Adobe Acrobat 5: The Professional User's Guide
1-59059-039-2	$49.95	Barnaby	Distributed .NET Programming
1-893115-09-7	$29.95	Baum	Dave Baum's Definitive Guide to LEGO MINDSTORMS
1-893115-84-4	$29.95	Baum, Gasperi, Hempel, and Villa	Extreme MINDSTORMS: An Advanced Guide to LEGO MINDSTORMS
1-893115-82-8	$59.95	Ben-Gan/Moreau	Advanced Transact-SQL for SQL Server 2000
1-893115-91-7	$39.95	Birmingham/Perry	Software Development on a Leash
1-893115-48-8	$29.95	Bischof	The .NET Languages: A Quick Translation Guide
1-59059-053-8	$44.95	Bock/Stromquist/ Fischer/Smith	.NET Security
1-893115-67-4	$49.95	Borge	Managing Enterprise Systems with the Windows Script Host
1-893115-28-3	$44.95	Challa/Laksberg	Essential Guide to Managed Extensions for C++
1-893115-39-9	$44.95	Chand	A Programmer's Guide to ADO.NET in C#
1-893115-44-5	$29.95	Cook	Robot Building for Beginners
1-893115-99-2	$39.95	Cornell/Morrison	Programming VB .NET: A Guide for Experienced Programmers
1-893115-72-0	$39.95	Curtin	Developing Trust: Online Privacy and Security
1-59059-014-7	$44.95	Drol	Object-Oriented Macromedia Flash MX
1-59059-008-2	$29.95	Duncan	The Career Programmer: Guerilla Tactics for an Imperfect World
1-893115-71-2	$39.95	Ferguson	Mobile .NET
1-893115-90-9	$49.95	Finsel	The Handbook for Reluctant Database Administrators
1-59059-024-4	$49.95	Fraser	Real World ASP.NET: Building a Content Management System
1-893115-42-9	$44.95	Foo/Lee	XML Programming Using the Microsoft XML Parser
1-893115-55-0	$34.95	Frenz	Visual Basic and Visual Basic .NET for Scientists and Engineers
1-893115-85-2	$34.95	Gilmore	A Programmer's Introduction to PHP 4.0
1-893115-36-4	$34.95	Goodwill	Apache Jakarta-Tomcat
1-893115-17-8	$59.95	Gross	A Programmer's Introduction to Windows DNA
1-893115-62-3	$39.95	Gunnerson	A Programmer's Introduction to C#, Second Edition
1-59059-009-0	$49.95	Harris/Macdonald	Moving to ASP.NET: Web Development with VB .NET
1-893115-30-5	$49.95	Harkins/Reid	SQL: Access to SQL Server
1-893115-10-0	$34.95	Holub	Taming Java Threads
1-893115-04-6	$34.95	Hyman/Vaddadi	Mike and Phani's Essential C++ Techniques
1-893115-96-8	$59.95	Jorelid	J2EE FrontEnd Technologies: A Programmer's Guide to Servlets, JavaServer Pages, and Enterprise JavaBeans
1-893115-49-6	$39.95	Kilburn	Palm Programming in Basic
1-893115-50-X	$34.95	Knudsen	Wireless Java: Developing with Java 2, Micro Edition
1-893115-79-8	$49.95	Kofler	Definitive Guide to Excel VBA
1-893115-57-7	$39.95	Kofler	MySQL
1-893115-87-9	$39.95	Kurata	Doing Web Development: Client-Side Techniques

ISBN	PRICE	AUTHOR	TITLE
1-893115-75-5	$44.95	Kurniawan	Internet Programming with VB
1-893115-38-0	$24.95	Lafler	Power AOL: A Survival Guide
1-893115-46-1	$36.95	Lathrop	Linux in Small Business: A Practical User's Guide
1-893115-19-4	$49.95	Macdonald	Serious ADO: Universal Data Access with Visual Basic
1-893115-06-2	$39.95	Marquis/Smith	A Visual Basic 6.0 Programmer's Toolkit
1-893115-22-4	$27.95	McCarter	David McCarter's VB Tips and Techniques
1-59059-021-X	$34.95	Moore	Karl Moore's Visual Basic .NET: The Tutorials
1-893115-76-3	$49.95	Morrison	C++ For VB Programmers
1-59059-003-1	$39.95	Nakhimovsky/Meyers	XML Programming: Web Applications and Web Services with JSP and ASP
1-893115-80-1	$39.95	Newmarch	A Programmer's Guide to Jini Technology
1-893115-58-5	$49.95	Oellermann	Architecting Web Services
1-59059-020-1	$44.95	Patzer	JSP Examples and Best Practices
1-893115-81-X	$39.95	Pike	SQL Server: Common Problems, Tested Solutions
1-59059-017-1	$34.95	Rainwater	Herding Cats: A Primer for Programmers Who Lead Programmers
1-59059-025-2	$49.95	Rammer	Advanced .NET Remoting
1-893115-20-8	$34.95	Rischpater	Wireless Web Development
1-893115-93-3	$34.95	Rischpater	Wireless Web Development with PHP and WAP
1-893115-89-5	$59.95	Shemitz	Kylix: The Professional Developer's Guide and Reference
1-893115-40-2	$39.95	Sill	The qmail Handbook
1-893115-24-0	$49.95	Sinclair	From Access to SQL Server
1-893115-94-1	$29.95	Spolsky	User Interface Design for Programmers
1-893115-53-4	$44.95	Sweeney	Visual Basic for Testers
1-59059-002-3	$44.95	Symmonds	Internationalization and Localization Using Microsoft .NET
1-59059-010-4	$54.95	Thomsen	Database Programming with C#
1-893115-29-1	$44.95	Thomsen	Database Programming with Visual Basic .NET
1-893115-65-8	$39.95	Tiffany	Pocket PC Database Development with eMbedded Visual Basic
1-893115-59-3	$59.95	Troelsen	C# and the .NET Platform
1-59059-011-2	$59.95	Troelsen	COM and .NET Interoperability
1-893115-26-7	$59.95	Troelsen	Visual Basic .NET and the .NET Platform
1-893115-54-2	$49.95	Trueblood/Lovett	Data Mining and Statistical Analysis Using SQL
1-893115-68-2	$54.95	Vaughn	ADO.NET and ADO Examples and Best Practices for VB Programmers, Second Edition
1-59059-012-0	$49.95	Vaughn/Blackburn	ADO.NET Examples and Best Practices for C# Programmers
1-893115-83-6	$44.95	Wells	Code Centric: T-SQL Programming with Stored Procedures and Triggers
1-893115-95-X	$49.95	Welschenbach	Cryptography in C and C++
1-893115-05-4	$39.95	Williamson	Writing Cross-Browser Dynamic HTML
1-893115-78-X	$49.95	Zukowski	Definitive Guide to Swing for Java 2, Second Edition
1-893115-92-5	$49.95	Zukowski	Java Collections
1-893115-98-4	$54.95	Zukowski	Learn Java with JBuilder 6

Available at bookstores nationwide or from Springer Verlag New York, Inc. at 1-800-777-4643; fax 1-212-533-3503. Contact us for more information at sales@apress.com.

Apress Titles Publishing **SOON!**

ISBN	AUTHOR	TITLE
1-59059-022-8	Alapati	Expert Oracle 9i Database Administration
1-59059-041-4	Bock	CIL Programming: Under the Hood of .NET
1-59059-019-8	Cagle	SVG Programming: The Graphical Web
1-59059-015-5	Clark	An Introduction to Object Oriented Programming with Visual Basic .NET
1-59059-000-7	Cornell	Programming C#
1-59059-033-3	Fraser	Managed C++ and .NET Development
1-59059-038-4	Gibbons	Java Development to .NET Development
1-59059-030-9	Habibi/Camerlengo/Patterson	Java 1.4 and the Sun Certified Developer Exam
1-59059-006-6	Hetland	Instant Python with Ten Instant Projects
1-59059-044-9	MacDonald	.NET User Interfaces with VB .NET: Windows Forms and Custom Controls
1-59059-001-5	McMahon	A Programmer's Introduction to ASP.NET WebForms in Visual Basic .NET
1-893115-74-7	Millar	Enterprise Development: A Programmer's Handbook
1-893115-27-5	Morrill	Tuning and Customizing a Linux System
1-59059-028-7	Rischpater	Wireless Web Development, Second Edition
1-59059-026-0	Smith	Writing Add-Ins for .NET
1-893115-43-7	Stephenson	Standard VB: An Enterprise Developer's Reference for VB 6 and VB .NET
1-59059-035-X	Symmonds	GDI+ Programming in C# and VB .NET
1-59059-032-5	Thomsen	Database Programming with Visual Basic .NET, Second Edition
1-59059-007-4	Thomsen	Building Web Services with VB .NET
1-59059-027-9	Torkelson/Petersen/Torkelson	Programming the Web with Visual Basic .NET
1-59059-018-X	Tregar	Writing Perl Modules for CPAN
1-59059-004-X	Valiaveedu	SQL Server 2000 and Business Intelligence in an XML/.NET World

Available at bookstores nationwide or from SPRINGER Verlag New York, Inc. at 1-800-777-4643;
fax 1-212-533-3503. Contact us for more information at sales@apress.com.

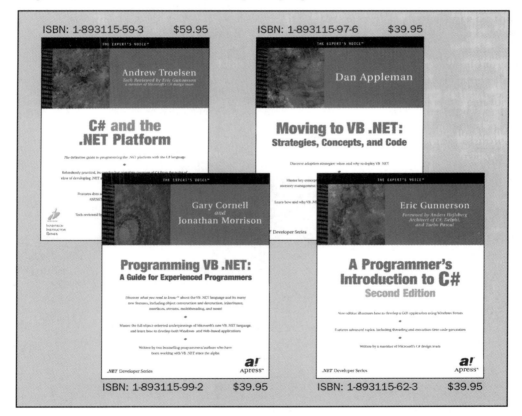

books for professionals by professionals™

About Apress

Apress, located in Berkeley, CA, is a fast-growing, innovative publishing company devoted to meeting the needs of existing and potential programming professionals. Simply put, the "A" in Apress stands for *"The Author's Press*™*"* and its books have *"The Expert's Voice*™*"*. Apress' unique approach to publishing grew out of conversations between its founders Gary Cornell and Dan Appleman, authors of numerous best-selling, highly regarded books for programming professionals. In 1998 they set out to create a publishing company that emphasized quality above all else. Gary and Dan's vision has resulted in the publication of over 50 titles by leading software professionals, all of which have *The Expert's Voice*™.

Do You Have What It Takes to Write for Apress?

Apress is rapidly expanding its publishing program. If you can write and refuse to compromise on the quality of your work, if you believe in doing more than rehashing existing documentation, and if you're looking for opportunities and rewards that go far beyond those offered by traditional publishing houses, we want to hear from you!

Consider these innovations that we offer all of our authors:

- **Top royalties with *no* hidden switch statements**
  Authors typically only receive half of their normal royalty rate on foreign sales. In contrast, Apress' royalty rate remains the same for both foreign and domestic sales.

- **A mechanism for authors to obtain equity in Apress**
  Unlike the software industry, where stock options are essential to motivate and retain software professionals, the publishing industry has adhered to an outdated compensation model based on royalties alone. In the spirit of most software companies, Apress reserves a significant portion of its equity for authors.

- **Serious treatment of the technical review process**
  Each Apress book has a technical reviewing team whose remuneration depends in part on the success of the book since they too receive royalties.

Moreover, through a partnership with Springer-Verlag, New York, Inc., one of the world's major publishing houses, Apress has significant venture capital behind it. Thus, we have the resources to produce the highest quality books *and* market them aggressively.

If you fit the model of the Apress author who can write a book that gives the "professional what he or she needs to know™," then please contact one of our Editorial Directors, Gary Cornell (gary_cornell@apress.com), Dan Appleman (dan_appleman@apress.com), Peter Blackburn (peter_blackburn@apress.com), Jason Gilmore (jason_gilmore@apress.com), Karen Watterson (karen_watterson@apress.com), or John Zukowski (john_zukowski@apress.com) for more information.